D0873332

THE STATION

Robert Byron was born on 26 February 1905. His family had a distant connection with the poet's family. He was educated at Eton and Oxford. He became a traveller with a passion for Greece. He wrote a number of travel books. At the outbreak of the Second World War, Byron joined the overseas department of the BBC and in 1941, while on his way to Meshed for the Intelligence Service, but under the cover of special correspondent for a group of English newspapers, his ship was torpedoed.

Robert Byron was only twenty-two when he wrote *The Station*, and yet it established him decisively as an original writer of challenging views and a vigorous and witty way of presenting them. In this elaborate account of his visit to Mount Athos with two Oxford friends, he made his first declaration of love for Byzantine civilization of which he remained to the end of his life a tirelessly enthusiastic advocate. Reviewing the book on its first appearance in 1928, Arnold Bennett wrote in the *Evening Standard* "*The Station* reveals a travel-writer of sly, urbane wit and all-inclusive observation, with a sense of style and a refreshing vocabulary," and the *Daily Telegraph* declared: "It is a volume that will bear reading again and again."

THE STATION

Athos: Treasures and Men

ROBERT BYRON

Introduction by John Julius Norwich

CENTURY PUBLISHING
LONDON
HIPPOCRENE BOOKS INC.
NEW YORK

Introduction copyright © John Julius Norwich 1984

All rights reserved

© The Estate of Robert Byron 1931

First published in Great Britain in 1931 by
Gerald Duckworth & Co. Ltd

This edition published in 1984 by
Century Publishing Co. Ltd,
Portland House, 12–13 Greek Street, London W1V 5LE

Published in the United States of America by
Hippocrene Books Inc.
171 Madison Avenue
New York NY 10016

ISBN 0 7126 0339 5

Cover shows a watercolour painting of Mount Athos
by Edward Lear courtesy of The Fine Art Society PLC

Reprinted in Great Britain by
Richard Clay (The Chaucer Press) Ltd,
Bungay, Suffolk

Here, in lush valleys, teem bees, figs, and olives. The inmates of the monasteries weave cloth, stitch shoes, and make nets. One turns the spindle of a hand-loom through the wool; another twists a basket of twigs. From time to time, at stated hours, all essay to praise God. And peace reigns among them, always and for ever.

CRISTOFORO BUONDELMONTI,

Traveller in the East, 1420

Contents

Illustrations

Introduction

WHEN ROBERT BYRON wrote *The Station*, he was twenty-two years old. Few other people write books when they are twenty-two, but then Robert Byron was not like other people. He had, moreover, written one book already. *Europe in the Looking Glass*, a typically ebullient record of a journey with two Oxford friends through Germany, Italy and Greece, had been published in 1926, when he was twenty-one. It is very much a young man's book—how could it have been anything else?—yet already on almost every page there are flashes of the biting wit, the astonishing power of visual observation, the faintly mannered style with its occasional fearless plunges into the purple patch, the perceptiveness so acute as sometimes to verge on clairvoyance (such as when he writes of Bavaria that "it is here, more than in Prussia, that the survival of militarism is to be feared") that were to be the hallmarks of his later voice.

I nearly wrote "his mature voice"; but Robert Byron, alas, never reached his full maturity as a writer. In February 1941 he was acting for the Intelligence Service and was on his way to Meshed with his cover—a group of war correspondents—when their ship was torpedoed off the north coast of Scotland. There were only two or three survivors who were picked up by a ship without radio communication, thus causing weeks of uncertainty for Byron's family. He died, probably by drowning, some two days short of his thirty-sixth birthday. What he might have achieved had he been granted a half-century or more of productive working life instead of a meagre fifteen years, we can only guess. Of one thing, however, we can be virtually certain: that the world of art history, and in particular the understanding of the art of Byzantium and of Islam, would have been profoundly changed.

To some extent, he had already changed it. In his two most important books, *The Byzantine Achievement* (which was published only a year after *The Station* and deserves republication more than any book I know) and *The Road to Oxiana* of 1937, he proposed theories which seemed in his day little short of revolutionary but which have now, thanks largely to his championship, become more or less accepted. As always, he overstated his case. In the early years of this century the general view of Byzantine art and culture was still that propagated by Edward Gibbon and, later, W. E. H. Lecky, who wrote in 1867:

> Of the Byzantine Empire the universal verdict of history is that it constitutes, with scarcely an exception, the most thoroughly base and despicable form that civilisation has yet assumed . . . There has been no other enduring civilisation so absolutely destitute of all the forms and elements of greatness, and none to which the epithet *mean* may so emphatically be applied.

Reappraisal, it is clear, was long overdue; and no one was better equipped for the task than Robert Byron. In both the present volume and in *The Byzantine Achievement* he performed it, magnificently. And yet, one wonders, would not his arguments have been still more cogent if he had been able to resist the temptation of simultaneously dismissing the art of classical Greece with the blistering scorn of which he was such a master—referring, for example, to its statuary as "those inert stone bodies which already debar persons of artistic sensibility from entering half the museums of Europe"? Perhaps so; on the other hand, this pugnaciousness was an integral part of his character, one that appeared—as his friends would ruefully admit—as much, if not more, in his conversation and behaviour as in his writing. He could not have eliminated it without in some degree being untrue to himself; and though his advocacy might have benefited, the book as a whole would inevitably have suffered—and would also have been, for the reader, a good deal less fun. Both in his life and his work he was always, despite his formidable intelligence, an unbridled force of nature. It was, in the last analysis, better that way.

The Station is a rotten title for a book. Obscurity, sometimes wilful obscurity, was ever one of Robert Byron's failings, and here he allows our bewilderment to continue until the very last sentence: "This is the Holy Mountain Athos, station of a faith where all the years have stopped". (Confusion of metaphor was another of his problems.) By this time, however, the purpose of the book is clear: to present us with a picture of Mount Athos and its inhabitants not simply as a piece of travel writing nor even as a study of a monastic society, but as a historical enquiry into the civilisation of Byzantium seen in its only surviving manifestation. As he put it:

> While the classical continues to suckle half the world on a voice of letters and stone [those metaphors again!] one fragment, one living articulate community of my chosen past, has been preserved, by a fabulous compound of circumstance, into the present time. Thither I travel, physically by land and water, instead of down the pages of a book or the corridors of a museum. Of the Byzantine Empire, whose life has left its impress on the Levant and whose coins were once current from London to Pekin, alone, impregnable, the Holy Mountain Athos conserves both the form and the spirit.

But although Byzantium may remain the underlying theme of *The Station*, the character and atmosphere of the Holy Mountain itself is too insistent to be ignored for long. You may, in the pages that follow, occasionally come upon a short passage of philosophical reflection, historical disquisition or critical analysis; much of the author's profounder thinking, however, he seems to have decided to leave over to his next book. What you will chiefly find is a rollicking travelogue, as three high-spirited young men, accompanied from time to time by others, move from one to the next of the twenty monasteries of the Holy Mountain. They examine its treasures, they photograph its frescoes, they make extremely bad sketches of the monasteries themselves and of those who live in them; but they also swim ecstatically off its sparkling, deserted beaches, complain vociferously about its unspeakably disgusting food and laugh themselves silly over their conversations with some of the dottier monks—behaving, in short, as any normal, healthy young visitor to Athos is bound to do. Several of these conversations are transcribed with relish. They may sound far-fetched to those without first-hand experience of the Mountain; to anyone who knows it, I can only say that they have the ring of truth. For an Athonite, life is very different from how it appears to us. Time has no meaning; the Son of God, His Virgin Mother, the Angels and the Saints are all living creatures of flesh and blood; of the outside world, many of the monks have almost as hazy a picture as we may have of Heaven or Hell.

I myself first read this irresistible book on my first visit to Mount

Athos in 1962—much of it by candle-light in some of the very guest-rooms that it describes. I remember my initial astonishment at how little they, and indeed the whole Mountain, had changed since Robert Byron's time—and then my almost immediate realisation that on Athos thirty-five years is but the twinkling of an eye, and that had I been able to make a similar comparison over two or three centuries my conclusion would have been much the same. A few buildings might have burnt down, a few new ones arisen; the monks might have been rather more numerous, their monasteries rather richer. But the beauty would have been unaltered, and that unearthly atmosphere which the total absence of feminity can sometimes render almost unbearably oppressive but which can on other occasions engender feelings of quite extraordinary serenity and peace.

All that worried me then was the future. Some of the larger monasteries still seemed relatively well populated, but in the smaller ones the same questions always elicited the same—or almost the same—answers:

"How many monks was this monastery built to hold?"
"Two hundred."
"How many has it today?"
"Fourteen."
"How old is the youngest?"
"Seventy-two."

Two of the three foreign monasteries, the Serbian Chilandari and the Russian St. Pantaleimon, were at that time expecting, rather surprisingly, transfusions of young novices from their respective homelands; though how these were going to settle down in their new and intensely reactionary environments seemed uncertain. For many of the Greek foundations, on the other hand, there seemed little hope. In former days not only was religious faith virtually unquestioned, but for many a Greek peasant the monastery offered far better prospects than he could otherwise have hoped for: free food and clothing for life, care and relative comfort in old age—to say nothing of his soul's salvation. By the middle of the twentieth century, all that had changed: education had been brought to the villages, and with it the seeds of doubt; increased mobility had provided new opportunities for work in the

Introduction

cities and towns; while the taking of monastic vows, which had once been considered a matter of legitimate pride not only for the taker but for his whole family, was now more likely to be greeted by at best a murmured expression of pity and at worst a ribald joke. (The Athonite reputation for homosexuality, largely unjustified as I believe it to be, has long been an article of faith among the sophisticated Greeks of today.) How, I wondered, could many of the smaller foundations— Castamonitou, Caracallou or Stavronikita to name but three—hope to survive even to the end of the decade?

But survive they have; and a friend of mine who returns regularly every year to Athos assures me that the monasteries are nearly all more prosperous now than they were when he first knew them. Thus *The Station* is not to be read as an account of a vanished way of life; on the contrary, it is as true to its subject today as it was when one of the most remarkable young men of his time sat down to write it. No better portrait of the Holy Mountain exists than this, written as it was nearly sixty years ago; nor is it likely to be surpassed in the future. Here, in short, is a classic. And a classic it will remain.

JOHN JULIUS NORWICH

Prelude

AN ENGLISH YEAR

LETTERS from foreign countries arrive in the afternoon. Each envelope advertises a break in the monotony of days; each reveals on penetration only one more facet of a standard world. But latterly another kind has come, strangely addressed, stranger still within. "We learn," runs one, "that you are safely returned to your own glorious country and are already in the midst of your dearest ones, enjoying the best of health. . . . PS.—We have experienced no cold this year hitherto." "I am proud," says another, "that the all-bountiful God has allowed us to see you again. . . . May he guard you from all evil, world without end. Send me from England ten metres of black stuff that I may make a gown." As the unfamiliar hieroglyphics resolve, memory evokes the senders, their fellows, and the weeks of their company. Till the whole excursion into their impalpable world stands defined as the limits of a sleep. But the experience, being personal, is framed in a larger retrospect. The colour of their environment lives by contrast with my own. Without that measure, its romance fades away.

Conveniently, as it happens, the period previous to this particular adventure from the earth falls within a year. It is precisely a period; because September witnessed my departure from a latitude whither, in the August following, I was to return. On the home journey we travelled from Constantinople; up the Black Sea by Rumanian boat to Constanza; from there to Bucharest; and on to Vienna, where an industrial exhibition, housed in three buildings each larger than the Albert Hall, consisted wholly of saucepans. There followed a few days in Paris. And so back to England, to a garden of Michaelmas daisies; with the bracken turning to gold, and thin blue columns of smoke filling the air with the scent of burning leaves. Cubbing had begun, disclosing those unknown hours when the dew sparkles thick in the hazy light and the trees and plants are twice alive. Ultimately the middle of November brought an upper floor in London, connected, despite the proximity of the Marylebone Road, with that zenith of residential snobbery, the Mayfair telephone exchange.

The house in which body and soul were now enshrouded was kept by Mrs. Byrne, an Irish Catholic. The upper floor had formerly been tenanted by a dotard, to whose tappings and ravings came responses in kind from an incurable ex-officer next door. But his death had coincided with my return to England. And, needing a room, I was immediately ensconced upon the bed which for six years had quaked beneath the struggles of the demented.

The other tenants, as they arrived, proved not less distinctive than he who had departed. Above, the Misses Jimmie led lives of mouse-like though sinister seclusion. While below, a Mademoiselle Péron, having a pale face and flamboyant hair, spent such hours as could be spared from the drama, in pacing the hall, sparsely wrapped in soiled cretonne. Her pom was the permanent inmate of this oil-clothed passage, where the air hung thick with kitchen whiffs and the odour of collected dust. To the intermediate and "drawing-room" floor she introduced a tenant of her own, an attaché at one of the Balkan legations. The common staircase thus became a channel of turbulent domesticity which spared its other patrons no embarrassment.

Outside, the fogs rolled up to stay and the organ-grinders gathered. Through the former only the blurred yellow stars of answering electric lights proclaimed the street's other wall. Of the latter there were often two, equidistant, mingling crises of discord with their own intrinsic melancholy. On alternate afternoons came an old man with bowler hat and concertina, whose répertoire, constant through nine months, started with a Highland jig, and, continuing with "The Lakes of Killarney" and "The British Grenadiers," ended on "God Save the King." Meals, other than a greasy breakfast, were to be had near by at a pleasant, economical restaurant, frequented, as I discovered, by people who did not wish to be seen. Since I myself, being inevitably tired and dishevelled, was in a like case, the annoyance was mutual. Later on, the clientele became uncomfortably swollen owing to the misadventure of one of the waiters' wives, whose dismembered person was discovered in a trunk. She had already forsaken her husband; in which example I had followed her on account of his persistence in speaking Italian. It was noticeable that the queue of cars outside the doors of the establishment was transformed by this circumstance from the £400 to the £800 class.

Christmas set in early. The small shops sported tinsel and stockings; the large, elaborate tableaux, ugly fancy dresses, and bazaars in cottonwool grottoes. In the country, hunt balls began. Staying in a house for one of them, I found myself alone at breakfast with a man whom I had previously insulted in print under the impression he was someone else. I explained this, and then, since the rest of the party elected to remain in bed till lunch, we discussed the army and Parliament as alternative careers. Being a soldier, he maintained that the former offered wider scope. At home we enjoyed our own ebullient function, attended by flutterings on behalf of the master's wife, whose official patronage had not been requested. Apart from the peculiar pasts of those who control them, the local packs of hounds are distinguished for hunting over country which contains a larger percentage of wire than any known area outside New Zealand. This, however, does not save them from focusing to themselves those latent social aspirations and malignities which are investing English country life with an artificiality comparable to that of London, and less excusable. It seems there are only a few who still comprehend the spirit of the countryside and the unconscious details that compose it: the trees and hedges closing to eternal forest in the blue distance; the whistle of a train down the wind; shadows of clouds running atilt the fields; the riders on the crest of a hill where a clump of beeches and a tussocky rampart of prehistory stand between them and the sky; the stripes of a newploughed field glinting in the leaden dusk of winter sunsets; the reins slipping through sodden gloves; and at last that elusive shiver, common to all countries, of the arriving night. The perception of such, of the happiness they give, is waning. It is the point-to-point that clamours on the morrow. Bookmakers and fish and chips; snuffling tents; champagne picnics; tweed skirt and plus four; shooting-stick and glasses; the altitude of behaviour in a cutting wind. Better take a walk up the back drive.

In London again, the New Year opened. Resentfully its first nondescript months allowed the days to lengthen. Birds twittered in the adjoining square. A dozen daffodils stood above the gasstove. It was imperative to seek the country.

Having in past years reached Ireland from Holyhead, the call of the unknown and the saving of 4s. 6d. now involved a night journey to Fishguard. The sea was calm; the train beyond, ramshackle and unreal, empty. Slowly we wound up the coast, the gulls crying unhappily over the sedges and sad, peaty hills stretching mysteriously inland. The fields, uneven and gorse-grown, seemed shrunk between their banks. A salt wind blew cold through the window. To one released from the turbid interiors of London these details obtruded themselves. At length the station was reached; a drive, a bath, and breakfast.

The sun shone, and all varieties of rhododendrons—huge clumps, single bushes, and cone-shaped, broad-leaved trees from the Himalayas—blazed their permutations of red, white, and purple. Tree ferns drooped; aloes poised grey armouries above the lawns; butterflies embarked on tentative flights. The house, of fabricated stone, sparkled like a porcupine of Gothic quills within its wooded cup. Beneath the trees, anemones and violets fought the moss. Primroses were on the banks; wild strawberry flowers between the brambles in the clearings. The sun lay hot on the face of the hill, calling the scents of the earth and its buds. Below, the tree-tops fell down to a river, which reappeared on the horizon to meet the sea. Here lay the town, Catholic cupola and Protestant spire distinguishable, with a many-arched bridge at the mouth and ships at anchor within the mole. Sometimes we motored; but to such objectives as a spit of sand, or a mountain where gold was found. At the foot of the latter the chauffeur uttered warning that those who ascended never returned. Throughout the afternoon we persisted, plodding from each promised summit to its superior, till there lay beneath us an enormous tract of land, turbulent and irregular, without habitation or cultivation, where five years ago the rebels killed any man who ventured. In the distance the hills rose to mountains again. Over them a storm was in progress. The colour of the land, of the sodden heather and soft brown virgin turf, had risen to the sky. There was a brown in the clouds; a brown in the gold of the misty rays that pierced them; a brown in the battle of the wind. Might the chauffeur, perhaps, have been right?

From here, after a day of poignant gloom in Dublin, I travelled west. The first house had been historically an abbey, displaying the form of such in every crocket of its eighteenth century exterior. The second was no less a castle. In the back parts the marks of Cromwell's cannon balls might still be seen. The nineteenth century, however, had witnessed a reversion to more chivalrous methods of defence. Each bedroom had been slitted anew with openings for the cross-bow; each archway punctured for the engulfing of unwanted guests in boiling oil. The garden, too, was peculiar in that not only was it extensively and emotionally romantic, but was impregnated in addition with the excited phantasy of the early Victorian engineer. The lake, instead of nestling, as lakes are wont, in a hollow, hung suspended on a platform. Separate streams, whose mingling waters might have been the delight of poets, were carried one above the other. A miniature suspension bridge, long-previous prototype of Menai and Clifton, spanned elsewhere the pellucid brook, riven immediately beneath to spume and roar in imitation of the lately discovered Zambezi. Fringed by bamboo, narcissi and grape hyacinths flowered in the grass.

It was now my intention to proceed to the north of Scotland. Yet another valued fraction of life's little day was mouldered in the Free State capital.[1] At six o'clock I boarded a steamer lying forlornly in the Liffey. And, after a strange meal of tongue and khaki pickles, at which the other passengers drank tea, I slept in solitary peace till awakened by the steward's announcing the banks of the Clyde. Only he whose reason has survived it, can grasp the implication of a Glasgow Sunday. To obtain a glass of beer it was necessary to affirm on paper my bona fides as a traveller and order a hot omelette. Late in the afternoon of the following day I arrived in the Highlands, having taken sixty hours to accomplish a single journey in the British Isles.

The colour of Scotland was the antithesis of Ireland, a liquid silvery light deepening the purple mountains to damson and the cold green of pines and firs to an equal tone. Snow lay still along the

---

[1] Travellers are advised to take consolation in a pink wax bust of Queen Victoria, with tow hair and glass teeth, exhibited on the ground floor of the Art Gallery.

summit of the Cairngorms. Over the heather the curlews wailed and the grouse called, "Go back, go back." On top of the hills, blue hares scurried in and out of the clouds. A pink granite obelisk commemorating King Edward's coronation also emerged, strangely urban at the height of 3,000 feet. At times we fished, struggling waist-deep in a current that was taking daily toll of similar invaders. To those who have not previously wielded a salmon rod in a gale, the experience is a memorable one. Only, however, when a third suit had been torn from my back by the flies' preference of tweed to fish, did I retire indoors, to spend the remaining days in a dinner-jacket.

Once more I returned to London—to find my sitting-room transformed, in the exuberance of Mrs. Byrne's good heart, from dull mustardy yellow to vociferous canary. With May and the coming of summer a new complexion overspread the routine of days. Pansies and bachelor's buttons twinkled in shallow boxes outside the greengrocer's shop on the way to the restaurant. Sunbeams crashed into the lumber-rooms of the dealers, bringing new life to furnishings not old enough to be antique. The paving-stones were hot; the shop-fronts let down sunblinds; from the road came the smell of basking tar and the fumes of exhausts. And when, having worked till half-past seven, the hour called to chase the gossamers of organised pleasure, there was a new thrill in thrusting the naked bosom of a stiff shirt upon the undarkened summer evening. The days, aided by the Government, had succeeded after all. Pale green feathered the tree-tops in the square. Railings and front doors bore the laconic boards of decorators. Enormous cars bowled through the streets. It was the Season, unanimously acclaimed, with the eternal optimism of the Press, as the most brilliant since the war. Débutantes were photographed; their idiosyncrasies, pet lizards and back hairs, noted. In the provinces, tired huzzifs consumed the details of their waistlines. In London they seemed frousled and uncouth, either speechless or prisoned in the opposite extreme of chatter.

An analysis of those metropolitan activities which provide the newspapers' dessert must infringe the moral copyright of too large a body of publicists to be attempted. To me, successive evenings seemed each a compartment; band of ballroom, gramophone of attic; each a dungeon of stereotyped outlook; one and all attuned to the quality of the buffet. A face, a charm, might salve the wreckage of the night; both probably were otherwise employed. Sometimes the compartments opened into one another, and the party succeeded and became an entertainment. Old ladies found vodka in the lemon squash, young ones men whose knowledge of the fox was hatred. Princesses ate free food that others might honour them with ribbons and stars. The joined of God came together, though the judge had put them asunder. Such occasions were rare. But each reinforced hope eternal of the next. At the brink of all yawned that festal pit, the night-club. Formerly, in those sparse hours snatched from the cold years of education, what ecstasy had filled these temples of illicit bibbing. Now, crouched over the spine of an eighteen-shilling kipper, the glamour had departed. And there was the morning to be faced, punctual and sane. Truly, my sympathies are with the law. Why, then, break it?

At each week-end, each attainment of a garden, the plants had jumped; some were out, others were dead; there was none of the customary imperceptible procession. From home I brought boughs of light green beech, which caught the children's eyes to the taxi roof, and embowered the room from floor to ceiling with the fresh-ness of a summer rain. Later came rhododendron and azalea. So the days lengthened and began to shrink again, till the eve of that incalculable moment, the eclipse.

My imagination had been fired. People whispered of a great black shadow that should come rushing over land and sea, trillions of miles to the minute. It was, they said, a sight that Englishmen had not witnessed for two centuries, and would not for another one. We should tell our grandchildren. Determining to tell mine, I telephoned to the owner of a car. At half-past seven in the evening we left London for the north.

It was ten o'clock when we reached Stamford. Stopping at the hotel for a slice of ham, we encountered an inebriate cleric, who, being a guest and therefore able to obtain it after hours, stood us a whisky each. More, he regaled our meal with tales of his youth; informed us, à propos his prowess at the butts, that he had been a "bogshootah at Caembridge in the year umptah"; and made much of the fact that in *his* parish the public-house was kept by the sacristan's sister, whose respect for the Church permitted her to take liberties with the law—one advantage at least of his profession. He, also, then decided to accompany us to the eclipse; but became disengaged from the dashboard where he was travelling, half-way down the High Street. Cheered by this jovial offspring of a sombre calling, we proceeded to Doncaster. There, in the small hours of the morning, we fell in behind the rest of England.

It was as though the Germans had landed in the South. Through the night, headlight to tail, a continuous queue of cars rushed feverishly towards the Orkneys; cheap cars, sports cars, limousines; bicycles, motor and push; every variety of wheeled automaton, directed by every variety of human being, blazing searchlights, flickering wicks, came tearing in pursuit of this astronomical phenomenon. By the road meals were cooking, bodies sleeping, tents encamped, motors overturned. Haggard policemen waved at corners. In the Yorkshire villages, the cottagers stood at lighted doors; hotel-keepers beckoned; garage proprietors thanked God. Viewed from a hill-top, the stream hummed back into the dark, mile upon mile, like a vast illuminated snake. The first glimmer filtered up from the Antipodes. We had motored from day to day. Then the lights of Richmond twinkled in the void. With the rest of the world, we took to our feet.

Lit by gas flares, we bore with the crowd to the appointed wold. Only Epsom has witnessed such a scene; and that by day. Beshawled matrons sold rasping tea with sandwiches that no mouth could encompass. Boys make jokes. Flappers shrieked. Hawkers bawled the menace of the *corona* and the efficacy of smoked celluloid to preserve the sight. Over the cold, sopping grass we trudged. A girls' school chattered hysterically on a wall; a widow stood apart, tense with the weaving of a mystic spell. It was light. Out of space hailed a friend who had motored with aged mother since tea-time yesterday, and was this moment arrived. It was lighter. We waited. We talked. Then the minute of the eclipse began. Half the hour passed in hopeless commonplace. At length a kind of scenic effect was set in motion. With a series of jerks the visibility changed. The cows galloped hither and thither in troubled herds. The crowd breathed, hallooed, and was silent. The jerks became quicker;

women gulped; parsons expired. Till suddenly a deep blue veil swept over the country and slowly lifted.

Hurrying down, we breakfasted at York and continued, stupid with sleep, to a neighbouring house for lunch. There my companion collapsed. I returned by train.

It was July. Parties had become freakish. Night upon night Mrs. Byrne stitched me into a new variation on the theme of a pirate king. Nor was there any symptom of cessation. None the less, nerves frayed and bank impatient, I decided to exchange the husks of the swine for more solid comfort. The rooms were re-let. I packed my chattels into boxes and trunks, suit-cases, cloths, and crates. And, with nineteen shillings' extra luggage crowded on the taxi, I bade Mrs. Byrne good-bye as she barred the egress of Mademoiselle Péron's pom upon the doorstep. There followed a month of peace at home amid the sweet soporific of phloxes, peace such that no single event has remained to chart it. Till the last days of preparation and purchase were come.

For through all this English year, a varied complement of days but coloured with the thread of a discontent, the sunlit image of a mountain had shone like the star to the wise men. It was arranged, throughout, that I should return; that I should assume, if only temporarily, my own enterprise in a world of arid sequences. In dejection the image had called hope. In presumption, rapture. Now it was at hand. Content stretched illimitable.

Chapter I

THE LEVANT

THE SUN, admitted at eight o'clock, struck the doors of the cupboard opposite with a meaning that sent a tremor through the nerves and a ball of air into the pit of the body. Over the bed the fringes danced response to a quickened heartbeat. For the day of departure had dawned; day, in another sense, of return.

That afternoon I proceeded to London, and arose next morning to shop. The manager of that imperial institution, Fortnum and Mason's, improvised poems on the contents of the saddle-bags. Six pound tins of chocolate, two of chutney, a syphon brooding like a hen over its sparklets in a wooden box, pills, toilet requisites and stationery gradually accrued, together with the ink in a tin case from which these magic words pour. But to devise chemical armour against the insects which await with hideous patience the infrequent tenants of those musty guest-rooms, defied the ingenuity of every pharmacist from W.2 to E.C.4. I am fortunate, however, in possessing some revolting physical attribute, which prevents me, though not impervious to tickling, from being bitten.

At 10.51 on Friday, August 12th, I left Victoria, surrounded by suit-case, kit-bag, saddle-bags, hat-box (harbouring, besides a panama, towels and pillow-cases), syphon-box, and a smug despatch-case that contained a lesser known Edgar Wallace and credentials to every grade of foreign dignitary, from the Customs to the higher clergy. Only as the train started did I discover the loss of the keys to these receptacles. Fortunately the carpenter of the Channel boat was able to provide substitutes for all but the suit-case. Meanwhile, troubles fell away as the pages of perhaps the greatest master of English fiction disclosed the appalling misdemeanours of Harry Alford, 18th Earl of Chelford. These were tempered with the items of the *Central European Observer*, a periodical new to my journalistic appetite, whose title had peeped like a succulent

[29]

strawberry from a cabbage-bed of Liberal weeklies and Conservative quarterlies.

The Channel was rough; but with the undoing of the luggage, the plying of the carpenter with beer, and the delightful spectacle of an arrogant humanity draped about the seats in green and helpless confusion, the passage passed unnoticed. Happiness untrammelled was restored at the sight of the rotund coaches of the *Train Bleu*. For itinerant comfort, the palm must ever remain with this serpentine palace. Curled against the garter-blue velvet of a single compartment, the French afternoon whirred past me in comatose delight. At length came Paris, the clumped ova of the Sacré Cœur standing high and white against copper storm-clouds. Slowly we shunted round the *ceinture* amid those intimacies of slum-life presented by the main line traverse of any great city: hopeless figures gazing in immobile despondency through the importance of the train at their own troubles; children roving the open spaces on tenement balconies; garments sexless, patched, one inevitably Tartan, listless on their lines; healthy plants and flowers rendered pathetic by environment; the whole gamut of man's misery, so it seems to the looker. At the Gare de Lyons the train doubled itself, gathered up its passengers, and started for the south.

Dinner was epic. Sleep cradled in the clouds. Morning broke with Avignon. And the sun rose over a barber's chair at Marseilles.

It remained to open the still fastened suit-case. Up a neighbouring street a locksmith of stupendous proportions and his shrewish wife set about to make a key for it. At the end of an hour their patience was exhausted and the upper catch was loosened from the lid by a drill. Now opened, it needed a strap to close it again, in search of which, to the speechless indignation of the shrewish wife, the locksmith and I left the shop. With the advent of the "zip-bag," rational instruments of cohesion seemed to have become extinct. We hurried from street to street, the locksmith scorning my idea of taking a taxi—he *never* did—and pausing now and again to direct my attention to a bevy of nude nymphs clinging by some process of stomachic suction to the boulders of a municipal fountain. Our quest fulfilled, I piled body and baggage into a diminutive motor, and, telegraphing to herald my arrival in Athens, descended to the docks.

The Levant

The *Patris II* lay silent and empty. I was shown my cabin, then left to explore its dark recesses. It was morning; the stewards were hardly aboard; and it was with difficulty that as much as beer and a sandwich were persuaded from the bar. But as the afternoon advanced, peace dispersed. Crowds on deck waved to crowds on shore, serried against the endless vista of warehouse brick. Two women fiddlers and a male harpist scraped discords to the hot air. Ten yards away, the faded rhythm of "Valencia" quavered from a ragged couple, haunted with memories of last year to which I was returning. A fat woman, the hazel of her bare arms emerging inharmoniously from petunia silk, began to cry. As the tea-gong thrummed we moved from the quay-side, threaded the enormous harbour, rounded the outer mole, turned, and sailed east.

The *Patris II*, a white boat, decorated by Waring & Gillow and sanitated by Shanks, is the pride of her line, which bears the same name as myself. First-class accommodation boasts a ladies' room in dyed sycamore and pink brocade, a lounge in mahogany, a smoking-room, and a bar. The passengers were mainly Greeks, attired in the crest of fashion, and each endowed with sufficient clothes to last them without reappearance through the sixteen odd meals of the voyage. White trouser and mauve plus four flashed above parti-coloured shoe; new tie was child of new shirt; jewels glittered; gowns clung; lips reddened; and all continued to ring the changes in face of the increasing heat; while I lay about, cool and contemptible, in one shirt and a pair of trousers. Music was unceasing. Two pianos and a gramophone ministered to "fox trrott" and "Sharléstoun." While below, in the bows, the incantation of strings impelled the steerage passengers to lose their small-moustached, black-coated selves in a more reserved syncopation. Something inexplicably haphazard pervades Greek dancing: the slowly moving ring of peasants on the sky-line; the inspired solo of an Athenian wine-shop; the applauded *pas-de-trois*, kicking up the dust of a café circle at a wayside station, with a great trans-European express caught up in amazement; many scenes were hailed from oblivion by the sad rhythm. Till the blare of jazz brought back the West.

First-class society resolved into groups. Seated at meals on the captain's right was Madame Venizelos, uttering words of patronage and comfort to such loose infants as toddled within her orbit. Paying court, on one side, was an ancient scion of the Athenian house of Mélas, a retired naval captain, bearing the magnificent appearance of an English duke of the 'forties, white beard and moustachios a-cock; on the other Sir Frederick Halliday, instrument of that permanent obstruction of the Athens streets, "Freddie's Police." The second stratum centred round a number of young men from the Greek colony in Paris, attired at all moments of the day for every variety of sport. At night there was dancing on the upper deck, which resembled a steeply pitched roof covered in treacle. Overhead, the southern moon hung like a huge gold lantern affixed to the mast, casting romance into the souls of the couples and a path of rippling light over the sea beneath.

The meals were served in the temperature of a blast-furnace, stirred to its whitest by the vibrations of electric fans. One and all were impregnated with the taste of candle-flame, the outstanding feature of that terrifying menace to the palate, "Greek food"— though to me familiar as the smell of a cedar wardrobe to a boy home from school. At my side, thoughtfully placed by the head steward, sat a compatriot, who, after thirty-six hours' unbroken silence, opened conversation with the words: "Do you perspaire much?" Himself, he said, he was resigned to a dripping forehead. Some people, on the other hand, exuded even from their palms. Throughout the voyage we kept our table animated with discussion of the absorbent merits of respective underwears.

The ship was timed to arrive at Piræus on Tuesday afternoon. Though we had left Marseilles punctually, it was not until the evening of that day that even the western coast of Greece appeared, a shadowy outline. Gradually the mountain gates of the Gulf of Corinth, giant cliff and weathered obelisk, stood softly from the rippled sea, each face a rosy grey, and a luminous blue lurking in the shadow of each easterly cleft. A white blur on the shore bespoke Patras. A three-masted sailing-boat rode by. Astern, the sun lay poised on an indigo hill, like a fairy tinsel flower on a Christmas-tree. A last glimmer trickled down the waves; then only a glow in the sky remained, deepening the hills and giving life to a star in the green opposite. Themistocles, the barman, jangling gin and vermouth, rooted the emotion in the senses. Darkness grew. The dinner-gong rang and rang again. At length it ceased, leaving its hearers filled with that spice of devil-may-care which only extended defiance of a ship's mealtime can induce.

The last evening on board was devoted to what the most sartorially sporting of the Greek youth termed *jeux de société*. Starting with a species of multi-lingual clumps and a system of forfeits which necessitated the demanding in marriage of the lady opposite, the night was finally launched on an orgy of hide and seek that was only cut short at one in the morning by the advent of the Corinth Canal. Towed by a small tug, the *Patris* slid slowly into this narrow, electric-lit groove. On either side rose walls of cleft rock as high again as the summit of her topmost mast. Great blasts of heat, conserved from the broiling day, fell down upon the passengers. Gradually, however, as we reached the middle and the bridge over which I had formerly motored to my first view of the Ægean, the novelty waned; and, of the crowd of passengers on the bridge, most were asleep before the passage was completed.

Piræus next morning presented the picture of webbed and inextricable confusion that large ports always do. Already, before the sun was up, an ominous shimmer, a kind of film, overlay the brown slopes and white houses enclosing the harbour. I was dressing leisurely when there irrupted Nicola, the unscrupulous henchman of an absent friend, shaved, freshly hatted, and leading by the hand a naval officer of inimitable smartness whom I had observed with awe arrive at the side of the ship in a launch. Having packed and breakfasted, I marched in sedate procession through the assembled passengers, already gnashing at the prospect of an hour's wait for doctor's and passport formalities, and descended by the gangway to the boat. Thus was the humble and meek exalted, to the envy of those who had despised him. The hands of the *douanier* were manacled by a *laissez-passer* from the Greek Minister in London. And in a few minutes we were making fifty miles an hour up the Syngros Avenue, the finest road in the world, as broad as Whitehall from the twin pillars of the temple of Zeus in Athens itself, to the sea two miles away.

The myriad blocks of the town, with the Acropolis perched on its untidy pedestal over to the left and the twisted, wooded spike of Lycabettus dominating its midst, vibrated a mirage of eggshell and white in the quickening heat. We reached the flat destined for my reception. In the absence of the owner, it had apparently become Nicola's perquisite; and a plethora of razor-blades, cake-crumbs, and permanganate of potash testified to his activities as a house-agent. For the moment, a bare-footed old demi-rep was preparing a bedroom, every pouch of her voluminous body quivering with resentment. But, appalled by the garbage of the kitchen, I decided to seek the advice of Lennox Howe, another resident friend. Between the splashings of his bath he offered me two rooms of his own apartment, uttering curdling tales of Nicola's nocturnal parties held in the very teeth of previous lessees. Thither, therefore, to the street of the little female fox the baggage was removed. And Nicola, who had broken, he said, an island holiday to meet me, was free to return to it, richer by 300 drachmas.

Howe's flat, situate in a basement, was cool even in the days that followed—the August tail of the hottest summer within living memory. At first I lay prostrate in the breeze of a fan, unable to move till the evening. At the back, a vine-covered courtyard gave access to numerous other households, whose washing and common idiot enlivened the scene. Lurked also, in its recesses, a tribe of lean and tawny cats, who came speeding day and night through the open doors and windows in horrible battle. Heedless of ground glass, arsenic, and entanglements of electric wires, their objective was the kitchen, where platters, cups, and lids of casseroles were flung remorselessly to the floor in their efforts to disinter the few provisions we could afford. Such was the savagery of their onslaughts that every night we stealthily deposited the more decomposed, and therefore magnetic, of the day's refuse in a near-by street. To these enemies were added gigantic insects, an inch and a half long, and clad in orange armour, that emerged from every crack in the plaster, rendering each doze and bath a period of suspense. Suggestion was immediately telegraphed to Messrs. Duckworth that the public must necessarily be attracted to a work bearing the stirring title:

'TWIXT CAT AND COCKROACH:

A Fight for the Union Jack in an Athenian Slum.

But, in view of the less exciting though more protracted events which have since occurred, the idea was not adopted.

For the greater part of 1926, between visits to Turkey and Byzantine monuments of Greece, Athens had been my home. There were calls to pay, acquaintances to cement, friendships to renew. At His Britannic Majesty's Legation the personnel had changed. But the Minister was on leave, and his mice were at play. Every evening we gathered on the Zappeion, the Hyde Park of the town, where the less exclusive population dines and drinks to the crash of bands among the trees and the harangues of professional orators. As the clock moved into the morning, and tired waiters piled the tin tables for the morrow, still the destiny of man waited our decision. The mainspring of argument was the first secretary, a Scot, struggling between the rationalistic cynicism of his generation and instinctive hope. One of his remarks remains in my mind: "It is only since they ceased to exist that God and Royalty have been genuinely revered."

The pivot of the morning was the English club, where ham sandwiches, gin fizz, and a variety of periodicals, from the *Pink 'Un* up, made it possible to recover from the dripping exhaustion of a hundred yards' walk. Thence, on the first day, I visited General Phrantzes, the master of the President's military household, to thank him, to whom I was indebted, for my reception at Piræus. He was installed in the old palace of King Constantine, a spacious, marble-cooled house, having Empire furniture and upholstered with a wealth of original Victorian chintz. Later I proceeded to the Foreign Office, to find George Mélas, formerly attaché in London. We lunched till five o'clock, drinking crème de menthe in deference to a sentimental past (despite the temperature of 105 degrees in the shade) and probing the ideals of Venizelism.

The grades of Athenian social life offer an intricate field for the anxious climber such as myself. In the eyes of the English colony the Legation is Mecca. But the present anti-social tradition of the British Foreign Office renders this an isolated goal rather than a posting-house to greater vantages. For, while winter brings the ordinary round of parties which form a Season and which even our diplomats cannot avoid, the summer is marked by a shifting of social gravities to the golf-club. It is this wired enclosure on the seashore, some five miles outside the town, that would claim the attention, if there were such a thing, of the *Tatler* foreign correspondent. There he might snap the Turkish Minister, dusky Falstaff, floating playfully among the *Americaines* after his nine-hole round; monocled counts from the Baltic States arriving in large motors; the Hellenic cosmopolis ignoring one another; and finally Phyllis, rock among quicksands, convoying her new princess or millionaire into a basket chair. In her other moments Phyllis dragoons a shedful of destitute refugees into weaving artistic tweeds, which she sells to her enemies. Gossip circulates, swells, grows titanic. From Oslo to Teheran the scandals of the old world are culled and digested, liaisons woven, marriages unpicked, as the sun falls over Ægina and the huge grey ridge of Hymettus assumes that virulent, blinding petunia which poets have so often mistaken for violet.

Stricken with the weight of unrequited hospitality, I decided, conjointly with Howe, to give a *masticha*—a form of entertainment peculiar to the Levant, and lately emulated by the Anglo-Saxon world in its cocktail-parties. Our establishment was set in activity, the unwilling labours of Augustina, the servant, being supplemented by the hands of sympathising friends. Wines from Crete and Samos, *ouzo* the national apéritif, gin, whisky, and vermouth, were ranged upon our tables; the folding doors thrown back; and our smiles extended to the reception of some thirty guests. The triumph of the party was the gin, regarded by Greek débutantes as a dilutant, to the excitation of their good humour. Everyone, having arrived at half-past six, remained till a quarter past nine, though it had been hinted in the invitations that the party would end at eight. What greater compliment could we have hoped?

With regret I saw my short stay in Athens drawing to a close. To me the town is a home—that squared modern town reviled of the cultured itinerant. There may I find refuge from the Anglo-Saxon canon. No need to be a gentleman or a good fellow any more. I become a person among persons, instead of a unit in a thousand teams. I can remain English without showing it. A world of friends displaced one of potential enemies. So it is all over the Levant. But Athens, though I am ill three days in seven, stands by herself, the changeless city of dust and politicians, fortress through millennia of the split straw, ill-watered, uncomfortable, but the city of individuals, where the pall of the West has not descended. Cursorily it seems a western town enough, conceived in the days of Otho, the Wittelsbach king of the thirties, when Queen Amalia sat in her Gothic grange upon a Gothic chair, the court wore national dress, and the Duchesse de Plaisance brought social convenances to the families that had led the Revolution and the merchants who had profited from it. Or the political observer may call it Balkan, riddled with intrigue. Yet what draught of happiness to encounter, straight from England, the exiled Dodecanesian leader Zervos, with the tale of his morning's adventure bubbling on his lips.[1] Here is history woven with the days, not years. But when other races fret and curse, the Greek smiles, soaring on a contempt for the rest of humanity so profound that even the taxi-driver, plainly directed, will take the unhappy passenger elsewhere, convinced that he knows best. And in the narrow Athenian streets, every doorstep and lintel of Pentelic marble, every cornice serrated with the acroteria that have descended uninterrupted from before Christ to the meanest hovel of the twentieth century, where is Europe? Before the sun is up the vendors are about, uttering the "cries of Athens" in the piercing semi-tones of a people who, like the Jews, are of no continent:

"Figs, fresh figs!"

"Pots and casseroles!"

"I buy old boo-oots!"

"Chairs to mend!"

"Lovely lace one drachma an ell!"

"Ice! I-ice!"

Every morning at eight o'clock the ice-man delivered his block. And, as he put it in the chest, still, almost beneath his breath, he wailed the chant, "Ice! I-ice—*Πάγος, ὁ Πάγος*," as though mesmerised with the beauty of his calling.

It is curious fact that, participating as we do in a system of education largely based on Greek literature, no attempt should ever be made to comprehend Greek psychology. The professional pedagogue, ranging himself in opposition to commonsense observation and the whole science of anthropology, affirms, with one snap of his bitten, ink-stained fingers, that the modern Greek is related

[1] He had gone to bathe before breakfast; and had found, on plunging in, the whole bottom of the sea covered with broken glass, placed there by the calculated animosity of the Italian Legation.

neither in language, body, nor mind to the ancient. Further, though the average reader of the classics experience no difficulty in reading a modern Greek newspaper, the pronunciation which he has been taught is one that not only no Greek can understand, but which denies, in addition, that very poetry of sound which Greek literature professes to reveal. Not, however, content with this purposeful obscurantism, the Anglo-Saxon professor, with the nauseating self-sufficiency of his kind, must even blame the native for pronouncing his language in the manner it demands. And while aware, if pretending to culture, that a cursive hand has existed for 1,000 years and more, he still forces his unhappy pupils to conduct their exercises in disjointed and uncouth hieroglyphics, thus wasting five minutes in every ten so devoted. A gentleman writes politely to *The Times*. And he receives in reply the ponderous sneer that the headmaster of Eton does not teach Greek in order that his pupils may enjoy the hypothetical advantage of reading the Greek Press in the vernacular. The humanities, in fact, will be enshrined for ever in as cumbersome and repellent a guise as the ignorance of the sixteenth century could devise. They will. But a scrutiny may be cast in passing, and not without relevance, upon the forces of their kingdom.

It is the privilege of the educated, immersed in contemporary duties, to fortify themselves upon the inspiration of the past. The majority has looked hitherto to that chaos of stone photography and sententious inquest on the nature of being, known as Antiquity. We, however, possessors of the twentieth century, have taken a step outside this limitation of spirit. We march hand in hand with science, the Benjamin of Victorian rationalism and now discarding its parent. The palings of the Mediterranean back garden are down. We have the earth instead. "Am I? Am I not?" ponders the second-hand philosopher, head bowed to the cabbages. "What matter?" comes the answer from astride the globe. "We run now with the soul, with the spirit that has escaped you, cobwebbed old man, paid instrument of enormous stagnation." But whither do we run? As I search, I too need my past. And I find it, now and perhaps for ever, in the Levant after all.

When, in A.D. 330, the year of the foundation of Constantinople, the Greeks took over the lease of the Roman Empire, the Christian religion had at length put them in pursuit of Reality. To analyse the affinity between the Byzantine civilisation that evolved, and our own requires more than this ultimate paragraph. But if, in the following pages, too great a hint of it obtrudes, let it be pardoned in the light of personal inspiration. For, while the classical continues to suckle half the world on a voice of letters and stones, one fragment, one living, articulate community of my chosen past, has been preserved, by a fabulous compound of circumstance, into the present time. Thither I travel, physically by land and water, instead of down the pages of a book or the corridors of a museum. Of the Byzantine Empire, whose life has left its impress on the Levant and whose coins were once current from London to Pekin, alone, impregnable, the Holy Mountain Athos conserves both the form and the spirit. Scholar and archæologist have gone before, will come after. Mine is the picture recorded. If patches are purpled with a tedious enthusiasm, or watered with excessive reference to the past, let the reader recall his own schoolroom and discover the excuse.

Chapter II

TRANSLATION

A IDED by my Greek tutor, I had contrived earlier in the summer to address a letter to the Œcumenical Patriarch of Constantinople, head of the Orthodox Church, to whom I was personally known. Couched in the phraseology of centuries, myself remaining his "Most Divine All-Holiness' faithful child in Christ," it was despatched, for fear of the inquisitorial Turkish post office, by diplomatic bag. The answer had preceded me, by the same means, to our Legation in Athens. It ran as follows:

"Basil, by the grace of God Archbishop of Constantinople, New Rome, and Œcumenical Patriarch.

"To the Most Honourable Mr. Robert Byron, the grace and peace of God and of our Saviour Jesus Christ.

"Having gladly issued, we transmit to your Honour enclosed herewith, our Patriarchal letter of introduction to the Synod of the Holy Mountain, for which you asked in your letter of the 20th ultimo.

"We pray for you all success in your scientific research, and all good fortune from God, from whom also may your years be of the fullest, healthy and joyful.

"1927, *July* 26.

"Of Constantinople.
"*Ardent suppliant of God.*"

Save for the last phrase, written in the Patriarch's own shaky hand, and the two logogriphs in facsimile, the letter was type-written in Greek. Of the same character was that addressed to the Synod.

"Basil, by the grace of God, Archbishop of Constantinople, New Rome, and Œcumenical Patriarch.

"Most holy *Epistatai* and *Antiprosopoi* of the Synod of the Holy Mountain, beloved children in the Lord of our Mediocrity, may the grace and peace of God be to your Holiness.

"He who formerly visited your holy place, the learned Englishman Mr. Robert Byron, anxious there to pursue his researches in Byzantine art, comes thither for this purpose, intending particularly to photograph the frescoes of the leading churches.

"We, therefore, gladly urge, through this our Patriarchal letter of introduction to your Holiness, that by your prompt solicitude there be afforded him everywhere a courteous reception and treatment, and simultaneously every facility for the photographing of the said frescoes, and generally throughout his scientific researches there.

"May also God's grace and his immense mercy be with your Holiness.

"1927, *July* 26.

"Of Constantinople.
"*Ardent suppliant of God.*"

The soul of possibly the most insignificant participant in the British Commonwealth of Nations drank deep of these eulogies. Further, a cloud was lifted. For the Patriarch had sponsored the practical object of the expedition, to which another member of the party was devoting time and money on my assurance of its feasibility. A more forcible recommendation to the secretive and independent monks than this, from the very pivot of Christendom, human insistence could not have obtained. A second letter was furnished by the Greek Foreign Office; and a third, to vouch for my companions, by the Metropolitan of Athens. Such a packet, surely, must substantiate our worth with every shade of monastic opinion.

[41]

To scraps of paper were added more material comforts: cans of an effective flea-deterrent; five dozen quarter-plate films of six pictures each for landscape; the works of Elinor Glyn in the Tauchnitz edition; and a small phrase-book, externally resembling a Bible, to bridge the gaps in my knowledge of the language. Saturday afternoon came. The suit-case, the kit-bag, the saddle-bags, the syphon-box, and the despatch-case were thrust through a window of the Prague express. And we steamed from the Larissa station at half-past six, my cabin-mate being an obese Greek who had brought his dinner in a bag and had already impregnated the entire coach with the fumes of resin-tainted wine. I was glad, therefore, to seek refuge in that of an American named Marten, whom I had been unsuccessfully trying to disabuse of a belief in the infallibility of Periclean art during a short acquaintance of three days.

After dinner—a parody of a meal—the obese Greek, whose liquor had now transformed the atmosphere of the compartment into that of a public operating-theatre, hoisted his rotund form into that lower berth which had cost me a quarter of an hour's rhetoric on the previous day to reserve for myself. I produced my ticket; the usurper was impelled up the carpet steps to a higher; and the attendant, tripping over the saddle-bags in the struggle to change the linen, became so enveloped in the sheets as to resemble a new-risen Lazarus. I slept, thereafter, with increased zest.

Dawn broke over the marshes and downlands of Macedonia, dotted here and there with the red-roofed boxes of refugee villages. Salonica was reached at eight o'clock. The London train was moving out. Marten and I spurred a two-horse cab to the harbour-front, where there stood, waving from the steps of the Mediterranean Palace Hotel, three figures. The long-planned rendezvous held good. Behold, bobbing on a surf of greeting, the party.

Foremost, like some mythical denizen of the seas twisted back in satisfaction upon the prow of an ancient galleon, was David, body akimbo, visage benign—a David of the font, and not to be confused with the pseudonym of a companion on a former adventure; on one side Reinecker, sparse and sallow, stifling a flow of eternal deprecia-tion; on the other, Mark, in plus fours, a waft of artificial heather in an arid land. In company with Marten, struck dumb by the babble of union, we sank to breakfast, while the concierge enquired our fathers' Christian names, and the porter, recognising me from last year, poured his blessings on "Mr. Robert."

Eggs materialised in metal pans. As we ate, Marten studied the party; and, summoning a similar detachment, I followed his cue. First sat Reinecker, separate from us in some degree: hardly English, intellectual, and student of art in that aspect; financially independent; and emanating from a large house of his own in Kensington filled with rare and austerely disposed Oriental potteries. In absolute contrast was David, one of life's familiar pillars from the days of battle at a public school; smoking in the bathing-place, drinking beer among the aspidistras of the adjacent pub; bawling at small boys in boats through a megaphone; rearranging a rather jejune collection of Egyptian figurines in a corner cupboard; and later at Oxford: studious and anthropological, buried in books, or snorting through the town in a motor that looked as if it had been made to transport a Boer family up country; sober always, even in insobriety; now, on the threshold of archæological distinction, unearthing clay fragments at Kish and Constantinople; or at home, flying the walls of the Heythrop country like a sedate heron; cenotaph of competence; monolith of equanimity. Third was Mark, another of school's mercies: of a frivolous nature, tempered with purpose; proud of Scotland, lover of the moors and all things Scottish; naturalist by descent, artist by choice; solitary by temperament; yet beacon-light of parties; careful of appearance; practising economy without stinginess; and, but for a visit to Spitzbergen and a month in the *château* of a French marquise, where there were caterpillars in the salad, untravelled. To him, after four days in the Orient express, the Near East came as a surprise.

Breakfast over, Mark and I proceeded to St. Sophia, the finest of the town's churches, to see the eighth-century mosaic of the chocolate-robed Virgin unattended in her vault of dull glowing gold. But we were not alone. For a vast concourse had gathered in homage to those who had fallen in the wars that Greece fought between 1912 and 1922. A service was in progress, and we were ushered, unwitting, to a railed and carpeted enclosure. There we remained for an hour in a poultice of humanity, while the Metropolitan, crowned and enthroned, led the service, and a civilian dignitary spoke interminable commemoration.

Salonica, despised of soldiers, is as curious a town as Europe can show. Achieving immortality with St. Paul, the outstanding event in its subsequent history was the immigration of an enormous band of Jews, driven from Spain with the Moriscoes at the beginning of the seventeenth century, to the ruin of that country's industries. And still the Jewish women, their red pig-tails knotted in and out of coloured ribbons, trail their full green skirts up the steps of trams and buses; still they utter imprecations which sound to the modern Spaniard as Shakespeare's jauntier passages to us: "Marry come up, sir conductor, thinkee this be a rightful recompense from two drachmas? 'D's teeth, 'd's wounds, sirrah! am I a pullet for the plucking?" etc. Still every variety of Hebrew jostles in the modern streets, from the Whitechapel vendor, with his bowler hat ingeniously shaped to accentuate the nasal curve, to the Elizabethan rabbi, fur-hatted, and gowned in a purple caftan surmounted by a high fur collar. Since the recovery of the town by the Greeks in 1912, it has regained something of that commercial importance which blazed the fame of its fair throughout the mediæval world. At the time of our visit preparations were being made to revive this institution. The municipality was engaged in raising the harbour-front. And, needless to say, the work reached the portico of the hotel simultaneously with ourselves. An unceasing train of carts jangled beneath our windows, crashes, oaths, and the ring of shovels intermingling. A strong wind was blowing. And throughout the hotel every vacant inch was coated with desiccated refuse. Mark, snoozing at midday through the noise of a stage battle, wished himself in the Highlands.

There arrived in the afternoon a resident acquaintance to visit us. It was to him, last year, that I had been indebted for my single venture into Salonica society. Though in no way connected with the Far East, he had lately engineered himself into the post of Japanese Consul; and, as he drove us out to inspect the British war-cemetery, the Rising Sun floated over the motor like a pennant at a tourney. Later we attended a dinner-party on the roof of the hotel, where a Tzigane band, passionately conducted by an ancient Russian, was playing jazz.

[44]

"Are there," I asked in a fevered impetus of conversation, "still many Jews here?"

"Yes," was the reply, "there's me—also Count Morpourgo across the table."

The evening, thus happily inaugurated, progressed upon the safer topic of American motors. Till at length a junction was effected between our table and that of the Governor of Macedonia, Monsieur Bouboulis. His Excellency was accompanied by two ladies: his sister-in-law, Madame Kotzias, who, having spent her most impressionable years at a girls' school near Woking, detested Britain to the point of inarticulacy; and an Alexandrine lady on whose fingers diamonds proportionate to her figure, were balancing like pigeons' eggs. The latter and I took the floor, or, rather, the plumbing, hoisting one another alternately from the gullies and ravines with which the roof was drained. At midnight we removed to the country, where we trotted over tiles; and then still farther inland; for the Governor made a habit of never retiring till 6 a.m. Next day we drank tea with Madame Kotzias at the Residency, where George I had been staying when he was murdered. This year, we learnt, she was divorced.

Roused early next day by the din of road-mending, I went creeping amid the tattered booths of the refugee town up the hill in search of antiques. It was here that I had noted, skew-eyed on a plush couch, a small painting of the Virgin, with jewels set in her celestial lights, that has since, after reproduction in *The Burlington Magazine*, passed into the possession of a curator of the Victoria and Albert Museum at a profit of 566.6 per cent. For the moment there seemed little to be found. Set about by an incoherent Levantine who announced his name as Haig, I penetrated in vain the kitchen of the Turk and the back-bedroom of the Armenian. Later in the morning, however, David, under the same guidance, purchased with infinite secrecy and at great cost a platter of almost prehistoric majolica, together with what appeared to comprise the only entire pieces of Byzantine pottery in existence. Having unearthed numerous fragments of this ware in the Hippodrome at Constantinople, David purposes to become its sole authority. Hence a pæan of triumph on his return to the hotel. Meanwhile, after having the greater part of my hair removed, I on my side had acquired a pair of sandals, a store of cigarettes, and a tin-opener. After lunch, and a comatose afternoon, we announced the moment of departure.

Then followed uproar with the concierge.

"Do you know," said he to David, incensed at the pile of news-papered crocks that had been dumped in the hall, "that I have known your antique agent for two years, and that he is a swindler?"

"Do you know," replied David to him, "that I have known you for two days, and dislike you intensely?"

"Thank you."

Eventually the luggage was piled formidably upon a hand-cart, and the last stage of a protracted journey was in train. Overhead the sky was black, the ships at the road's edge dancing up and down in a chill wind, and large drops of water deliberately and impertinently falling on our panamas. Far down the quay the famous White Tower stood out, the colour of its name against an inky firmament; while over it, from the sullen horizon of water to the raisin-coloured inland peaks, glittered the arch of a rainbow. Ultimately all was safe on board. And at half-past seven, in a stormy glow that cast searchlights of miraculous colour on the encircling hills and the now enormous town surmounted by its castle, we sailed out of the harbour, seated on smutty coils of ropes in the stern of the *Nausica*.

The steward, anxious for the comfort of his only first-class passengers, enumerated the intended dinner, imitating the wing-movements of a chicken in explanation of the word κοττόπυλο. He also pointed with pride to a peregrine falcon which he had shot in Cephalonia and which now stood, wings outspread, upon a lichen-covered loglet, the glory of the central table.

And so, after a year's plan and counter-plan, the last hours were reached. That we were still on earth was recalled by the sudden stoppage of the *Nausica's* engines, leaving us in mid-sea for an hour at the mercy of the fortunately inactive elements. Over a last bottle of beer we said good-bye to this last tossing straw of our world. We slept. Till, when barely light, there appeared, framed in the cold circle of the porthole, the dark outline of a long finger of land, twisted by imperceptibly darker shadows into deep ravines and curving bays. At its end, cut in terraced silhouette against the frigid gleams of the lower sky, reared a vast steeple from the livid grey sea. As the sun, risen a fiery ball above the rim of the world, warmed the cold light, silhouette gave place to hazy pink. Here and there twinkled the white blur of a monastery down at the water's edge or perched up among the woods. The Holy Mountain! And ourselves the pilgrims.

As the *Nausica* drew in, the peak disappeared behind the towering semi-circle of a small bay. At its inmost point, dwarfed almost to invisibility by the tree-covered surroundings, stood a few buildings. This was the port of Daphni. Two boats appeared, in one of which was a Greek police officer, who demanded our passports. He made some hint that these must precede us to Caryes, the capital of the Mountain, while we waited here below. But the letter from the Foreign Office silenced him. His whole obtrusion was an innovation, the price of the Greek Government's having ratified the autonomy of the community and its constitution, the oldest in Europe. Finally, with a wrench which was, to me who knew, more vivid than to the others, we descended the gangway with our possessions and rowed to land. Last year a welcome had awaited us in the person of Father Boniface, deputed keeper of the port by his monastery of Xeropotamou, to which it belongs. Now, however, he had been recalled.

Having disposed of the policeman, it remained to transport ourselves immediately to Caryes, the village-metropolis, situated two and a half hours' ride away over the other side of the ridge: that ridge, forty miles long, which is the northernmost of the three fingers that jut like a mutilated hand from the north-east angle of the Grecian coastline. For it was there that we must present the Government of the Mountain with our letters of recommendation, to receive in return another, without which no monastery could admit us to its hospitality. Tethered beneath a tree we espied two mules, of which their owner, an Albanian in a plate-shaped straw hat, informed us that we could only have one. It transpired, after infinite argument, that there was, in fact, no actual obstacle to our having both. They were led to the miniature wooden warehouse at the end of the jetty, and loaded.

Mark and I went on ahead; he hunter of the minutiæ of creation, pouncing upon strange butterflies, leaf insects, and dung-flies; I, gazing at the olive-leaves glinting like sheaves of silver spear-heads against the blue of the sea beneath. The sun shone powerfully as the large white cobbles of which all the Athonite paths are made wound up through the olive-groves and woods of maples and Spanish chestnuts; over shady bridges spanning non-existent rivers; past stray shrines and marble basins catching ice-cold mountain streams for the delectation of the traveller; one and all emblazoned with a cross or the legend of a saint. After three-quarters of an hour's climb we halted, panting, at the pillared entrance of Xeropotamou, a large monastery to which as yet we possessed no right of entry. But the porter, a twinkling old monk, produced, in answer to our request for water, *ouzo* in addition.

"Ah! delicious!" I said. "Much better than at Salonica."

"Tchah! the *ouzo* of Salonica is lemonade."

Reluctantly we continued; and, reaching the top of the ridge, 3,000 feet up, amid pines and firs, caught our first view of Caryes on a gardened plateau beneath, with the sea in the distance. As we entered the narrow streets half an hour later, an air of activity, almost gaiety, seemed to prevail. Shops were open; tiny restaurants crowded with black figures, gowned and bearded, munching at wooden tables. In the streets, multi-coloured blankets, fruit and vegetables, saddle-cloths and saddle-bags, were focusing knots of haggling monks arrayed in every variety of surtout, from the ragged garment of the stage beggar to the *soigné* silken gowns of stately old men, owners of authority in their monasteries or the capital. It was market day. And the town presented a far different appearance from its ordinary. Formerly, scarcely the sun itself might shine, as we found ourselves within the twisting, vine-hung thoroughfares, where no wheel had ever bowled, and here and there a sombre trailing figure turned wide eyes to the clatter of hoofs. Even now no women gossiped, no children played, nor animals disported. Only perhaps a cat stole by, or far off, a hen, muffled in shamed seclusion, heralded an egg.

The luggage was unloosed upon the floor of the single inn, where several parties of monks, in from the country, sat at their midday meal. While Mark and Reinecker inspected the stew-pans of the kitchen, containing meat unappetising enough to gladden a militant vegetarian, David and I walked next door to make the acquaintance of the civil governor, Monsieur Lelis, to whom General Phrantzes

had given me a letter. We found a small, kindly man, an official of
the Foreign Office, who three months ago had been diverted from
a special mission to Paris to fill this lonely post. He seemed to
enjoy conversation, and we discoursed upon the health of the outside world, the fate of Sacco and Vanzetti, and the waning dominion
of the Charleston. For the first month, he told us, he had enjoyed
his stay here. Thenceforth the lack of rational converse had affected
his nerves. He had lately taken a trip to the summit, which he had
failed to reach, owing to a buzzing in the ears and a bleeding at the
nose, due to the height. He then invented for our apprehension, a
legend of wholly imaginary precipices, representing the last 1,000
feet as a dangerous glissade on which one false step meant death.
As it is impossible to roll a yard without being hooked up on the
jagged, vertical strata, his tale left me unmoved.

We returned to lunch, which was helped, after all, by yet one
more bottle of beer. And then lay down to sleep, spreading our
overcoats upon a balcony festooned with orange-trumpeted creepers
and overlooking a panorama of olives and cypresses. The sea was
visible below, and in the distance the summit, remote grey white
above the highest point of the ridge, twirling and casting loose every
vagrant cloud in an elsewhere cloudless sky. As we dozed, a cat,
bearing in its mouth a mangled entrail with a tenderness eloquent of
a determination to save it for another time, trailed over our feet
with a malformed kitten at her heels. At four we rose, extracted
some letters from the post office, where the star and crescent of the
Ottoman Empire still blazoned every pigeon-hole, and betook ourselves to the police station. Primarily mystified by the double
surnames of Mark and David, the officer almost collapsed under
the strain of discovering our professions. I informed him that we
had none. This is my usual policy, as often it is inadvisable to admit
the wielding of a pen. The occasion reminded me of an incident at
Smyrna, when for half an hour I blocked a ship-load of impatient
passengers by refusing, as there, of all places, was necessary, to
divulge my share in the world's work. The calm of the Turk rivalling
my own, matters were brought to a complete *impasse*. A solution
was only found by an exasperated Frenchman's rushing forward and
exclaiming in a voice of loathing and contempt, "*Rentier? Vous êtes
rentier?*" To which I admitted that my parents enjoyed an exiguous

income sufficient to keep the wolf from the door and a servant to open it.

A similar situation threatened to arise at present.

"We have no professions," I said, "but write down what you like."

"What?"

"Although we have no professions, you can, if you wish, invent some."

"?"

"Electricians, painters, taxi-drivers, soldiers, bank clerks, clergymen, café-keepers, archæologists——" I suggested.

"Are you *all* archæologists?"

"ALL."

And he wrote:

"Archæologist.

"Archæologist.

"Archæologist.

"Archæologist."

With a straightening of ties we approached the Synod house. The moment for me, who was responsible to David for the success of a prospective publication, was one of crisis. The seat of government was contained in a broad-eaved house of two stories, washed raspberry colour, and set, amid beds of hollyhocks and harpaliums, between two courtyards. These were connected by a mews-entrance passage that ran underneath it. Mounting a flight of wooden stairs, I handed our letters to a member of the Synod guard, who was attired in the old national dress of white tights and pleated linen kilt, embroidered jacket, flowing linen sleeves, and a red cap adorned with the silver eagles of the Orthodox Church and the letters A.O., for "Ἅγιον" Ὄρος, which means Holy Mountain. After a short interval, we were ushered into an oblong room. Opposite the door, against a wall pierced by three windows, sat the black-gowned secretary at his desk. And near him, on a brown wooden throne, the *Protepistates*, the elected head of the entire community, who this year was Father Daniel of Iviron, dignified, silent, and bespectacled. Broad Turkish divans ran round the walls. The majority of the Synod, which, containing a representative from each of the ruling monasteries, numbers twenty, was absent, the places of some being marked by piles of letters. Coffee and Turkish delight were handed us as we sat, myself maintaining a desultory conversation with a monk whom I remembered, but could not name. At length, fired with an inspiration, I enquired if they had seen the portfolio of Professor Millet. No, they complained, though for months at a time he had enjoyed their hospitality, no copy had reached them. He was waiting, I suggested, till the whole series was completed.

"I will fetch it."

"We will go together," said Daniel the *Protepistates*, rising. Taking his silver-topped wand in his hand, and followed by a tiny Rip van Winkle of the Synod Guard, he led the way. As we processed through the streets, monks squatting at their wares sprang to their feet. Returning with the heavy tome, we handed it round, while the secretary produced the synodical letter which he had inscribed on paper printed with the eagles of the Byzantine emperors. I humbly begged that our desire to photograph the frescoes, seconded by his All-Holiness the Patriarch, might be mentioned for the persuasion of the individual monasteries. It was, he said, already. The four members of the *Epistasia*, the executive committee of the parliament, drew from inner wallets the four quarters of the seal of the community, struck anew in 1912, when, after 482 years' Mahommedan suzerainty, the Mountain had returned once more to the Christian governance. The secretary joined the pieces to a stem, stamped the letter, powdered the impression with gold, and folded the whole in an envelope, which he handed us. With bows and varied thanks, we filed out.

The Albanian muleteer, according to instructions, was waiting outside, and had been waiting, moreover, for an hour. In the teeth of his imprecations, we proceeded again to the Governor. And he also, with that palsied deliberation which characterises the clerical operations of the Levant, wrote us a circular letter. Meanwhile the muleteer was shouting outside: the luggage was loaded. Pausing yet again to buy two gaily striped saddle-bags in which to convey the syphon and numerous loose books, we at last descended from the town by a path leading in the direction of the sea. Five minutes brought us to an old balconied house which was surrounded by a fenced garden, and approached beneath a spreading mallow-tree covered with the flowers of its familiar field counter-part.

This was the Lavra *konak*; the Lavra being a monastery, and a *konak* signifying, in Athonite parlance, the residence of a monastery's representative on the governing body. In this case it was Father Evlogios, who had shown me much kindness last year. I had written to him from Athens announcing our arrival, for which he had prepared both the Governor and the Synod, besides despatching the two mules to meet us at Daphni. *Ouzo*, coffee, cold water, and *glyco*—that inestimable preserve of cherry, grape, or orange, too rare to deserve the appellation jam—were handed on a tray, to the confusion of the others, who were unacquainted with the attendant ritual. But our host's congratulations on my acquisition of Greek were shattered by the irruption of the muleteer, whose patience was now beyond control. Regretfully we departed, promising to meet again. Mounting each a mule, we rode for two hours downhill among the trees and shrubs. Above us the summit, free of the clouds that had encircled it, stood into the sky, a pinnacle of naked fiery rock deepening from rosy gold to red-hot purple as the evening drew on. Eventually the monastery of Iviron appeared beneath us at the edge of the sea, backing its balconied faces of yellow and chocolate against the wooded cleft down which we came.

As we arrived, darkness fell suddenly. In the confusion of unloading, the muleteer inadvertently handed David seventy-five drachmas too much change, which the excess of his charges enabled us to keep without scruple. I, meanwhile, had been called inside by the advent of a white-bearded *epitropos* in rustling silken crêpe and tall cylindrical hat—worn at every appearance in public by every monk above his knotted, uncut hair—to whom I made conversation on a window-settee. The room in which we found ourselves, lit by a hanging lamp in the centre, was hung with weird, cracked portraits of foreign royalties, mostly the later Russians, but including, besides one in peruke and tricorn, the Kaiser and Edward VII. At length, in the middle of a story about an English aeroplane that had landed during the war on the park-like strip of grass between the monastery and the sea, dinner was announced. The food was good, and the wine, the guestmaster warned us, would go to our heads if we drank too much. Mark made signs to him that it had already gone to mine: with the result that, for the rest of the evening, my glass was only partially filled. Retiring to our bedroom, we settled ourselves with pillows and sheets upon two iron bedsteads and a range of spacious divans. The day had been tiring. Conscious all over, of a strangeness, we fell into our first sleep on the Holy Mountain, to the twittering of frogs and the flutters of singed and drunken moths.

Chapter III

GOVERNMENT IN THE FOURTH DIMENSION

THE EARTH is behind us. Prostrate in the guest-room at Iviron, we lie upon another plane of existence, back in that mysterious, immaterial *regnum* from which the mind cast loose with the Renaissance. It is a world peopled in physical truth with the bodies ascribed to El Greco's astigmatism; where the ghosts of the departed flit wireless-like among the woods and the marble troughs—sun-spotted, happy ghosts perching on cruciform signposts nailed to trees, shooting out of caves, sentinels on gaunt crags, contained even, in the very aged, within human bounds. How comes it that this fragment of a life which once held sway over all the Greek seaboard endures unaltered since its foundation, the most remarkable testimony to Europe's evolution on the face of a Europeanised globe? Who will say but that this talk of a theocracy at our very door is not some antiquarian figment, sprung from a technicality of word rather than fact? Its continuity must be demonstrable, together with a proof of independent administration in the present. Nor will the sceptic, whose thesis is the exaltation of living, be content with either, till accompanied by a showing of those mystic emotions which call flesh and sense to a profession of their own denial. At the hazard of tedium, let the eye inspect this interim. The rest is the stucco of a day. Here is the concrete.[1]

In the earliest Christian times, the Mountain was already, for appearance and security, the chosen of hermits. Legends survive of this period, beginning with that of the visit of the Virgin herself. History opens in the ninth century with the arrival of Peter the Athonite, a substantial person who after fifty years' battling with wild beasts, both of mind and forest, was discovered by a hunter. He was followed by St. Euthymius of Salonica, who, having for-

[1] There is no up-to-date bibliography of Athos. The most accessible is that of F. W. Hasluck's *Athos and Its Monasteries*, compiled in 1912.

[54]

sworn the world at the age of eighteen (leaving a daughter, Euphrosyne, to carry on his family), at first moved on all fours and ate grass. He then retired to a cell, whence his companion was driven out by the vermin, but which he only exchanged after three years for a position on a pillar. Soon after, a friend of his named John Colobos founded a monastery at the northern and mainland end of the peninsula, receiving a chrysobul from the Emperor Basil I the Macedonian, which appointed him and his foundation protectors of the Mountain and its hermits, as against the inhabitants of the neighbouring town of Erissos. This document is known to have been dated prior to the year 881. A portion of it was formerly in the library of the monastery of Philotheou, whence it is thought to have been transported to Leningrad. Its importance lies in its constituting the first official recognition of the holy men's title to the proprietorship of land.

But dispute ensued on this very ground: Which holy men? The hermits or the monks? And in so doing symbolised the basic issue of the ecclesiastical problems of the time. Hitherto the profession of monasticism had demanded simply individual retirement and the practice of such ascetics as the spirit moved. The common rule of life initiated by St. Basil in the fourth century, while strengthened in western Europe by the ordinances of St. Benedict, had fallen into desuetude in the East before the Hellenic instinct for private self-assertion. But in the eighth century Theodore of Studium had attempted the reintroduction of a coherent form of communal living among the numerous bodies of hermits within the jurisdiction of the Orthodox Patriarchates. Between the new monastery of Colobou and the solitaries of the southern end and actual peak a controversy now arose that symbolised this deeper issue in the question of the actual proprietorship of the land. It was settled in favour of the hermits in a second chrysobul granted by the Emperor Leo VI the Philosopher, who reigned between 886 and 911. That they were already possessed of a central organisation at this time is proved by the title of First Quietist, attached to the representative whom they sent to Constantinople to conduct their appeal. Henceforth this head of the community was known as the *Protos*, or First. From him, by bureaucratic descent, springs the *Protepistates* of to-day. Thus, though there were yet on the Mountain proper no actual monasteries, the middle of the tenth century found it under the legal proprietorship of holy men, and administered by a central authority resident in Caryes. There, in the Synod's archives, the documents of the Byzantine emperors which were to give meaning to Article 62 of the Treaty of Berlin in 1878, are still preserved.

But the system of ordered monasticism, as visualised by Theodore, was to triumph in the end. The piety of the brothers Leo and Nicephorus Phocas, prominent functionaries at the Byzantine Court, had been attracted to the Mountain, and the project conceived that their boyhood's friend, Athanasius, should found a community at their expense. In 961, Leo visited Caryes, and financially assisted the enlargement of the Protaton, which was then, as now, the central church of the Athonite community. Two years later Nicephorus became Emperor. Athanasius, having calculated to receive him as a brother, was indignant. But he was persuaded to undertake the foundation which the Emperor not only endowed, but rendered independent of all but imperial control. Thus the seed of autonomous administration was legalised. Following the analogy of the previous century, a rivalry immediately arose between the Lavra—as Athanasius' foundation was called—and the scattered inhabitants of the rest of the Mountain. This was carried in 972 to Constantinople, where the Emperor John I Tzimisces, murderer and successor of Nicephorus, handed it to the judgment of a Studite monk. In accordance with the Studite ideals laid down by Theodore, the position of the monastery was confirmed, its emoluments being increased by the new Emperor. Simultaneously, the powers of the *Protos*, and the assembly of hermit-leaders that was already holding regular sessions in Caryes, were defined. But with this reinforcement of the Lavra the predominance of loosely scattered groups of cells was doomed. Before Athanasius' death, at the close of the first millennium after Christ—due to the collapse of a dome which he was helping to build—three more monasteries proper were in being. Of the twenty that survive to-day, eight followed in the eleventh century; two in the twelfth; one in the thirteenth; four in the fourteenth; and one in the sixteenth. By the typicon of the Emperor Constantine IX Monomach, issued in 1046, the cells of the hermits were finally subordinated to their present state of dependence on the larger foundations. Hence the term "Ruling Monasteries."

From now till the sack of Constantinople by the Latin Crusaders in 1204, the history of the Mountain is illumined by a single incident. Towards the end of the eleventh century, Vlach shepherds, who had obtained leave to supply the monks with milk and wool, were discovered to be purveying their wives and daughters in addition. Uproar followed; the Patriarch's signature was forged to restore discipline; and half the monks deserted their monasteries in company with the shepherds. The stricter fathers then demanded the suppression of the beardless, as well as the female element. And, to preserve the Mountain from total desertion, the Emperor Alexius I Comnenus, asking if he were Herod that he should murder children, stifled the enthusiasm of the reformers by threatening to cut off their noses. Then came the sudden tragedy that wrecked the complicated and magnificent civilisation of the mediæval Greeks. In the division of their empire that followed the Latin conquest, Athos fell, with the "Kingdom of Thessalonica," to Boniface of Montferrat. It was placed by Benedict, papal legate to that transient conceit, within the jurisdiction of the Bishop of Sebaste, who built himself a castle on the promontory as a base for systematic plunder. But, in deference to the representations of the Latin Emperor, Henry of Flanders, Pope Innocent III restored the ancient status of dependence on none but the head of the state, accompanying his edict by sententious comments on the Mountain's arid soil but spiritual fecundity. Such the position remained till the recapture of Constantinople by the Greeks in 1261.

The following century witnessed the partial subversion of the old rule of Athanasius enjoining upon the monks a community of property, in favour of one under which private wealth was permitted. The difference has since become known as that between the cenobitic and the idiorhythmic way of life. The chief implication of the latter is that the occupants of a monastery, being some rich and others poor, necessarily lose their footing of equality. But that wealth must necessarily offer more scope for useful activity to the intelligent is in this context often forgotten. To contemporaries, in whose eyes monachism was not designed for useful activity, the idiorhythmic system gave offence. In 1394 a strong protest was despatched from the Patriarch Nicias against the possession of property, the maintenance of private kitchens, and protracted absences in the outer world. At this time also were regulated the contributions due from each monastery to the upkeep of the machinery of government in Caryes and the central church of the Protaton. Ten years later, however, the new mode of life was finally and categorically condoned in a chrysobul of the Emperor Manuel II Palæologus, that enterprising monarch who travelled in the West and spent Christmas at Eltham with Henry IV. In return for this concession, the Emperor rewarded himself with the revenues of the monastic estates. In 1430 the Turks took Salonica; and the monks, by hurried submission, were able to retain their autonomy intact. Eight years later, representatives of the Mountain were found at the Council of Florence in active opposition to the proposed union of the Greek and Latin Churches. Constantinople fell in 1453. And, with the extinction of the Byzantine autocrats, Athos was placed, like the rest of their unhappy world, within the temporal jurisdiction of the Œcumenical Patriarch, who was, in his turn, responsible to the Sultan for the government of all the Greeks within the Ottoman dominions. Thus the community remained, its administrative independence unimpaired, till November 2nd, 1912.

From the fifteenth to the end of the eighteenth century there is little to record. In 1574 the Patriarch Jeremiah sought to remedy the financial plight of the monasteries by calling upon the Constantinople Trade Union of Furriers to audit their accounts. It was now that the number of ruling houses was fixed at twenty. In the seventeenth century a Turkish governor, corresponding to a French *sous-préfet*, made appearance as adviser to the monastic authorities. In the eighteenth came the great revival of wealth and letters throughout the Greek world that led to the Revolution. This was preceded in 1783 by the typicon of the Patriarch Gabriel, defining the powers of the *Epistasia*, the executive committee of four, as opposed to those of the whole deliberative assembly. But the nineteenth century had not entered its second quarter before the Mountain was subjected to ruinous penalties by the abortive rising of 2,000 monks in sympathy with their compatriots on the mainland. Legend has it that a cross of light appeared on the summit, bearing, as to Constantine 1,500 years before, the words: "ἐν τούτῳ νίκα—by this conquer." A crushing indemnity was extracted by the Turks; a garrison of 3,000 soldiers quartered in the monasteries; and the community reduced to such straits that, of the seven thousands of monks formerly in residence, only one remained. Gradually, however, the financial position improved. Though it received a blow in 1861, when the Rumanian Government, at their wits' end to infuse life into a still-born state, confiscated lands of the Athonite monasteries worth £120,000 a year. This action, though legally indefensible, did not lack the precedent of the Greek Government itself, which had pursued a similar policy under Count Capo d'Istria in 1834. But on that occasion so much of Greece was still Turkey that the Athonite monasteries suffered comparatively little, their estates being mainly in the north. Then, in 1878, the Holy Mountain entered on a new stage of its history, when, for the first time, its autonomy was recognised by international treaty at Berlin.

The latter vicissitudes of Athos, and their ultimate and satisfactory conclusion, have been so interwoven with the Mediterranean policy of Tsarist Russia that their tale is reserved for Chapter XI. After the Great War, which closed for Greece in catastrophe, the Hellenic Government, faced with the problem of supporting a million and a half destitute refugees, confiscated all the landed property in the kingdom. With the rest of the proprietors, among them British subjects, the Athonite monasteries suffered. But the extent of the measure hangs in the balance, reasonable compensation having been promised by the Greek Government in 1926—though not yet paid. At length in 1927, the constitution of the Mountain, based on nine centuries of precedent, obtained the ratification of the Hellenic sovereignty. It is possible, therefore, to give an account of the Mountain's administrative machinery which bears the stamp of finality.

The rule, or, more exactly, precept, of life enjoined by Athanasius in 969, and adopted by subsequent foundations on the Mountain, was not original, sixteen of the clauses being identical with those laid down by Theodore, Abbot of St. John of Studium in Constantinople in the first years of the ninth century. Theodore's ideal was tinged with the Latin concept of usefulness. Under his ægis, it is thought, was systematised the cursive handwriting which supplanted uncial, and which had, proportionately as far-reaching an effect on the distribution of books as the invention of printing. Hence it was that the practice of calligraphy and painting was early pressed upon the Athonite monks. The prohibition of slaves, of private property, of grand clothes and elaborate food, of cafés and houses of ill-fame, was common to both. The two latter indicate the enormous size to which, even within the crowded precincts of the capital, the monastic foundations of the time were apt to swell. In the paragraphs dealing with slavery, there is nothing of humanitarianism. A superfluity of domestics was deprecated solely as a luxury.

It is interesting, also, to note that as early as Theodore there was prescribed that absolute exclusion of the female sex which, surviving in the twentieth century, has afforded the Mountain its greatest publicity. "Have no animal," Theodore wrote, and Athanasius echoed in less explanatory terms, "of the female sex in domestic use, seeing that you have renounced the female sex altogether, whether in house or field, since none of the holy fathers had such, nor does nature require them. Be not driven by horses or mules without necessity, but go on foot, in imitation of Christ. But, if there is need, let your beasts be the foal of an ass." Hard words—to deliver the fathers and their friends to the mule for ever. But Theodore scarcely foresaw, nor Athanasius after him, that they would be applied with the preposterous inconsequence of later Byzantine Christianity, to a fertile 120 square miles. By the middle of the eleventh century complaint was already launched against the herds of cows on the Mountain; on the ground, mainly, that Caryes threatened to develop into a commercial centre. Regulations were therefore established for a weekly market only.

Tradition assigns the female rule to another source. The Empress Pulcheria, it is said, having founded the monastery of Vatopedi, was summarily bidden remove herself by the Virgin, jealous, after the fleshly manner of Greek deities, of this encroachment on her preserve. It is on record that Stephen Dushan, King of Serbia, brought his Queen on a pilgrimage to Athos. But the rule was scrupulously observed by the Turkish governor of later days, whose harem remained forlornly in Constantinople till the two years' tenure of his office were over. It remained for an Englishwoman, Lady Stratford de Redcliffe, to achieve the first historical infringement. As an official of the Constantinople embassy wrote later, she ought to have known better.

With the coming of the idiorhythmic system and private property, the path to God of unadulterated mysticism was complicated by works and ethics. And it was the idiorhythmic monasteries that contributed to the intellectual revival—the founding of a school and printing-press—which marked the eighteenth century. To-day, from the point of view of cleanliness and order they are often the better managed, and have been, when their resources allowed, the most active in works of assistance. Iviron, beneath whose roof we lay, maintained until the end of the nineteenth century, when it ceased to be necessary, a hospital for lepers. And it was this monastery which, in 1880, presented the Patriarchate with the large and valuable site of the enormous red-brick Greek school which dominates the more crowded quarter of Stamboul. To the building itself another Athonite monastery, Vatopedi, contributed £3,636.

In the fourteenth century the change was marked by the abolition of the office of abbot in favour of two trustees, known as *epitropoi*, aided by a council of elders. Even in those monasteries that retained the older cenobitic rule, the power of the abbot was now subject to limitation at the hands of a similar body; although, in matters spiritual, it was emphasised. These conditions prevail to-day. The tenure of the abbot is for life. His advisory council is chosen in some monasteries by himself, in others by the fathers in corporate session. In the idiorhythmic houses, the monks are divided into two grades, and it is only from the higher that the elders are elected. These frequently maintain in their cells pupils whom they train to step into their shoes when they die. But in each monastery the system varies.

The outstanding distinction, however, between the cenobitic and the idiorhythmic lies in their methods of finance. In the former, before the confiscations, it was the custom to send monks as overseers, who might ensure the arrival of the revenues from the various farms and plantations owned by the monastery on the mainland. These then found their way into the common purse. In the latter the estates were put up to yearly auction among the elders; and the highest bidders, having paid a lump sum into the treasury, could often, with the aid of cheap Albanian labour, make for themselves 100 per cent profit on their outlay. The younger monks of these foundations and those of the lower grade, receive a small payment for their services toward the upkeep of the monastery, and are given wine, two pounds of bread weekly, and occasional vegetables. Clothes, books, and extra food they must buy themselves. It is plain that the system, though pleasant in prosperity, is not adapted to communal economy. And in times of stress it has always happened that many of the idiorhythmic monasteries have been obliged to reconstitute themselves cenobitic. The position is exemplified at present by the monastery of Stavronikita, which, although it formally announced in 1926 that it intended to close down, contains instead of one kitchen, fifteen, and as many comparatively wealthy elders.

The generosity of the Greek Government, however, allows the Athonite community privileges which to some extent ameliorate a financial condition by no means desperate, though unsatisfactory in comparison with the prosperity of the years before the war. The monasteries are exempt from death-duties. And all exports and imports are free of duty. The latter alone are calculated at seventy million drachmas annually—approximately £194,500—the customary taxes on which must necessarily deprive the budget of a country containing scarcely seven million inhabitants of an important sum. On the exports from their estates on the Mountain, together with the income from previous investments, the monasteries are now dependent. To quote two random figures: In 1925, 268 tons of nuts were exported, in addition to wine, oil, wood, and charcoal. And it is calculated that the Lavra alone derives an annual revenue of £2,750 from its forests. Scientific planting is considered superfluous. In light of which, it may be noted that an Austrian expert, on a recent tour of inspection, expressed the opinion that the afforestation was as good as any in Europe. The total yearly expenditure of any single monastery is hard to gauge. That of Iviron was assessed, before the war, at between £6,000 and £7,000. But it is now, as the *epitropos* was at pains to inform us next morning, considerably less. The Russian Monastery computes to-day that containing as it does, 600 monks, £13,700 is the minimum to which annual expenditure can be reduced.

Leaving aside the somewhat complicated regulations which bind the smaller communities of cells known as *skitai* and *kellia* to the Ruling Monasteries, there remains to give some account of the central administration at Caryes, the origins of which, as has been shown, date back to pre-Athanasian times. On May 10th, 1924, the Holy Synod of the Mountain, following an extraordinary session, submitted to the Greek Foreign Office—the department is significant—a final draft of the Athonite constitution, as it has come down to them. This has now received the ratification of the Hellenic state, and is incorporated in the letter of the Hellenic constitution. The following most important sections may serve to illustrate the fundamentals of the cratic government in our time:

> *None but the twenty Ruling Monasteries may possess property on the Mountain.*
>
> *No increase in the number nor change in the status of the monasteries is permitted.*
>
> *All who embrace the monastic profession on the Mountain are deemed Greek subjects.*

These clauses have relation to the three foreign monasteries, Russian, Serbian, and Bulgarian. But their full import will only be understood after reading Chapter XI.

> *Justice is dispensed by the authorities of the monasteries, save in penal cases, which are referred to the civil courts in Salonica.*
>
> *The representative of the Greek state on Athos must uphold the orders of the Holy Synod, provided these accord with the present constitution.*
>
> *Every decision of the Synod that does not run counter to the constitution is obligatory on the monasteries.*
>
> *The administration of the properties of the monasteries is consigned to the fraternity of each individual one.*

The actual government of the Mountain, which has functioned uninterrupted over a longer course of years than any in existence, is divided, like others, into the legislature, or Holy Synod, and the executive, or Holy *Epistasia*. With the latter we were already acquainted.

The Holy Synod numbers twenty members, each monastery sending a representative on the 1st of January to sit for twelve months. These reside in the different *konakia* maintained by the monasteries in Caryes, one of which, it will be recalled, had been the scene of our visit to Evlogios. It is responsible for the security of the monasteries and the maintenance of order; has the right to investigate all who disembark on the Mountain; and to expel those whom it considers undesirable. In the event of a criminal act, the civil authority cannot intervene without its consent. It must sanction the election of, and invest with office, all abbots and *epitropoi*. Finally, its interference in the domestic affairs of a monastery, though irresistible when invoked, is permitted only in the most exceptional cases.

The decisions of the Synod are enforced by the *Epistasia*, the origin of which is to be found in the chrysobul of Constantine IX Monomach, dating from 1046. Its full organisation was completed in 1779, during the term of Patriarch Paisios. The twenty Ruling Monasteries are divided into five groups of four. These groups are chosen in annual rotation, each of the monasteries which they contain sending a deputy chosen for his "experience, education, and powers of oratory." Save in the case of the *Protepistates*, he may, if it is desired, represent his monastery on the Synod in addition. These four possess the four quarters of the composite seal of the community, with which they must impress all the correspondence of the Synod. Their chairman is the *Protepistates*, who is the chief monk of the community, but can only be a member of the leading monastery of each group. They enjoy also a kind of mayoral dignity, being responsible for the cleanliness and lighting of the Caryes streets. They possess a general medical authority, regulate food prices, forbid the opening of shops during vespers, or on Sundays and official holidays, and cast a stern eye upon the preparation of non-ascetic foods on Wednesdays, Fridays, and other fast days. They must maintain a proper decorum, suppressing all songs, plays, barrel-organs, smoking, improprieties, and drunkenness. Nor, as we were later to discover, are these duties a sinecure. In case of need, the *Epistasia* acts through the Synod Guard, employing in the last resort, the state police, of whom there is a small resident force commanded by one bored officer. These latter possess a tiny prison in Caryes, tenanted from time to time by holy smugglers.

There exist on the promontory some 5,000 monks. This figure may be compared with those available at previous dates. By 1489, the monasteries alone, exclusive of dependent cells, contained 2,246. This, at the end of the seventeenth century, had increased to approximately 4,000. Following the Revolution, there remained but 1,450. In 1849 there were 3,000; in 1903, 3,260; though the whole monastic population of the Mountain, including those outside the monasteries, by then numbered 7,432. In 1913 the total within the monasteries rose to 3,742; while, including those without, it fell to 6,345. To-day, at 5,000 all told, the depletion is due mainly to the Russians, who have decreased since the war by over 1,000. The variations of the figures of the Lavra will testify to the vicissitudes of an individual monastery. Starting under Athanasius with eighty, it was immediately increased, upon the fresh endowment of the Emperor John I Tzimisces, to 120. In 1046 it held 700; in 1489, 300; while in 1677 and 1678 there appears a discrepancy between 600 and 450. With the Revolution the inmates sunk to 60. In 1903 they rose to 165. And they have now returned to their original quota, in the neighbourhood of 100. Novices are recruited by the Mountain as a whole at the rate of from 100 to 150 a year, exclusive of 40 or 50 Russians.

It will be seen from these statistics that the Mountain is no mere coccyx on the body politic of Europe, but an organism in which the germs of life are as vigorous as when first implanted. And it may be enquired, Of what nature is the attraction offered by the cloister to the man of the twentieth century? The cynic, the materialist, and he who boasts his common sense, will reply: Indolence and shelter. Nor will they be wholly at fault. But their perception is not acute. Institutions are not borne flourishing through a thousand years on such ideals alone.

In the composition of man there is body, there is reason; so with the animals. And there is something further, which the animals do not share. This, the essence of all true satisfaction, takes the form of a quest. In some its impulse is negligible. In others it dictates the whole course of existence. Of the latter there are, in the main, two sorts. There are the humanists, who hold to the fullness of living, whose faith rests implicit in the virtue of the earth to set the seal to their desires. For them their Absolute is inseparable from that alliance of the physical and transcendental which the language terms Beauty. And, secondly, there are those for whom no physical interpretation, no channel other than the direct, can suffice. These are the religious whose goal takes form in God. The border-line between the two is ill-defined. But they constitute, none the less, cardinal classifications of human temperament.

It is clear that for the first, the humanists, religion will frequently mean nothing; and that in no circumstance will it conjure in them the fundament of emotion that it does in the second. But it is the tragedy of contemporary transition that for the second, the in-stinctively religious aimed towards an Absolute external to the earth, there exists, in many cases, no religion adequate to the direc-tion of their imaginings. Thus it happens that in both—in the inspired of earth and likewise of heaven—there has arisen no mere negative distaste for Christianity, but an active detestation. This is born, for the humanist, of the belief that religion of any kind degrades man by directing himself from himself; for the religious, of the canting phrase and withered fable, beneath which, as memory tells him, the emotions of childhood were stifled and unpicked.

To approach those humorous and kindly men, the monks of Mount Athos, in a temper of psychological understanding, it is necessary to forswear, if only temporarily, the sting of these preju-dices. Let the humanist realise, atheist though he be, that the religious seeks, after all, only the same as himself by other roads. And let the religious who is agnostic visualise to himself another Christianity, far different from that which has been extended and distorted through four centuries of uncongenial logic; a Christianity not yet moulded by Latin materialism to the convenience of an institution; not wrung by civil wars, combed with the burrowings of sectarians, and balanced between the parties of the state like a boulder on a needle; but a single path of exploration, unclouded by doubtful ethics and hieratic blackmail, toward the eternal El Dorado. Such was the Christianity that conquered, and such, on the Holy Mountain, it has remained.

This inflexibility of approach, passion "to be one with the nature of God," takes, in its most intense manifestations, the form of mysticism. And on Athos it is the mystic that has left his imprint, has invested the very air with his outgivings. For him, to pure contemplation is added a coadjutor, such as the humanists find in beauty: "Refusing to be deluded by the pleasures of the sense world, he accepts instead of avoiding pain, and becomes an ascetic; a puzzling type for the convinced naturalist, who, falling back upon contempt—that favourite resource of frustrated reason—can only regard him as diseased."[1] To some the virtue of pain, the divinity of human suffering, is apparent, to others not. But analogy may be pointed in the opposite sphere; for few will deny that the world's greatest artists have been those that have experienced it.

In the mystic, all the senses are fused in the impetus of one inconceivable voyage. "I heard flowers that sounded, and saw notes that shone"—a literal testimony of the past (eighteenth century), and an epitome, for all the reader knew, of the trend of modern science. It is the forces of the mystics with which the visitor to Athos, unwittingly perhaps, finds himself in contact. Only once has the Mountain, in this respect, attracted the attention of contemporaries. In the fourteenth century, the Hezychasts, as they were called, claimed to envision, through perpetual contemplation, the light of the Transfiguration. This appeared owing to the accident of their sitting with heads bowed, in their navels, a fact which has brought them the contempt of posterity. In the controversy that followed they were championed by Nicolas Cabasilas, Archbishop of Salonica, a sincere literary exponent of the maligned phenomena which reason was already discrediting. And it so happens that there survives in the church of the Protaton in Caryes a contemporary portrait of this—almost the only mystic of the later Byzantine Church whose name has descended to history. In this face, painted as though by a French impressionist, the mute history of the Mountain may be read through a thousand years.

[1] Evelyn Underhill: *Mysticism.*

Chapter IV

SEAT OF ANGELS

ON THE last day of August we issued from the commonplace of sleep, to discover with surprise that the barrier between ourselves and the accustomed had emerged from myth of yesterday into disconcerting reality. Trooping down to the shore, we stood poised on one edge of the sea, with the sun, opposite, on the other. An ecstatic calm, smoother than pearls, overspread the water, broken by the black figure of a shrimping monk, gown tucked above his knees. Behind, above a broad field scattered park-like with occasional trees, reared the monastery, topped here and there with little leaded domes and resembling a great country house. The beach was stony, and sank with exasperating sloth. Once out, it seemed impossible ever to come in. We floated, as the Mediterranean allows, vertically, standing at attention and peering down to the rocks beneath the water for the octopi and dogfish with whose tales the monks seek to deter the visitor from these rash excursions. Ultimately, we returned to coffee and ablutions, the latter performed at a corner sink in the passage. The *epitropos*, full of kindly attentions, assured us of a boat to the Lavra. Before it could be ready there was half an hour in which to examine the monastery.

In so short a time we could see no more than the buildings. Though the third oldest foundation on the Mountain, dating from about 980, only the original church remains, the rest being mainly a decorative bastard classical, in particular one enormous tower, resembling a malformity of a Wren steeple and bearing on its topmost tier a coloured clock-face attended by a life-size figure to strike the hours. In every corner of the spacious court, flagged and grass-grown, stood oleanders clothed in flowers both pink and white, and orange-trees dripping little green fruits. The monastery, as its name 'Ι Βήρων, implies, was founded by Georgians, with money granted to Thornic by the Emperor Basil II Bulgaroctonos in return for his aid in suppressing the rebellion of Bardas Sclerus. The second abbot was Thornic's nephew, Euthymius, who wrote the first translation of the Bible in Georgian language. This manuscript, together with numberless others of unrivalled importance for the study of Georgian history, was conserved until 1913, when, according to *The Times* of September 13th, the Greek monks, at the height of their anti-Slav agitation, burnt the whole collection. Whether this was so, we had no time to verify; nor to inspect such as may remain of the forty crosses seen by Dr. Covel in 1677, "all studied and set out with diamonds, pearles, etc., some of very great bignesse and value." The monastery was formerly rich, having received a donation of house property in Moscow from the Tsar Alexis in 1654, whose health had been restored by an *eicon* specially prepared by the monks for the purpose. An electric plant had been installed, to which the fittings bore witness. But whether it ever worked is not recorded.

The moment of departure arrived.

"Everything is changed; we have no men," apologised the *epitropos*.

"What matter?" said I. "We can carry the luggage ourselves."

Feeling that, in fact, it did matter considerably in such heat, we transported the luggage to the portico, where it was roped to mules and led down to the arsenal, as the monastic ports, fortified against pirates, are termed. A boat scarcely larger than a child's canoe was awaiting us. After some delay another was substituted. And, propelled by two men, we launched out to sea, sped by a concert of good-byes.

The water was unrippled, the sun blazed, as gradually bay after bay, point after point, stretching down from the backbone of the ridge, hove into view and passed. All the land was furred with trees and shrubs, thick and ceaseless, stopping short of the water in white-veined cliffs of grey and green marble, which in their turn continued into the fathoms, every crevice of their submarine world revealed by the sun as an aquarium by an arc lamp. As we moved along, buildings stood at distant intervals: the monasteries of Philotheou and Caracallou turreted above the water; Mylopotamou, standing out to sea upon a rock, delectable retreat of exiled patriarchs, where hermits recuperate from the rigours of their process; and, inland among the woods, the lonely tower of the Amalfitans, reminiscent of the Italian venturers who sought the trade of the East and prayed in their spare hours with the rest of the mediæval world. Slowly the ridge rose higher to the summit, Athos itself, with its gaunt hinder precipices brooding and imminent, and the pin-point peak flitting in and out the clouds. At intervals in return for ginger-nuts and cigarettes, the oarsmen gave us to drink from water kept miraculously cold in an earthen amphora beneath the seat.

It was three hours, and one o'clock, before we rounded the southern end of the peninsula and beheld the arsenal tower of the Lavra dominating a harbour enclosed within an artificial castellated mole. A monk, resident in a house attached, informed us that his fellows in the monastery above were now asleep, but that he would telephone at three o'clock. We decided, meanwhile, to lunch off our own provisions. The dishes, spread upon a suit-case and manipulated with a damascened clasp-knife belonging to David, consisted of the following:

Pâté de saumon aux truffes
Galantine de poulet et de jambon
Biscuits petit beurre
Pâté de foie gras
Noisettes de gingembre

———

VINS
Eau de siphon à la maison,

the latter deriving from a canopied fountain a little way up the hill. This inimitable meal was followed by a siesta within the shade of a mulberry-tree, whence both myself and the "Honourable Robert Curzon, Junr." in the forties, had previously eaten. Below us, the arsenal tower, approached only by a rickety footbridge, gleamed white against the deep blue sea. This idyll, pillowed among black ants and every genus of dried prickle, was interrupted by the news that the telephone was broken. David and I therefore set off up the hill to present our letters of recommendation and beg mules for the transport of the luggage.

Seat of Angels

The monastery entrance was approached by an enormous domed portico inset with panes of early nineteenth century coloured glass, and sheltering a sugary *Panaghia*[1] of the same date. As we sat talking to the porter, a crowd of young monks appeared, among them the guest-master who had attended our wants last year —a man of extraordinary resemblance, both in feature and expression, to the well-known bust of Pericles. These were followed, creeping round the corner like an ancient musk-rat, by Father Nicodemus.

"Hail, my father, how are you?" said I. "Do you remember me?"

He did; and, stretching his wicked face, tufted with pallid red hairs, to a smile, he took the letters which the Governor and the Synod had written us. A monk then led us across the courtyard and up to a large room, apparently already tenanted. Awaiting coffee, we sat outside on a balcony. Last year, at this the chiefest monastery, the circumstance of my name and the political parentage of a companion had brought us a magnificent reception. The *Synodico*, reserved for great officials of the church, and lavishly furnished with carpets, cruets, and clocks under domes, was placed at our disposal. The Union Jack, blazoned on a red ensign, was hoisted from the balcony. And a carillon of bells was pealed as I walked with stately tread by the side of Nicodemus, in veil and orders. More, I was presented with an address, in which the last paragraph affirmed that though "to-day you quit our monastery, you leave indelible memorial upon its history. We who have had the good fortune to entertain you shall pray always that the Great Pilot of the Universe, God, may fortify your powers and prolong your years to the welfare of your nation." It was upon such assurances as these that David and I had planned our enterprise. We were now upon the threshold of three of the most important cycles of frescoes on the Mountain. What if the doors should be closed against us?

There emerged from the guest-rooms, as the afternoon wore on, a noted Athenian professor of sacred iconography, unshaven, collarless, and wearing a black bombazine coat; two Germans in khaki Norfolk jackets, whose clothes exemplified their national genius for counteracting the shape of the body; a very old man in

[1] Virgin.

[71]

frock coat and evening collar, attached to the Patriarchate in Constantinople; and finally a monk, not of the Mountain, tall and well groomed, whose bun of hair behind must have been the envy of the smartest horse-woman. These were followed by Father Procopius, the guest-master, a monk of long, ascetic face, speaking like a rusty gate and clothed in a faded purple cassock patched in black.

"It is impossible," I said, "for us to share a room with these others."

"To-morrow," he replied, almost with tears, "you will be alone. They are all going."

David and I then descended to the refectory, that he might gain some idea of the work to come. There issued from the buttery a French-speaking monk. In him we confided our hope of permission to photograph the paintings.

"You should go and see the doctor," he answered, "the Doctor Spyridon. He will do everything. He is more even than the *epitropoi*."

I recalled him as the foremost of our previous hosts. Hurrying back to the guest-house, we unloosed the parcel of sacred books which David had purchased as potential bribes from an Anglo-Catholic Woolworth's in the Oxford High Street; dedicated an illustrated manual of *Cathedral Architecture* to Nicodemus, and another on *Anglican Vestments* to the doctor, and went rushing down the courtyard, where we encountered Nicodemus on a bench. He received the gift with polite suspicion. The doctor lived up an outside flight of wooden steps, that rose from beside a bed of blood-red tobacco-flowers. We found him in undress, white beard awry, greasy white locks trailing on his shoulders, and hands folded on a pumpkin paunch. He was seated on a semi-roofed balcony jutting from the outer walls of the monastery, high over the olive-groves and, as it seemed, the sea. Flowers and clumps of basil, in round tins washed blue, stood about him, red, yellow, and green against the different blue of the far-off water. His sitting-room was decorated with photographs of prominent ecclesiastics and occasional pieces of embroidery, to one of which were pinned the white wings of a dove. Peaches, coffee, and *ouzo* were handed by a lesser monk. The following conversation then ensued:

[72]

"Hail, my father, how are you?"

"Hail! How do you do? It is good to see you again."

"I am delighted to be once more on the Holy Mountain."

"It is lovely here, is it not?"—waving his hand out to sea.

"Very lovely. Do you know, my father, that we are writing a book?"

"A book?"

"Yes. The English public ignores the very existence of Byzantine art. We will show them."

"You will show them?"

"We are writing about the frescoes. The finest frescoes in the world are on Mount Athos, and the finest frescoes on Mount Athos are at the holy monastery of the Most Great Lavra. We want to photograph them."

"Ah! Photograph them! Those in the refectory?"

"Yes, but those in the church as well."

"In the church? Why not the refectory?"

"Those in the church are better. We want England and the entire world to talk of the frescoes at the Lavra. Those in the refectory are interesting but not beautiful. We have come all the way from England to photograph those in the church."

"All the way from England," he echoed reflectively.

"Tell us, my father, will there be difficulties?"

"I do not know. I will ask the *epitropoi*. Come round to-morrow morning and have coffee with me early."

"Early? At what time?"

"Oh, early, as the sun rises."

"But at what hour?"

"At eleven by Byzantine time."

"That is seven by Frankish?"

"Yes."

"Thank you very much. We will hope for news in the morning. Good night, my father."

"Good night."

Fevered still with uncertainty, we returned to the guest-house as it grew dark. Dinner arrived; and with it all the raw hideousness of the true Athonite meal burst upon the uninitiates. Is it that our palates have changed? For in previous centuries travellers spoke of these unchanging dishes with relish and appreciation. Thus notes Dr. Covel of his experience at the Lavra in 1677: " . . . the best monkish fare that could be gotten was provided, excellent fish (severall ways), oyl, salet, beanes, hortechokes, beets, chees, onions, garlick, olives, caveor, Pyes of herbs, Φακαίς, κτωπόδι, pepper, salt and saffron in all. At last conserved little oranges, most exquisite, good wine (a sort of small claret) and we alwayes drank most plentifully. . . . He is no Greek that cannot drink twenty or thirty plump glasses at a setting." A more accurate analysis of the Mountain's resources at the present time cannot be penned. Though in the word κτωπόδι not everyone perhaps has sensed the awful threat of octopus. Belon, writing over a century earlier— in 1553—corroborates these details, and adds one more of profound and unswerving truth: "*Ces Caloieeres* (monks) *commencent tousiours leur repas par oignons avec des Aux.*" Even the Virgin, we suspect, during her mortal visit, started her meals with *hors d'œuvre* of chopped onion and garlic.

Even during our state visit the food at the Lavra had been nasty. The others, who had sneered at my warnings over the comparative normality of dinner at Iviron, now paled before the grime of cloth and napkins; spoons, knives and forks slimed with grease; the inevitable *hors d'œuvre*; soup of haricot beans; those unmentionable vegetables, resembling large cut nails and filled with pips tasting of stale pharmaceutical peppermint; and an omelette of whipped oil. The Germans told a story that lasted three-quarters of an hour by a Turkish grandfather clock in the corner that had hailed from Croydon in the eighteenth century; at which David, who speaks German, grew more and more morose; while Mark, who does not, emitted peals of glazed and meaningless laughter. At last we retired, two to a small room of which we had extracted the key from Father Procopius; the others to keep company the Germans. On approaching the beds, flocks of red bugs might be seen frolicking over the striped holland of cement mattresses. Fountains of blood—we wondered whose—squirted from their bodies as we pressed them flat like gooseberry skins. Indeed, it has become our intention to add yet another to those charming publications which reveal the intimacies of nature and God's hand to the little ones. A new generation of children, instead of being shown the seashore, shall

"Ramble Mid Maneaters on the Mountain." In the case of those still hidden, our Athenian deterrent proved efficacious.

Next morning we went, as arranged, to the doctor's. But the confusion entailed by translating our own time into one which varies daily with the rising of the sun, made us late, and he was already gone to the monastery council, to plead, we hoped, our cause. At eleven we returned, to find that he had succeeded. He led us to the council house, where an *epitropos* rang an outside bell. Another monk appeared, to whom he gave orders, which were communicated to the sacristan. The key was fetched; the doors opened. But as David, loaded with tripod and plates, was about to enter, a diminutive and bespectacled fanatic shot into the doorway, where he remained, arms outstretched, making passes with his fist at the camera. His fellows were less impressed than we, and hustled him away. Thus at last our objective was reached and concern dispelled.

That day the other guests departed. Henceforth, for five more, the two rooms were ours alone. So also, after a few jokes and presents of cigarettes, were Father Procopius and his underling, Father Bartholomew. The food changed; we provided butter instead of oil; and we insisted on its being served hot. The "small claret" flowed, diluted in the midday heat from the syphon. Occasional Greek guests, coming and going, were forbidden our privacy.

The form and atmosphere of each individual monastery present a varying study, according to whether it is idiorhythmic or cenobitic, to its traditions, and to the personal characteristics of its elders, abbot, or *epitropoi*. But all have certain features in common. And to describe the Lavra is to describe the prototype of them all.

To picture the foundation of Athanasius as it stands and has stood for all but 1,000 years, towers and storehouses, church and chapels, refectory, library, treasury, and guest-house, fountains, shrines, trees, flower-beds, and endless rows of cells, all grouped within a fortified enclosure—imagine the stupendous peak risen 6,500 feet from the water; and on a spur, where it splays out to stabilise the impact with this other element, a sloping platform still a steep 500 feet above the shore, planted with gardens. This is the site. Look down from above, where the salad-green vines drop their clusters

[75]

of cold blue grapes against the red earth; where peaches, figs, and walnuts flourish by a mountain stream, dammed in a reservoir to work a mill; there appears, amid an ocean of olives spired with the dark points of cypresses, a small embattled town. Come near, to the four-pillared portico, where the crimson oleanders fringe a broad-roofed verandah buttressed out of the hill, to shelter the monks at evening. Enter the double doors, clamped with plate upon plate of blue-washed iron. Salute the porter in his lodge, round which variety of necessaries, tasselled rosaries, black monkish slippers, bread-moulds chip-carved into the eagles of the Church, and Canadian salmon, are for sale. Twist a corner up a narrow slope. Penetrate yet another plated door through the inner wall. And here is the courtyard, a thin rectangle, some 400 feet by 150.

At the back, white against an overhanging scrub-grown hump, itself a mountain fastening all the clouds that pass, the square serrated tower of the Emperor John Tzimisces stands from the wall, approached by a labyrinth of wooden stairs and eremitic balconies. Viewed from the top, the plan of the buildings is revealed, enclosed between the long irregular lines of cells tiled with stone slabs that gleam silver in the sun as they convolute away. In the centre stands the refectory, cruciform and bellying with age, its lichen-covered roofs reaching almost to the ground. Tradition ascribes to its site an ancient temple of Minerva, to which a few worn and inappropriate capitals give evidence upon its loggia. Within, the walls are adorned with horrifying martyrdoms, together with more familiar scenes: the Last Judgment, hell mouthing flames in rivers; the Last Supper, serene within the apse; and, upon the opposing end walls of the transept, a tree of Jesse, and the death of St. Athanasius—the latter Giottesque in its dignity and feeling. The prevailing colours are reds and greys upon an indigo background, all overlaid with the darkening haze of candle-smoke. The monastery being idiorhythmic, however, many centuries have passed since the monks have habitually dined in common at the horseshoe marble slabs grooved for gravy, which stand in a double row on thick, squat bases surrounded by seats of solid stone topped with board. The ceiling, of painted planks, is slightly coved, and adorned with coloured baskets of fruit in the Turkish classical manner.

Over the entrance presides the Virgin, hard and austere, set in an aura of cubiform grey on a gentian ground. Between her and the church opposite stand the two cypresses, giant bushy cones planted one by St. Athanasius, the other by his coadjutor, Euthymius of Daphni. These spring each from a stone ring, three feet high and one thick, which is washed in the ubiquitous Greek blue, colour between bluebells and a pastel sky. In the centre is the phiale, a deep leaden dome upheld by an open ring of pillars with Turkish capitals, which are balustraded at the bottom with ancient panels of Byzantine relief. With the exception of the latter, this structure, "the handiwork of Mercury and Atzali," dates from 1635; as also the painting within the dome, which, though presumably restored, since it is open to the air, carries the symbolic anti-naturalism of the monastic artist to a fabulous pitch. The subject is the baptism of Christ. From a circular composition of the company of angels in the centre, golden doors open to emit a tongue of geometric flame, bearing a dove to the head of Christ, enrivered in the Jordan. In the circular frieze that continues round the lower part, formalised vermilion horses prance against mountains alternately of bright orange and deep purple. The whole is made doubly brilliant by the violence of the white high-lights.

Underneath this dome is its *raison d'être*, the fountain, in this case—for all the monasteries possess phiales of one kind or another—one of the most remarkable objects on the Mountain. From the centre of an enormous monolith basin, some eight feet in diameter and of extreme antiquity, rises a bronze tube bearing circular tiers of expectorating beasts, and surmounted by a horned eagle, wings outstretched. The whole character of this conduit, which has in all, twenty-eight jets, is strongly reminiscent of the Iranian and Sarmatian wrought metal ornaments unearthed in South Russia and the Caucasus, the finest animal representations in existence. Indeed, the traditions that the Athonite fountains embody is one of extraordinary interest. The idea of water-healing originated in the fourth century; and, with the rebuilding of St. Sophia by Justinian, a huge fountain was erected outside, whence the population of Constantinople used to collect the water for the cure of their maladies on Epiphany Eve. A survival of this was the famous ceremony of the blessing of the waters conducted at the Russian court

[77]

on the same date. Later it was at such phiales as the Lavra's that the Byzantine Emperors were wont to receive the rival teams of the Hippodrome before the races. A detail of one of them, in the precincts of the imperial palace, bears a curious likeness to the present; "On the cornice which surrounded the phiale stood cocks, goats, and rams of bronze, vomiting water into the bottom of the basin."[1] That of the Lavra is painted primrose yellow. As if to add to the babel of motives—Turkish, Byzantine, and Iranian—two ancient marble dogs, seated beneath, smile and twist their flat-nosed faces in a manner which can only be described as early Chinese.

Behind the phiale and the two cypresses stands the church, built by St. Athanasius and later repaired at the cost of his life. From the centre rises a broad, shallow cupola, flanked by two sub-sidiaries, each bearing leaded, shell-like domes, and surmounted by elaborate wire crosses. The building is washed the colour of a dying crimson-tinted wallflower, the cupolas being picked out in white, as also the splayed stone foundation which runs like a bench round the bottom. Entrance is effected opposite the phiale. But the old *narthex* (vestibule), where formerly the visitor was shown the cell and library of St. Athanasius himself, was demolished in 1814, and the present conservatory of coloured glass substituted. This is supported on a white marble base, sparsely carved by an Armenian with mystic symbols. Horribly frescoed within, it conceals a pair of magnificent Turkish baroque wooden doors, deeply undercut to represent the eagles of the Orthodox Church, below which the church that they adorn is transformed into the semblance of a triple-towered pagoda. These are painted gold, brown, mustard, orange, and deep blue, on a background of white. They give entrance to the church proper, and it was here that David encountered the fanatic.

Inside, the paintings, dated from 1535 and very restrained in colour, occupy, as the rule prescribed, every inch of the walls. But the general effect is spoiled by the high grey marble *eiconostasis*, picked out with gold, which divides the apse from the nave. To the right and left are two chapels. In the former, delicately sprung from four pillars of deeply marked pink marble, lies the tomb of

<hr>

[1] J. Ebersolt: *Le grand palais de Constantinople.*

St. Athanasius of Athos, covered with a modern silver sheath and hung about with trinkets. Opposite is the chapel of St. Nicolas, containing its old seventeenth-century screen of carved and gilded wood, and frescoed by the "hand of the most good-for-nothing Frangos Catellanos of Thebes in Bœotia"—so he signed himself in 1560. The nave is supported on four pillars, above the two foremost of which stand portraits of the two great soldier-Emperors of Constantinople, who were the monastery's original benefactors— Nicephorus II Phocas and John I Tzimisces—each crowned and invested with the imperial robes: the former with long hair flowing upon his shoulders, lover, fighter, mystic, the very quintessence of the mysterious Byzantine character; the latter bearing in his hands the church, from which may be seen the *narthex* as it originally looked, and the habitation above of its sainted architect. Frequently repainted, though probably with that extreme accuracy which characterised the monkish restorers, it is possible that these were, in their original versions, almost contemporary portraits. As such, their interest for the historian is enormous.

It is difficult, without a long study of the subject, to give an account of the numberless *eicons* which adorn the churches and chapels of the Athonite monasteries. Alone in the world, the Holy Mountain bears adequate witness to the magnificence of technique and colouring which this lesser province of the Byzantine Renaissance attained. Of those at the Lavra, the two great pictures of Christ Pantocrator and the Virgin on either side of the *eiconostasis'* central doors are sheeted round the figures with silver gilt, wrought in a filigree of such intricacy as to produce a texture rather than a design, and studded with plaques of Byzantine enamel gleaming like a kingfisher from its depths. Similarly ornamented, though smaller, is the picture in the back of the bishop's throne, a tall canopied erection of carved and gilded wood dating from 1635. The majority, however, are unmetalled. And it is these which, as paintings, attract the greater interest. One in particular, behind the altar, is noticeable for a Latin scutcheon represented as attached to the cross below the feet of Christ crucified.

Our rooms lay on the left, near the entrance, leading off an arcaded verandah on the first floor, which possessed at one end the inevitable marble sink. The building was old, having been built as a hospital in 1580. But five years later—on Friday, the 15th of July, 1585—"there was a great and most terrible earthquake, which destroyed the dome of the Lavra and the cupola of the hospital (now guest-house). . . . The sea was so disturbed that the water in the harbour retired without to its mouth." To this circumstance, perhaps, was due the subsequent transformation.

Its decorations were of a singularly modern fashion. Round the verandah ran a dado painted to resemble black and pink marble bordered with porphyry. The ceiling was of boards alternately chocolate and dull yellow, which were interrupted by a diamond-shaped panel of blue powdered with brighter yellow stars. Realism was enhanced by a clock of one dimension near the door, whose hands stood everlastingly at thirteen minutes past eleven. The large, low room within, furnished with an L of broad divans, and having five windows in the farther wall overlooking all the sea to Thasos, was divided at the near end by a row of three pillars, whence sprang coved ceilings decorated with borders and arabesques of mulberry-red and brown. The pillars were boldly marbled in grey and black, and bound with primrose bands in lieu of brass, the bases and capitals prominent with fictitious reliefs. Around the walls hung matchless prints of the Hellenic history in the nineteenth century: George I mid plush and palms of frightful prominence; Queen Olga rigid in coronet and bustle; the granting of the constitution; and the raising of the standard of Independence. In the middle two tables, draped and fringed, groaned beneath a permanent cruet and our own transitory comforts.

Chapter V

VISITING

$\mathbf{T}$HE HABITS of frivolous children of the world were powerless against the traditions of half the Christian era. And our days assumed a complexion of monastic regularity, both in the ordering of their hours and the sobriety with which we set each to his avocations. The morning opened as a rule with myself, a small sleeper. At half-past six, assuming a dressing-gown of green silk for the benefit of passing monks, I paddle along the verandah to the kitchen; there to find Fathers Procopius and Bartholomew presiding over an enormous wood-burning range, the chimney of which protrudes from the wall in the form of a black canopy.

"Good morning, Father Procopius!"

"Ah/Ah," he replies on two different notes, "good morning. Have you slept well?"

"Very, thank you. Can I have some hot water?"

"Hot water?! Ah/Ah"; and with never-failing surprise he twists the tap of a sooted cauldron to emit a thin boiling stream into a pewter plate, hand-beaten and marked on the rim with a criss-cross pattern. Thus fashioned are all the utensils of the Athonite kitchen, stewpans, ewers, and basins; likewise even the drinking-cups attached to the roadside fountains. The less pretentious vessels are of pottery, roughly glazed and decorated at intervals with large eyes of colour. Though wholly modern, they differ in no respect from those which David had lately disinterred from Constantinople Hippodrome. While it might equally be supposed, out of their context, that they had been designed by Picasso. Holding the plate by means of one of a row of kettle-holders ranged neatly on a shelf, I return to the sink which projects from the balcony, offering a fine view to the courtyard. The tap, fixed in a backing of carved marble, shoots Niagara into the pit of the stomach. From

[81]

the plate I shave. And monks beneath slacken their footsteps to gaze upon this curious operation.

At length we all dress, and return to the kitchen bearing a box of ginger-nuts; in response to which Father Procopius leads us to his inner cabinet, "the housekeeper's room." As the insistence of our needs became irresistible, he conceived a devotion for us, after the manner of a good-hearted fowl—dour perhaps in appearance, and appalled by the eruption of a brood of unmanageable ducklings, but determined to do her duty by them. Eventually, with the sly look of the true housekeeper, he goes to a cupboard. *Ouzo* is fetched from a shelf, the distillation of his heart.

"Your health, father!" Or, as it is literally said, "Your hygiene!"

"Your health!"

Bartholomew then appears, bearing coffee; his gait and beard are those of Henry VIII, his speech faster and more indistinct than that of a Frenchman in a railway accident. After a discussion of the sea and the weather, and a council on lunch, we return to our occupations.

David, in any case, must betake himself with camera to the church. Its keeper, dubious at first, became more reconciled to our unhooking of lamps and balancing on the elbows of stalls after I had surreptitiously presented him with a packet of cigarettes enclosed within the sheep's clothing of a medicine-box. It happened that we remained over Saturday, when the church is cleaned in preparation for the morrow. This the sacristan and his myrmidons were doing by spreading damp sawdust over the floor to suck up the dirt, then sweeping it away again. Could we wait a quarter of an hour, till it was finished? David, whose temper had been deranged by the food and the refusal to allow him to penetrate the *eiconostasis* to photograph an Ascension, brushed them aside. Stumping over the sawdust, he launched out upon the portion of the floor already swept, trailing clouds of the adhesive cleanser in his wake. But the monks, instead of annoyance, exhibited only mirth at so ridiculous a sight. Diving for his feet, they pinioned him till every trace of the offending dust was removed. The work of both parties then continued. A monk was always at hand to guard us from stealing the objects without price contained in the church. In this capacity even the fanatic reappeared, seemingly penitent for his outburst, and deeply interested in the lens of the camera, while we stood ready to fasten his arms in case of assault. It appeared, indeed, that our having obtained permission to photograph in the church caused some sensation, as I was perpetually hearing snatches of conversation in the courtyard linking my name with this unholy work. Meanwhile Mark and Reinecker were sketching; and myself, if not assisting David, noting the colour and form of the paintings upon which he was engaged. Lunch was usually at 11.30—a late hour for the monks, who like to be asleep by then, and a concession to our barbarous inconsequence. Afterwards we also slept till the close of the afternoon service at four. From then till dark the work continued again.

Our friend the doctor had gone to Caryes on business. But a frequent visitor was his Elisha, Father Dorotheos Benardos, a vain youth of twenty, who was now in sole charge of the doctor's little house and balcony. He arrived one day bearing in gift a quartet of books on the Athonite constitution; and proceeded to stay, two gold front teeth gleaming like a lighthouse from his bearded lips and a smell of stale garlic exuding from his person. At length, too tired to concoct further conversation, I prevailed on Mark to draw him, and translated the intention. His demeanour was immediately that of an embarrassed typist apprised of her success in a beauty competition.

"Oh, good gracious! Do my portrait? And without a veil? I've only got my old hat on. And no gown. Can you lend me one? No, of course not. . . . I forgot. Shall I sign it when it's done? Where would you like me to sit?"

Swishing about the room, he came to rest on a Windsor chair, profile to the window. He straightened his cassock; he arranged his feet. And finally, removing his cap, he loosed upon his shoulders a flood of black frizzy hair.

Earlier that morning, on my visiting the doctor and finding him gone, Dorotheos Benardos had opened his soul to me on the balcony. He had lived, he said, in Piræus, and had been on the Mountain four years. But he had not forgotten Athens. And then, as if to prove it, he started a recital of the town's pleasure resorts—Phaleron, the Zappeion, and Kephissia—as an exile in the colonies might sigh over the lost days of Earl's Court exhibitions and the river at Maidenhead. A silence fell between us at this painful juncture.

Then he turned to me and said:

"*Ἐλώ εἶμι κοσμικός*—I am a man of the world."

A day or two later he began again:

"A few years ago a man died here who had a number of English medals." (Greeks frequently obtained them in the war.)

"Medals?" I replied, not wholly understanding the word.

"Yes, medals," he repeated, drawing imaginary ribbons on his chest. "When you return to England, will you send me some?"

"Send you medals? But how, and for what reason?"

"Why not? Can't you go to the Foreign Office in London, and have them sent to me?"

"But why? You have done nothing."

"No, but I will. I will do great things. I love England."

"You must do them first. Besides, the Foreign Office does not distribute medals."

"The Foreign Office does not distribute medals? Who does?"

"The King."

"Have you visited the King?"

"No."

"I visited our Kings three times." Pause. "But when you get back, you will send me those medals?"

"No."

Silence. Each gazes at the sea, breathing hard.

"What can I do to be famous? I do want to be famous."

Thus sped the days. But towards evening, the sun having fallen preternaturally early owing to the imminence of the hill behind, the personalities of the party, sharpened by fatigue and the prospect of food, assumed a prominence of which the overpowering background was apt to deprive them. For the first half of our stay the great expanse of sea overlooked by our five windows was unruffled, assuming as the westerly night surged up, a solid and unearthly calm, flecked only by currents acres in extent. And once, caught on Thasos, three puffy clouds, pink with the reflected sunset behind us, sent three definite reflections forty miles over the sea to the shore beneath—an uncanny spectacle, as though this giant space was but a mirror. Then, swiftly, darkness comes; the solitary hanging lamp is lit; another wheedled out of Father Procopius for a nail in the wall. And the party is alone with itself.

Mark, a cheeping chorister of our schooldays, has retained, despite the blottery tenor that has displaced his treble, a habit of uttering with the suddenness of a ship's siren, the less interesting of Schubert's ditties. To David, spasmodically musical, each burst is of greater variation from the author's prescription than he can endure. Seeking retaliation, he hits upon those emunctory sounds that frequently result from a surfeit of radishes. And Father Procopius, tottering through the door, finds himself, often as not, deafened between an exhibition of competitive street-singing and the echoes of a vomitorium. There follows food, to which the saddle-bags contribute biscuits, chutney, and tinned appetisers, more delicate than sustaining. During the meal argument arises. Reinecker betrays the trust in rational thought that characterises the war generation. I, incapable of logic, take refuge in insult. David, mistaking the two or three months' schedule of our present venture for a life based on consciously reasoned motive, hurls the accusation of such upon me. Receiving a blow in return, he decides to leave for England next day. Then goes snorting to the smaller bedroom to develop the day's plates. This occupies an hour. Mark, chippy with sleep, gyrates to and fro, till the plates are heard washing in the sink outside. He then picks his way through a garbage of broken glass and scrumpled paper, cursing to bed.

As the work in the church progressed satisfactorily, we fixed our departure for Monday. The Saturday previous, day of David's misadventure with the sawdust, Mark and I decided to occupy that odious period the afternoon, as is customary, by walking over to tea with a neighbour. The latter in this case was the Rumanian *skiti* of the Prodrome, or Forerunner, as the Orthodox Church calls St. John the Baptist, situated an hour away. It was extremely hot as we climbed upward from the monastery, shoes torn and feet bruised by the irregular white cobbles of this most typically Athonite road. Enquiring the way of a passing muleteer, we eventually turned off to the left towards the sea again, guided thither by a cross stuck on a tree revealing the monogram of the Saviour and the objectives of the confluent paths. At a long trough, shaded within a wood of ilexes, we drank and bathed our faces. There then appeared a white quadrangle of buildings, having over its gateway a high tower. Vespers were in progress. But a monk with a broad flat face wholly unlike that of a Greek, beckoned us within the church, where we remained for an hour, unwilling listeners to the nasal Balkan chanting. The building was erected in 1857, and contains only one feature of interest—a wonder-working *eicon*, painted by the Angels in 1860.

We were entertained, when the service was over, by a Greek-speaking monk, shrunken and ill, who said he had asthma and needed a doctor. We suggested Spyridon. But he had already visited him. We then discussed his foundation. The first Rumanians came here in 1820. There were now about fifty; which was, he pointed out, very few, considering that in Turkish times nearly all the Athonite monasteries had been re-endowed by the generosity of the trans-Danubian Voivodes and Hospodas, the only Christian princess who preserved their old Byzantine status of semi-independence under the Ottoman dominion. Indeed, since the Balkan wars it has been a grievance against Greece, and one that has lately come to a head in an official interchange of notes, that Rumania should remain distinct from the other Balkan states in not sending recruits to one of the Ruling Monasteries. It is desired that the present *skiti* should be advanced to such a status. This request, however, neither the ecclesiastical nor lay authorities can grant.

Our asthmatic friend begged us to stay the night. It would have pleased us to do so. The rooms seemed clean, that in which we sat being adorned with a print of the massacre of Smyrna in 1922, in which the martyrs of the twentieth century were depicted falling into the sea with haloes affixed to their bowler hats. But the others were expecting our return. And after visiting the monks at supper in the refectory—for the *skiti* is cenobitic—we took our leave, fearful of the shutting of the Lavra doors. "Lock-up" takes place in every monastery at twelve o'clock by Byzantine time—that is, between seven and eight. Oppressed with the setting of the sun, we quickened our tread, barging into bushes and tripping over stones, like two Aberdonians on a comic postcard. On return, we discovered David and Reinecker had struck up a friendship with the gardener. Having eaten themselves into the initial stages of dropsy, they had brought away for us a tray of grapes, figs, peaches, and even a melon. Their intention had been to bathe; but, finding themselves anointed with the sewage of the arsenal, they had retired in disgust and encountered their benefactor half way up the hill. He talked to us all, next day—an old man with white beard and a sunburnt pippin face rendered wholly different by contact with the soil from the inhuman visages of his fellows, always in the clouds.

That evening a storm broke, lightning flashed, the building creaked, and the windows threatened to blow from their frames. Sunday dawned overcast, rain dropping. And it seemed as though the *damnosa hereditas* of the English race, the English Sabbath, had followed us even here. Oppressed with this feeling, we changed our clothes instinctively for better. Without, the wind howled and the sea, a deeper blue, rolled white horses. In the afternoon we went to church, having first watched the ceremony of its announcement; a monk in a pleated gown marching round the church beating a metallic savage rhythm on the *semandron*, a piece of hardened wood six feet long and carried on the shoulder. As the rhythm gathered, other monks assembled, hurriedly slipping into gowns and veils as they arrived, like undergraduates late for chapel. With them we entered; endured the service more for politeness' than religion's sake; and, after it, proceeded to the farther end of the courtyard, to be shown the books and treasures. These were kept in three separate compartments, guarded by iron doors.

In the inspection of manuscripts, my enthusiasm, subverted by ignorance, flags. The library of the Lavra, however, contains none of importance, though a late Byzantine *herbarium*, profusely illustrated, offered a certain entertainment. But in the treasury, opened by two keys in the keeping of separate persons, our attention was alert. There was an excitement in the handling of a chrysobul with golden seal and actual scarlet signature of "Andronicus faithful in Christ King and Emperor of the Romans the Palæologus," complete. Many book-covers, reliquaries, patriarchal crowns, patens, chalices, and crosses were exposed to view in glass-fronted cupboards—some indifferent, some of pre-Turkish times. But one object alone preoccupied us: the Nicephorus Phocas Bible. The far-famed stole said to have been worn by the

Emperor, is scarcely earlier than the eighteenth century. But of this book, and of its companion reliquary, the royal deed of gift, dated 970, is still preserved at Caryes to attest the authenticity.

Of the reliquary we were unfortunately ignorant, and there is, I believe, no recorded instance of a visitor's having seen it during the present century. Description, however, is extant, and may be quoted, as relative to a world masterpiece, beside which the great Bible, now, by permission of Nicodemus, actually within our hands, ranks only second. The case, which encloses a piece of the Cross seven inches long, is of silver gilt, approximately a foot and a half by a foot and opening on top with folded doors like a triptych. These are set with enormous *cabouchon* jewels—diamonds, emeralds, and rubies, as well as pearls, which alternate with medallions of saints in enamel. There are twelve rows of eight each; and the two largest pearls measure over an inch and a half across. With the exception of the loot stolen from Constantinople during the Fourth Crusade, and now in the treasury of St. Mark's, such objects are unknown in the West. And even those cannot compare, either in age or workmanship, with the ones at present under review.

The cover of Nicephorus Phocas' Bible, measuring about twelve inches by nine, forms one side of a contemporary manuscript of the Gospels, to the front of which have been added three or four pages in uncials that would seem to date, at the latest, from the eighth century. It is curious that these alone did not attract the attention of those earlier travellers, to whom anything in the nature of Byzantine art appeared "ugly" or "in bad taste," and who have passed the book without mention. The metal itself is of that exquisite colour, a pale, sour gold, which silver gilt achieves with age. The stones inset include, beside the more precious varieties mentioned above, cornelian, amethyst, garnet, lapis, and beryl. At the corners are four huge crystals, beneath which are visible the sacred monograms of Christ and the Virgin. Below the feet of the Christ is a cushion, patterned in dark grey on white enamel, similar to that upon the open pages of the book held in the left hand. At the shoulders, on either side, are the half-lengths of two saints in brighter enamels. The halo is composed of two rows of small grey pearls.

But, apart from the intrinsic beauty of material and workmanship,

the gorgeous austerity of the relief itself constitutes the real
æsthetic value. It is hard to analyse, this supreme mastery of semi-
sculpture possessed by the mediæval Greeks, so unlike, so superior
to the glucose formulæ of their ancestors. It would seem to lie
in the combination of a supreme purity of design with an extraordinary manipulation of surfaces, the infinitesimal angularisation of
every contour. In this province the Byzantine craftsman is distinguished from his fellows of all ages.

We lingered over the examination. For it seemed as though it
were possible, in handling this memorial to that compound of
sophistication and the supernatural which invested the capital of
the Eastern Empire, to imbibe, personally, something of its spirit.
At length it was returned to its cupboard, and, crossing the courtyard to where we espied Nicodemus on his bench, we thanked
him for the monastery's hospitality and requested mules for the
continuation of our journey. The malignity of his countenance was
dispersed in smiles; and, enquiring, after the work, he beckoned
us within the council-house, complete with telephone and monkish
secretary, where the pealing of the bell brought us the usual tray
of restoratives. Having retrieved our letters of recommendation,
we repeated our thanks and returned to dinner.

A feeling of sadness now overcame us, and Father Procopius too.
Apéritifs came in dozens, followed by an omelette into which
Bartholomew had cooked his very soul. The evening ended with
ineffectual vows to pack at once against an early start. Outside, the
wind was still howling, sending flickers down the lamp-chimneys
with each gust. What hope for the morrow, with all dependent
on the weather?

Chapter VI

THE DISTANT, WATERY GLOBE

Thare es also another hill that men calles Athos; and that es so hie that the schadowe theroff rechez unto Lempny, the whilk is therfra nere lxxvii. myle. Abouen on thir hilles es the aer so clere and so sutill that men may fele na wynd thare: and therfore may na beste ne fewle liffe thare, so es the aer drye. And men saise in thase cuntrees that philosophirs sum tyme went up on thir hilles and held to thaire noses spoungez moisted with water for to cacche aer, for the aer thare was so drie. And also abouen on thir hilles in the powder thai wrate letters with thaire fingers, and at the zere end thai went agayne and fand the same letters that thai had writen the zere before als fresch as thai ware on the first day withouten any defaute. And therfore it semes wele that thase hilles passez the clowdes to the pure aer.

"THE BUKE OF JOHN MANDEUILL,"
First circulated about 1360.

NICODEMUS had arranged that we should start at dawn; and the fear that we might not wake was eliminated by a violent chanting which began at 3 a.m. in a chapel on the verandah, the doors of which, at our very ear, we had formerly conceived to denote another guest-room. The very irritation of being thus woken now precluded our arising. And the muleteer, arriving for the luggage, found us still in bed. But as the volume of the service grew, each larynx stretched to burst, we were obliged to shave, half-clothed, scarcely ten yards off the open doors of the chapel. Meanwhile the muleteer stood by in readiness for each of our thirteen pieces of luggage as it shut. A present of 1,000 drachmas, average of half a crown each nightly, was pressed into Father Procopius' hand, accompanied by the formal utterance of "a present for the church." And he, overwhelmed with the aggregate of what was not in fact a large rate of donation, rose to his private cupboard and filled a bottle with his personal *ouzo*, to keep us warm during the coming day and night. He was now torn with remorse to recall the food he had provided, and enumerated its horrors in a litany of penitence, with which we could only concur. It came to us that, had we been able to deposit our offering at the beginning instead of the end of our stay, things might have been different. But there lies the charm of the Mountain: there is no distinction between rich and poor. All are equal suppliants of a hospitality, the nature of which no external authority can dictate. It is this, let us hope, that may preserve it from the track of the globe-trotter. He will shrink from difficulty of the language, the nauseating victuals, the inhabitants of the beds, the indescribable sanitation, and the absence of wheeled locomotion. And from his wife, at least, usually the worst of him, Athos is safe.

The muleteer was counting the luggage.

"You must have another animal," he said, blenching. "Go and ask Nicodemus. He is below at the council-house."

"Come with me."

He came and made the request. Nicodemus uttered refusal. To which I, a little annoyed, replied:

"If the holy monastery of the Most Great Lavra is unable, or does not wish, to give us the necessary mules, are there any here for which we can pay?"

He was stung to apology.

"But we do wish. Only they are busy, getting in the wood."

Nevertheless, he gave us another.

A minute later, as we were loading, a young monk of sparse beard and tattered gown ran up and shook me by the hand.

"How do you do, Kyrie Vyron?"

"Is it possible? Andreas?"

Here was good fortune. Andreas, occupant of the dependency of the Lavra named Kerasia, situated abut 2,500 feet above the sea, for which we were bound, had guided us to the summit last year. Would he do so again? Certainly. He had with him a friend, a monk with Kaiserish moustachios, who hailed from the monastery of Gregoriou and also recognised me. He too was living at Kerasia. They had come down to the Ruling Monastery on business, and would start back with us at once. With a last good-bye to Father Procopius, we clattered out through the low fortified gateways.

Since there were only five mules, and two were needed for the luggage, I walked on in front with Andreas, discussing trees, snakes, and birds, as in turn they obstructed or fled from our path. Myrtles, dwarf oaks, rock holly, and various shrubs to which I could put no name, gradually gave place, as we moved higher, to groves of ilexes, gnarled and shady, varied here and there with oaks that might have been the envy of an English park. Andreas said that he had been on the Mountain eight years, having been brought here by his uncle. Did he like it? "*Etsi ketsi*"—so-so. He would go away when he was tired. Formerly he had been attached to the English consulate. The consul was a fine man. Did I know him?

It happened that I did; and the fact awoke in me a reminiscence. Finding, during a stay in Athens, that I needed a new passport, I had applied to the consulate for one, which was inadvertently issued without being stamped. The result was that, on returning to Constantinople, whither I had removed a fortnight later, after a visit to Broussa, I found myself in imminent danger of arrest for being in possession of British credentials under false pretences. Relief from the predicament seemed to lie with the British consulate in Constantinople. But the state of this proved worse than the last. Our boat to Constanza, with £60 worth of railway tickets across Europe depending on it, was timed to leave at eleven o'clock. The staff arrived in driblets from half an hour to an hour late, the man we needed last. Then he who had the keys refused to surrender the passports to the man upstairs who had the stamps. We, meanwhile, tempers beyond control, ran swearing from basement to attic of the highest building in Péra. At length the man upstairs resorted to the telephone, which the man below approached with a stream of oaths. The man above then wished, he said, to know who was master in this office. If he was not, he'd know why not. No more! Have the goodness to send those passports up in double quick time. . . .

Thus do Englishmen, white men all through, assume the characteristics of the Orientals around them. Nor even now were our troubles at an end. Arriving at the Customs, with a quarter of an hour in which to board the boat and nine pieces of luggage, we found three officials in glass cases, each approached by a queue of twenty people, stamping passports with that febrile sloth which the Turkish race shares with the hour-hands of watches. Desperate, we exhibited handfuls of Turkish pounds, advertising in four languages that whoever should succeed im placing our passports to an official's nose should receive them. The result was magical; but the effect upon the already exasperated crowd of Albanian *hodjas*, Balkan mothers, and mackintoshed English misses, was explosive. Rising as a man, they shattered the glass cases about the heads of the officials, sending a hail of broken glass across their necks and ears and the enormous documents over which their hands were creeping. And what, in this ruthless cruel East, lain low beneath the shadow of a drunken tyrant—what happened? Not one of the officials even raised his eyes, far less diverted his nib, from the paper on which he was engaged.

As the path rose to a rocky gate cut in the spine of a huge spur that went curveting up to its own peak before dropping to the sea, Andreas and I stopped. From here we could look along both sides of the triangle in which the promontory ends; back east to where the Lavra had now disappeared; and west along a series of giant glissades of white stones waiting to precipitate themselves upon the sea, where its blue edge encircled every cape and inlet with the graduations of a peacock's tail. Round us blew a cooling wind in great gusts. After ten minutes the others caught us up. And another two hours' ride along what has been described as a mere cornice brought us to Kerasia.

Two fat old monks, toothless greybeards, gowns and caps green with age, rushed out on to the little balcony beaming greetings upon me whom they remembered. And we sat as before, beneath the same bottle-gourd hanging from the same shady creeper, eating a delicious *glyco* of green oranges. This year, it being a month later, the grapes were ripe; and a great bowl of them, tasting, though no one will believe it, of wild strawberries, was placed before us. The others were charmed at this hospitality. But I, mindful of a former bill, ate with two minds. The outlying communities are not bound to hospitality, as in the case of the Ruling Monasteries. Hence our relations were now commercial.

[93]

Below us shone the green domes of an elaborate building, relic of the Russian attempt to overpopulate the peninsula, now containing only ten occupants; "and those," said the Greek monks gleefully, "with no food." Further still, down a woody cleft bound in with white crags, stretched sky and sea a blue sheet, horizon the stitching of a join. How precipitous and how far the descent was only borne upon us by the appearance of a passing steamer, no larger than a boat of pins and matches in a child's bath.

The question was now of mules. Andreas had said they abounded. But it appeared, once we had arrived, that those of the Holy Apostles—the name of this particular cell, which was one of a group—were out at work.

"Listen," I said. "We start in two hours' time. If there are four mules, we will take them. If there are not, we will go on our feet. But one we must have to carry our coats and food. Find it."

Delivered of this injunction in the tones of a bull, we proceeded to lunch—an excellent meal of tinned *hors d'œuvre* and bottled breasts of chicken. The red wine of Kerasia is the best on the Mountain, very strong and made from the strawberry-tasting grapes. The greater part is sold to the monasteries, the Lavra alone buying 20,000 okes, the equivalent of 5,680 gallons, annually. The manufacture being actually in process, the earthen floor of the kitchen was guttered with red wine, which oozed from a vat ten feet high. Garlic was presented us, in the form of tulip bulbs, non-odoriferous and, judging from the donor's face, of Elysian delicacy. We therefore ate it, to our future regret. After half an hour's sleep on carpeted divans in a room of odious squalor, though adorned with yet another English eighteenth-century clock, we rose to announce departure. Andreas, it is unnecessary to say, had chosen the hour fixed to go in search of the mule. But a display of artificial temper sent his friend running down after him. Together they returned, successful. Overcoats, saddle-bags, and the despatch-case were affixed, and, accompanied by the two monks, we cavalcaded down the garden and out into the woods.

It was one o'clock, and the sun was at its height. The path wound steeply up what appeared from below a titanic white wall stretching into the sky, with the tall trees along its upper edge dwarfed by distance to the semblance of an imperceptible scrub.

The mule's legs being, after the nature of Athonite quadrupeds, pre-hensile, it had the advantage of us, as we fastened upon roots and boulders with every device of human composition. I had pre-viously ascended in the dark. It had been cool. And the invisible obstacles seemed negligible after the priming draughts of Kerasia wine. But now, at the very solstice of the day, its fumes only served to retard us. Bodies, fat with spurious luxury and clerkly inaction, poured frigid streams of perspiration from spine and forehead, experiencing acute discomfort at the unwonted effort. Gradually we separated, David and myself first, then Mark, lastly Reinecker.

As we rose, the trees grew bigger and more buttressed against the incessant storms; conifers appeared among them; and, as in a German fairy-book, symptoms of charcoal-burners—great tripods of branches and black heaps shaped like hives, ten feet at the apex. Despite the sun, it became cooler. And as we emerged from the trees that topped the precipice upon a further slope of rock and scrub, the vegetation assumed an autumnal complexion: bracken brown; hips and haws ripening on unfamiliar thorn-trees; and everywhere patches of giant autumn crocuses, mauve and spotted. Behind and below, vast peaks that had formerly towered above us were shrunk to a mere pattern of two dimensions. The horizon was half-way up the firmament; and, as we moved, rose with us.

We had climbed more than two hours, monks and mule follow-ing, when we reached the *Panaghia*, church and hospice combined, a squat grey building grown from the rock, with an imperceptible dome humped out of its stone-tiled roof. The land beyond the door-way seemed to slope down again, since no more could be seen. But it was surprising, on stepping casually to the edge, to find the rim of the sea five and a half thousand feet immediately beneath. The door stood open. Running inside, I unearthed from a cupboard a long cylindrical pot on the end of a rope, which, thrust down a well in the floor, provided us with much-needed water, flavoured with refuse and hairs though it was. After five minutes' rest, David and I, accompanied by Andreas' friend, started on the last thousand feet.

"The highe pique or Peer thereof," wrote Sir Paul Rycaut of the Mountain in 1679, "is . . . as uneven, craggy, and horrid as

[95]

Caucasus; but somewhat beneath it is covered with trees, shrubs, and boscage. . . ." The latter, with the exception of a last zone of gaunt jagged pines, we now forsook. Then even these were below us. Only the naked ivory shoulders of Athos gleamed sheer and white against the bold blue sky, tipped like a glittering minuscule of sugar with the little beehive church of the Transfiguration. Above us eagles, their under-wings spotted in the manner of aeroplanes, circled and hung, uttering soulless cries in the cold azure. A game-bird whirred from our feet. The crocuses, larger and brighter, starred the ground in purple groups sprung from between the myriad teeth of the marble.

The monk, in silent boast, sped like a mountain goat caparisoned in crêpe, up the twisting vestiges of path. David and I, debilitated by the rarity of air—"*les aviateurs prennent leur précautions à deux mille mètres*" had been the Governor's remark—plodded unhappily behind, panting as we had not panted since we shared the same game of football. I suggested a rest. But David, eyeing the monk two corkscrews above, said: "I have a certain pride in these things." So we struggled break-neck up the sun-kissed marble, vaguely shadowed with leafless prickly vegetation in its crevices; and still the church receded beyond the range of hope and vision. A peculiar trembling overtook the legs. We felt we should now be reduced to locomotion on the stumps of our knees. "Shall we stop a minute?" said David. And, with a call to the monk, we subsided.

Thus proceeding at intervals of a quarter of an hour; with the slopes beneath become vertiginous in their enormity, falling, as it seemed, unbroken by a single foothold to the peacock blue rim; with spates of perspiration suddenly escaping from our hats to deluge neck and ears; with the sun, sinking behind the pendent brow, leaving ambushed blasts of frozen air in the shadows; with the *Panaghia* scarcely visible, a mere grey excrescence on its ledge—we reached a point where church and summit were no longer within sight. Ten more minutes, said the monk. Five. And then, defiling up between great rocks, their further faces dripping liquid gold, there rose before us a straight white wall and tiny dome.

Beyond, a void.

In 1926 we had ascended, as we thought, to see the dawn. Andreas, incensed at being woken by forcible shaking from his icy board in the *Panaghia*, had run his fastest. It was dark; and, imagining each twist to be flanked by a precipice of unholy depth, we had rushed with him, sick with the effort, until the motionless silhouette of goats, grouped Mappin-terrace-like against the exiguous light that now filtered through the black, proclaimed the top. The cold was ghastly. Andreas, rending some portion of the church furniture indistinguishable in the half-light, lit a fire in an angle of the building, at which we crouched disconsolate. This was in contrast to the procedure of Athelstan Riley in the Anglo-Catholic 'eighties, who, finding himself "in a cloud, and it being very chilly . . . lighted the lamps of the *eiconostasis* and sang the Magnificat"! Despite his example, we remained outside, an hour and yet another hour, as slowly, imperceptibly, the day lightened. To quote from the recorded impression of the time: "The clouds seemed in a turmoil, tearing and swirling on, disclosing and shutting the tantalising vision of a sun beyond. In a final agony the great black bank was rent. And for one half-minute there lay beneath us the whole sea, and the other two of the three fingers of land; the wooded Athos twisting like a furry serpent back to the mainland; the bay of Salonica and the Macedonian hills; Greece; Europe; and all the kingdoms of the world and the glory of them. The sun shone, and the golden morning seemed to penetrate the brain and suffuse the whole body. Half a minute—then with a rush of cold wind the curtain fell. And, picking up our sticks, we started downward through the dead grey mists, to breakfast at the *Panaghia*, 1,000 feet below."

What wonder, then, that I must see the view again, remaining, if necessary for ever, till the clouds disperse? The others, sceptical of the effort entailed, had croaked prognostications of the weather. But God was with us; and the rainy canopies which had overshadowed the whole southern end of the peninsula for the last forty-eight hours had dissolved even as we climbed. David and I, turning the corner of the church, gasped as we looked down the Mountain's back.

Reared a mile and a quarter off the globe, we might, had we wished, have put out a hand to pluck the sky, have palmed away a cup of blue. For that broad illimitable space was now reality, possessing an interesting and unsuspected texture. Its scope had shrunk. All around the horizon of land and sea had risen to three-quarters up the range of vision, and in so doing, assumed new character, as when a face, seen only in profile, is turned to the front. To the east, whence we had climbed, tiny contours uttered Lemnos and the Asia Minor coast: the plains of Troy, whence Tozer saw this platform of ours "towering up from the horizon, like a vast spirit of the waters, when the rest of the peninsula is concealed below." In the north, all the coastline of Thrace, Cavalla, and Dedeagatch wound away to the junction of the Dardanelles, with Turkey's remnant hovering in soft uncertainty. In the west, battling for definition athwart the cadent sun, the other two fingers of Chalcidice, Longos and Cassandra lay one above the other in the sea; and over them Olympus and the line of Greece. While, farther south, another transient shape proclaimed Eubœa and the satellite Sciathos, which means, in Greek, "Shadow of Athos." Thither, in the morning, the shadow stretches. Had it been the dawn we witnessed, instead of hazy sunset, we should also have seen, as all the Orthodox world knows, Constantinople, the great capital. We looked; but the flat dome of St. Sophia rose only in the mind. Christ saw the town, no doubt, the old Byzantium. For the Orthodox world knows, too, that it was here the devil led him.

Below the church, distance galloped down the gilded crags to peaks beneath, where tattered breaths of cloud hung forgotten to their spurs. Until, infinitely far, the tree-clad spine of the peninsula began, twisting its serpentine course up the vertical panorama; land meeting water with cape and cleft, a warm glow to each face; the monasteries clinging pale and diminutive to their sides. As the forty miles stretch out, only a shadow in the haze remains, outlined in the silver gleams of the farther sea; spreading then to a farther shadow—the mainland.

Wedged in a niche of rock, I sat agaze, an arctic wind shrivelling the clothes, numbing the hands, and rushing up the legs. The others had arrived, even now scarcely reconciled to their exertions: Mark busied with some Alpine weed, Reinecker remarking upon the merits of the romantic landscape. Gradually the cold, hitherto spasmodic, became universal and intense. A darkness was present in the sky. David and Reinecker first, then Mark, monks, and mules, turned and went. I could not.

But it was necessary. With a glimpse at the church, built in this version by the Patriarch Joachim III the Magnificent to the glory of God, and at our names, which we had pencilled last year in an indiscoverable corner as monument to our first pilgrimage so long as we should still have strength to return—and which, despite the experience of Sir John Maundeville's philosophers, had survived— I too turned my face east. I turned to go. But stood, rooted. For there, out upon the water, moving with an impetus almost visible up toward the cold lowering horizon, lay a grey elongated cone. The shadow: which "rechez unto Lempny, the whilk is therfra nere lxxvii myle." Slowly it was dissolved in the approaching night. A film crept over the peacock rim. Rigid with cold, I threw myself in the wake of the others, reaching the tree zone as the darkness really fell; and stopping with them to drag down the rest of the slope limbs of battered pine in preparation for the night.

We discovered, on reaching the *Panaghia*, that Georgi, the goatherd, had not returned. On arriving last year at midnight, a giant figure, axe aloft, had hurled itself upon us from the door, accompanied by the hot snarls of dogs. But on enquiry if he was a brigand, he had subsided. We had met him to-day on the way to Kerasia: a Viking of a man, with auburn moustaches and streaks of gold in a brown beard. He had a new coat. Formerly his clothing had consisted of a woollen garment so ragged that, but for the adhesive qualities of his largely visible body, it must have dropped in a thousand shreds upon the floor.

"What is that?" he said in greeting, noticing the top of Father Procopius' bottle sticking from my pocket.

"*Ouzo.*"

"Indeed."

And, without further word, he pulled it out, smelt it, took a swig, and put it back. He might or might not be back, he said, a little worried lest our wants should remain unsatisfied without him. This, however, was not the case.

Hauling in the pine-branches, some of them so large as to need our assistance, Andreas and his friend lit a fire beneath an arched stone chimney at the end of the upper room—upper by reason of its position on the hill. It was an enormous fire, casting a readable light throughout, and so hot as to be unapproachable. Despite the chimney, the room was filled with clouds of smoke, which gathered in a pendent layer eighteen inches thick under the ceiling. A store of branches was got into the room beneath; water drawn from its well; and the wooden windows tightly closed with chunks of rock against the cold. We settled down to dinner.

It was a curious scene, this long, low room: the roaring bonfire leading the shadows in perpetual dance; dying now to a red glow; leaping up to light the edges of faces, arms, and shoulders; the ceiling hidden by a cloud, mobile with compression of arriving smoke; the floor occupied by two enormous platforms, two feet high and twelve across, with between them from door to hearth an aisle of the same width; all of thick, rough-hewn planks, dark and worn, those of the platforms mounted on peeled logs shiny with age. And ourselves, spread apostle-like over these strange furnishings amid overcoats and saddle-bags: David, broad and complacent, efficiently opening a tin of Wiltshire ham; Mark nibbling frivolously at a truffle; Reinecker delving in the biscuits; myself apportioning chocolate for the "pudding." And in a separate corner the monks, hair loosed on their shoulders: Andreas balancing cloak-wise a khaki coat with collar and cuffs of frayed cinnamon velvet; his friend huddled in a rug, red within, outwardly printed with the spots of the leopard. All through a thickening haze. The smoke pall falling lower. And the cold from without penetrating those parts of the body farthest from the fire.

Pulling on an extra pair of trousers and a jumper, I looked outside. The moon, in medium phase, cleft a trench of light down the sea to the very base of the Mountain, thus clearly defined in its titanic remoteness. Above rose the summit, colour of the embedding stars, with the gaunt black trees straggling ineffectually over its beginnings. And from the demure cabin of man, distinguished only by the one horizontal line of roof in a world of verticality, a sudden stream of sparks, fiery red among the cold lights as though from a railway engine on a frosty night, blew from the chimney, and, passing over the precipice, lost itself.

The night passed, if not in peace, in warmth; for, whenever the fire died down, a monk arose, returned with half a tree, and heaped it on to the embers. Sleep was evanescent. For myself, a pillow was forthcoming in the despatch-case; and with grisly irony a pillow-case, provided by the afterthought of fond parent, had inadvertently accompanied it. Head ensconced on this travesty, it remained to settle the body. To lie on a bare board in an overcoat that can be doubled at the supporting hip is not in itself an insupportable hard-ship. But when, at every point where flesh, armoured no matter how, touches the wood, a ravening multitude of fleas rises to the attack, slumber is necessarily spasmodic.

With the first glimmers of morning we rose, to find the sun beneath us down the precipice, fighting its way above black billows of cloud that came curling at our feet. Our faces, ghastly in the dawn, were rendered more horrible by a grey coating of wood smoke. The monks were impatient to start. Having eaten some biscuits, we thrust things into their bags with the unseeing inertia that follows a broken night, folded the pillow-case, and set off down. On the way I suddenly remembered that my mother, incensed, after hearing my accounts, that in a genderless age she should still be prohibited from this last stronghold of decency, had implored me to bring her some plant, "something living of the Mountain." It seemed that the crocuses, envied of botanists and growing at an altitude whose rigours must be comparable even to those of the English winter, were crying for the purpose. Grasping pseudo-trowels of living marble, we gouged a dozen sepulchred bulbs into a biscuit-tin. Planted in a special bed, their leaves at least have risen to the spring. But whether they will flower awaits the autumn.

On reaching Kerasia, there emerged from a row of French beans Father Basil, a crafty, auburn-bearded monk the genuineness of whose greeting reconciled me to the memory of how formerly he had sought to turn us from the door till assured of our financial worth. The morning was spent in writing letters; since David, being on the point of arranging his marriage, had resolved to send Andreas' friend, at the cost of 7s. 6d., on a mission to the Caryes post-office. These finished, we lunched. Last year, appalled by the unkemptness of the kitchen, we had taken spade, dug onions and potatoes straight from the ground, and fried them ourselves. Behold now the same in the hands of Basil. "An English dish, gentlemen." There was

also an English knife, which a fair-haired monklet of fourteen informed us had been with them thirty years.

At three o'clock, five mules, over the price of which a small
monk in a white sweater had worsted us, were loaded with the
luggage and ourselves. The bill was paid, Basil uttering not a whisper
of dissent as the fictitious items were removed. And we embarked
on a ride of such hair-stiffening precipitousness as still to take away
the breath at the memory of it, of the thumbscrews of agitation
induced by the sight of camera and plates slithering across vertical
torrent beds, each clutching hoof sending cascades of shale falling
half a mile to the sea beneath. We were too tired to walk, and
suffered ourselves to be hiccupped over these tortuous ledges,
new and marvellous views revealing themselves at each turn, the
wooden saddles digging spine or stomach according to the up or
down, and the three monks, Basil, Andreas' friend, and the little
Crab-apple in the white sweater, shouting directions to each other
with weird inversions of normal intonation.

At one point, negotiating a lesser version of the Khyber Pass,
David and I dismounted to compose an art-view of David, poised
pilgrim-like upon a walking-stick, gazing out to sea. This elaborate
and beautiful process occupied a certain time, during which the
mules, spurred by the malice of their masters, redoubled their pace.
Wishing to come up with them, costing, as they were, 4s. 9d.
apiece, we hurried and we shouted, to no purpose; till at last we
bawled with open mouths, bringing pieces of the Mountain crashing
about our heads, trees from their roots, clouds from their moorings.
Like Egyptian acrobats on the pyramids, we hurtled from boulder to
boulder, retrieving in our course a mackintosh and overcoat fallen
from the mules' backs. They had stopped. Did we pay, I can-
nonaded, for mules in order to walk? Was he a thief? Had he no
eyes with which to attend the coats? In answer to which Basil
smiled gently through his auburn beard. Whereat, like the doomed
Moriarty high up on a mountain-ledge, I forced him backward
to the very lip of eternity, fingers twitching for his beard, simulating
the lust that overtakes a Turkish soldier at the plucking of a hirsute
prelate. Certainly, he said, he would take care of our possessions
during the remainder of the ride. He had not really understood
before. Mark, meanwhile, unfamiliar with the modes of the

Levant, sought agitatedly to pinion my arms against an earnest homicide.

We topped the *skiti* of St. Anne, where formerly we had slept the night in the roof of the church. It is here that the left foot of the grandmother of God is preserved, "a most miraculous and odoriferous relic." And, after a two hours' ride, we came in view of St. Paul's. No sight on the Mountain can compare with the first vision of this monastery from the path to Kerasia. Even Reinecker let escape a tribute to its bewildering beauty. Tucked in an angle of stupendous cliffs, the massive foundations rise imperceptibly convergent to square blocks of cells, backed by a curving, serrated wall which fits to the rock behind. While from it a square and slender tower, colour of pink putty, like all the other stone, aspires to help the landscape in its composition. For this is but the pivot of the scene. Below runs a river-bed, strewn with Leviathans of the ice-age, dry now, but tearing cataclysmic to a group of boat-houses and the sea, twenty minutes away. And above, whence the river comes, rears the whole peak of Athos, snowy, luminous grey against the blue, falling in darkening, gashed escarpment to the building and the cypresses about it. The monks put on their gowns, changed their soft caps to hard, and tightened their belts. I gave them cigarettes, and thus made peace. Crossing the river-bed, we approached the monastery.

Chapter VII

TO METHODIUS

SEATED on a bench above the path sat a fat monk with a white beard, shaded by a mulberry-tree. As we approached, he descended in welcome.

"Whence are you?" he asked. "French, Germans, or Americans?"

"We are English."

He then espied the luggage. "So that is how they travel in England," he remarked. And conducted us forthwith to a high guest-room smelling of a disused nursery. Here we awaited, with more than usual expectation, the reviving tray. Over the door hung a fine early eighteenth century *eicon* of the *Panaghia*, her dress of rose-colour shaded in chocolate, and enclosed in a light wood Gothic frame crossed at the corners, redolent of the nursery Landseer. A series of windows opposite the door, draped as though pertaining to a romantic bedchamber of the Second Empire, permitted the full glare of the falling sun. Outside, a balcony poised us above the slim green cones of cypress-trees, themselves balanced only on a ledge of rock and fostered by the monastic sewage that poured at intervals down a wooden shoot. Doves were fluttering from branch to wall. Rapt in contemplation of the arsenal tower on the shore, it was only David's elephantine tread which brought to our notice the fact that the balcony was threatening to part company with the wall.

Within the room, a series of prints so typical as to merit description, told the great incidents of Greek history. There was the series of ironclads such as the *Averof*, named after their millionaire donors; a mythological matron, in a classical helmet, uttering a tear at a rustic cross bound in blue and white ribbons and inscribed *ΕΙΣ ΤΟΥΣ ΠΕΣΟΝΤΑΣ*—To The Fallen—1912, a souvenir of the First Balkan War; Kolokotronis, also in a classical helmet (specially

[104]

manufactured in England and brought out by Byron), leading his Klephts on horseback in the War of Independence; Kanaris, the admiral, gorgeously moustached; Germanos, Archbishop of Patras, raising the standard of revolt in 1821, at the hill-bound monastery near Calavryta; the scene outside the Royal Palace at the deposition of 1861, linen-kilted warriors prancing in exaltation, with the departing Otho and Amalia vignetted in one corner, the arriving George and Olga in another; and the great Patriarch of Constantinople, Joachim III, entitled, although a king had reigned in Athens eighty years, "*Le Grand Chef de la Nation.*"

The guest-master, Father Methodius, a young man of weak disjointed body and smiling face, brought us at length refreshment. The *ouzo*, distilled, he said, from figs, was such that only a hurried draught of water prevented its permanently scalding the roots of the tongue. There is a sinister reticence in the appearance of Greek drinks. It happened one June afternoon that I was led to pay my respects to His Beatitude Meletios, ex-Patriarch of Constantinople, Patriarch-elect of Alexandria. A natural timidity was not dispelled by his appearance: enormous corkscrew moustachios of silver descending over a beard that reached his pectoral cross; voice deeper than human; and the stature of a giant, which alone had saved him in 1923 from the hands of the Turkish mob, when he clung to each successive baluster from the top to the bottom of the Patriarchate, while the dragoman telephoned for the allied police. The usual tray was handed. Seated shyly on the edge of a chair, I perceived a thimbleful of orange sediment which seemed to denote one of those innocuous and sticky fluids dispensed in temperance canteens. Unheeding, I swallowed. And, to the Patriarch's surprise, in place of the abstruse political problems which he was expecting to discuss, I rose from the chair and rushed weeping about the room till the agonies of what I had thought to be my last drink on earth subsided.

Our rooms were clean and airy, being furnished with blinds, proper beds, elaborate gilt mirrors, cupboards, and even clothes-brushes and combs. This was the Ritz itself after our latter experiences. Mark, besotted with the sudden luxury, displayed a housewife's pettiness over the possession of large and small drawers, access to the mirror, proprietorship of the window-ledge, and proximity of the spittoon—a brazier-like vessel containing white powder and a kind of basting-spoon to inter contributions. These are to be found in all decently appointed guest-rooms and churches, adding, in the latter case, much to the poetry of the Orthodox service.

We then decided to bathe.

"You have only one hour," said the gatekeeper, a severe old man. "The gate shuts punctually at twelve"—this meaning seven. "It takes twenty minutes to the sea." Hurrying down the hill, we plunged into the water—a sheet of apricot with a boat and two monks, tall-hatted and upright at the oars, silhouetted against the sunset. I swam to a cave I knew and sat in it upon the cool green stones beneath the water, as though in a beryl. Having dressed, we realised that the hour was gone, and set off back at a run. But our progress was impeded, as we approached the monastery, by the sudden conversion of the path into a river by the unlocking of some upper sluice, in order to wash away the numerous droppings of the mules with which the day's work had coated it. Taking to the vineyard walls in the manner of suburban cats, we were in time to find a wicket still open, framing the black figure of the porter, watch in hand. But our exhausted appearance extracted a smile of indulgence. Rising to our rooms leading off a long, stone-flagged corridor, we found Methodius scouring the crannies to announce our dinner.

It may be, even at this early stage of our sojourn, that that hypothetical entity, the reader, is already stirred to nausea by incessant reference to the palate. It may be; but all the more shall he forgive, as buoyed on the content of a normal meal, the port burning on his gums, he turns these lugubrious pages of rancid fish and heathen vegetables. He shall more than forgive; every fibre of his emotions shall respond to ours. And when, with no trace of hesitancy, we award the crown of gastronomy and the very mantle of Mrs. Beeton to Father Methodius, a thrill shall course the marrow of his bones. As Clarendon to Falkland, the author to Methodius of St. Paul's erects this obelisk of prosody.

Dinner began with tomato soup containing clouds of macaroni stars; continued with potatoes fried in paprika sauce; onions fried; potatoes baked; and ended with cheese, grapes, peaches, and coffee.

Next morning we were wakened early to be shown the relics while
the priest was still at hand after the morning service. The first of
these was a piece of the Cross, encased in magnificent gold filigree
studded with coral and dating from the year of Queen Victoria's
accession. This was followed by a piece of the gold offered by the
magi; together with a substantial portion of the myrrh, which is
reported by the Jesuit Braconnier, in the opening decade of the
eighteenth century, to have been presented to the monastery by the
Princess Maco, daughter of the Serbian despot Ghika and wife of
the Sultan Mahommet the Conqueror. Last came an *eicon* of the
Virgin, almost indistinguishable with age, which had refused to
ignite when Theophilus, the iconoclast Emperor of the ninth
century, made holocaust of its fellows. And in the fullness of time
it had arrived at that sanctuary of maltreated pictures, the Holy
Mountain. Though whether of its own volition, riding on the waves,
as they usually did, or by the hand of man, we did not discover.

Each monastery exhales its own atmosphere. Even in the forties,
St. Paul's was noticed for its cleanliness. After the haphazard
squalor of the Lavra, its ordered passages, their shadow lifted only
by an occasional stripe from an open door or uncurtained skylight,
were a tribute to the cenobitic rule. The main buildings, despite
the singular beauty of their grouping in the dark angle of the
Mountain, date from no earlier than 1902, the older having in that
year been destroyed by fire. Tall and plain, they are supported
within, up to the first floor, on blue iron pillars to form a kind of
cloister. The church, ornamented inside with grey mottled
Athonite marble, was built in 1844 at the expense of Sophronius
Calligas, a wealthy Constantinopolitan. It is large and, in view of
the date, fortunately unfrescoed. Without, it carries unbroken the
Byzantine tradition of fluted cupolas and leaded domes. Some of the
buildings were still in process of reconstruction. And this activity,
noticeable elsewhere, was in outstanding contrast to last year.
Then all had been complaint; there was neither money nor labour;
no one knew what the government might do next. Now the position
was regulated, and would continue, after all, as before.

It remained to enquire about the photographing. Behind the
monastery rises the old hinder wall of ochreous pink stone, with
each of its narrow crenellations surmounted by a queer tile of

sliced stone resembling a pecking bird. And on it sits the tiny barrel-vaulted chapel of St. George, scarcely twelve feet high and twenty long, where hang in ruinous disorder, the finest frescoes on the Mountain. Thus placed, right beneath the summit, with every winter storm crashing down upon its roof, it will admit, say the monks, of no further repair. Yet the paintings on the inner side of the roof are already gone, rotted by the damp. The others remain insecurely fixed, with great cracks rending the plaster, ready, it seems, to fall with the next thunderclap. Will nothing ever be done to save them?

Let him who still conceives of Byzantine painting as a hieratic degradation, imagine a Giotto unsweetened, as Giotto already was, by Italianate naturalism, painting in the luminous colours of El Greco—those cold blues and clarets, olive-shadowed yellows, and pure, clear greens of under the sea; lit with angry brilliance; geometric in form; yet in austerity sympathetic, in power gentle. It is these, the very flower of the Byzantine Renaissance—not only the link between European art and the East, final explication of El Greco, but in themselves divorced from history, masterpieces for the world—that are threatened. Americans are expending £1,000,000 to convert the most picturesque quarter of old Athens into a pillared playground for cats, that they may unearth yet another shoal of those inert stone bodies which already debar persons of artistic sensibility from entering half the museums in Europe. And here, for the want of a few hundreds, paintings which historically throw an entirely novel light on the origins of European painting since the Renaissance, and æsthetically exhibit an astonishing and moving affinity with the goals of modern art, must perish.

Methodius assured us that the photographing presented no difficulties. The chapel was always open. He would conduct us to it himself. This he did, by a series of buildings and staircases, each floor of which was distinguishable in our subsequent journeys unguided, by the absence or proximity of its sanitary arrangements. Indeed, during the remainder of our stay we came to rely more and more upon the nose as an instrument of exploration.

David settled, I approached the tower, erected, according to a Slav inscription over the door, in 1522, and enjoying on Athos the prestige of Magdalen's in Oxford. By the lintel of the entrance hung a hornet's nest, the occupants of which seemed peaceful, though they emerged in such numbers as to drive me hurriedly inside. A series of steep, straight flights of steps, enclosed at one side between the outer and an inner wall, led from floor to floor. These had formerly been tenanted; but the rooms were now in an alarming state of disrepair, their floors creaking and trembling like a mystery-house at a circus. The roof proved a steep four-sided cone, on which I picked my way as remote as possible from the gaping gutter-holes in the battlements. It had been my intention, wedged in a crenellation, to attempt a downward photograph. But the looseness of a coping-stone upset my nerve. I descended, to find lunch, at 10.30, on the table.

As we slept during the afternoon, Andreas' friend arrived from Caryes bearing letters and a wholly unintelligible telegram for David, unsigned, with no clue as to its place of origin. Among others, a screed of panting indignation was addressed me from a friend whose projected stay in a Lundy Island lighthouse had been made impossible by his parents' learning, from the gossip-column of the Secretary of State for India's daughter, that while the party was in residence the licensing laws would not be enforced.

As we read, the monk waited for his money, seating his uncleanly draperies on Mark's pillow. We had agreed that he should receive 160 drachmas, half of which had already been paid to Basil as a guarantee. We now gave him 110, thus including 30 extra as a tip.

"But," he answered, "remember what you said."

This supposed dictum was the outcome of an incident of the day before. On the way down from the summit, the mule, which he was leading, had stopped to drink at a trough which owed its construction, according to an inscription, to the activity of such and such a monk by means of a συνδρομή.

"What does συνδρομή mean?" I asked.

"A συνδρομή," he replied, "is when someone goes from one person to another demanding and receiving money for a purpose. It is what you are going to do among your friends for me, is it not, so that I can buy some new clothes? As you see, these are all torn. I have been here four years now, without new ones. In the war I fought in Asia Minor, and escaped to the coast by Broussa in 1922."

To which pronouncement my sole words had been: "When so many were killed, you were very fortunate."

I now turned on him, pointed out that he had already received more than he bargained for, and threatened, if he did not cease, to take it away again. Accepting the offer of some cigarettes, he retired.

There arrived in the evening two more guests: a Greek occupying some professional status in Salonica, of which we could not fathom the meaning; and a tall Czech, adorned with a raw shaven head, whose beard and moustache were trimmed with nice precision to a seventh of an inch all over.

"*Ach!*" he shouted excitedly, meeting Reinecker, who looks foreign, in the passage. "*Sind Sie ein Deutscher?*"

"*Nein,*" was the reply. "*Ich bin Engländer.*"

"*Ach so? Von London?*"

"*Ja.*"

"*Sind Sie auf lange hier?*"

"*Zwei Wochen—die anderen sechs oder sieben.*"

"*Also, haben Sie Bekannte hier? Was treiben Sie? Studieren Sie? . . .*"

And so on. Five minutes later, David, Mark, and I, unaware of his advent, met him at the dinner-table. Reinecker mumbled a formula of introduction, whereupon, observing his mode of hair-dressing, we opened conversation with such German as we could summon.

"*Ah, monsieur, pardon!*" he replied, with stumbling deliberation. "*Je ne parle pas l'allemand. Je suis Czecho-Slovaque.*"

This sudden decision relieved us of the embarrassment of his conversation. For his French was of an incompetence which prevented his uttering unless addressed. Later, meeting him at the sink, I twitted him on not speaking German from patriotic motives, to which he replied that he had never learned it, colouring to the lie. I was tempted to ask if his Czech was as bad as his French, but refrained.

Next day, finding him in the passage as Methodius was calling us to lunch, I accidentally translated the summons, since he spoke no Greek, into German. Upon which he bowed stiffly.

During dinner that night we were entertained by Methodius, who told us the story of basil, the sweet herb; how the Empress

Helena discovered this little plant sprung from the blood of Christ
on the site of the Cross, and brought it back with her to Constantinople, since when it has flourished on window-sill and balcony
through all the Greek lands.

Our fellow-guest from Salonica exhibited a facetious good
humour, comparing me to Mangas, a kind of mythical Hellenic
naughty boy whose peculiar attributes of comicality I could not
recall. As the meal continued, his voice grew louder, his dis-
quisitions more dogmatic. He was a typical Greek of the middle
class, enthralled by politics, religious believer in the Hellenic
destiny. Anglophil, anxious to be of assistance, boundlessly conceited, yet, save when enlarging on a favourite subject, unobtrusive.
During a conversation, I mistook the meaning of a word for another
outside the context in which he had used it. This led him to a new
field.

"Every word in Greek," he said, "has ten meanings, and every
meaning ten words. You need to know each one. Greek is the most
beautiful of all languages. The Bible and all the holy works were
written in it."

"The Gospels, for instance," I interpolated, wishing to seem
intelligent.

"Yes, Matthew, Mark, Luke, and John the Theologian all used
it. Yet they were not Greeks. But the Holy Ghost descended with
the gift of tongues——"

"Ah! Of course, the *Holy Ghost* was Greek."

Whereat Father Methodius, handing a dish of stuffed tomatoes,
exploded into giggles; and the guest, his peroration marred,
groaned, protesting and reiterative, that this was not the case. I
recount the anecdote with pride, as it is not easy to hoist a Greek
neatly on his own petard.

Another curious figure at this monastery was Father Zenobios,
tiny and wizened, of great age, and speaking English in a pathetic,
shrill voice. The other monks used to push him about, regarding
him as not wholly in possession of his faculties, and, though lovable,
tiresome. Born over three-quarters of a century ago in Cephalonia,
when the Union Jack was still floating over the Ionian Islands, he
had remained a British subject. His career in the world had started
as a stoker on a ship of the Union Castle Line. After fourteen years

of this, he became a stevedore, working at Gravesend and Green-hithe. He knew London, had driven something in the nature of an engine at Newcastle, and visited India, Australia, and South Africa, his journeys in the latter including both Kimberley and Bulawayo. For the last twenty-five years he had enjoyed the peace of Athos.

"I love England," he told us. "I pray for her night and morning."

It eventually transpired that the photographing on which David was engaged was strictly forbidden, owing to the distaste experienced by the abbot on a former occasion, when some of the *eicons* in the church had been reproduced in a newspaper. As, however, he was away, there was nothing to prevent our continuing the work. He was returning on the morrow in company with the governor. And it became plain to us that Methodius was anxious to know the date of our departure, as we were occupying the best rooms and he wished to have them ready cleaned for the reception of a more distinguished guest. His attitude of apology for this seeming inhospitality was so genuine that he could hardly frame the words of enquiry. Could we not return after three or four days? In his agitation he served lunch at half-past nine.

But we had already decided to leave that evening. And, writing a note which he should deliver to the Governor, we pressed Methodius' hand with profound gratitude for this respite of comfort. We had been actually very tired on arrival. Now, restored, we could face further obstacles bravely. The luggage was being loaded in the courtyard under the superintendence of the steward. With a last promise to return, if not now, next year, we clattered out of the gateway and down the road to the sea.

Chapter VIII

DISCIPLINE

IT IS NOTICEABLE, as the visitor's boat is impelled up and down the waves by some jocund octogenarian whose peaked shade against the glare of the sun on the water resembles the helmet of a Spanish trooper, that the promontory of Athos is composed of marble. Both cliffs above, and rocks below the surface, fluted and pillared in fantastic diagonals, are inlaid with white veins, whose petty twists interrupt the grandiose conformations of the waves' battery. The marble is both green and grey. And from the stone jetty of St. Paul's arsenal, where the end had fallen into the mouth of the tiny harbour as though to ambuscade the lobsters, there could be seen, as we swam about, a dull green cape jutting from the "boscage" of the slope above, not a quarter of an hour away. Beyond it the coast-line continued unbroken. Conceive, therefore, our astonishment when there materialised, on rounding this corner, a large bay. And in its farthest recess, shouldered on a shrub-grown, overhanging cliff a hundred feet above the sea, the high wall and fantastic jutting balconies of Dionysiou.

As an adjunct to the English home a wholesome discredit attaches to the balcony. The architectural phantasmagorias of outer London —Belmont, Bellevue, and Bellavista—rise in the imagination, protruding their banistered platforms to the tune of dormered roof and Rhenish tower; or, in the earlier phase, when architecture was "free" like last year's poetry, and Ruskin held the torch of taste, arcaded in Venetian Gothic, Torquay marble pillarette and passion-flower capital sustaining cloister to the bathroom window. Nor may utility be permitted to compensate æsthetic doubt. In both inner and outer London, from the hooped embrasures of Mayfair and the stuccoed balustrades of Kensington to the last row of latter-day Morden, it is *vulgar* to sit upon a balcony. The City holds the same canon. What blithe advocate has yet dared sniff the morning sun from the turrets of the Law Courts; what hapless clerk from the

[113]

Assyrian crow's-nests of Adelaide House? Nor are provincial towns less squeamish. And in the country the balcony is superfluous, Either the sun shines, when we rush into the garden to see it. Or else it does not, when we stay indoors. The balcony, in fact, remains the instrument only of suicides. Each one is a lasting memorial to the postman who met his death in Northumberland Avenue through impact with a lady in search of her Maker.

But in southern climates it is different. And on the Holy Mountain, more particularly in such monasteries as Dionysiou, that are cramped for space, there is no domestic function that the balcony does not fill. It has swollen to the dimensions of rooms and wings, windowed and roofed, but no less balconied for that, strutted out on slender wooden brackets. It is often the habitual means of communication between one quarter of the monastery and the other. It supports the household offices, that their refuse may descend unhindered to the rocks or sea below. And for the individual monk it is, above all, his home and his castle. Here, when his position in the monastery admits his possession of one, grow his pots of basil and his flowers. Here he sits on summer evenings, with only the sea between him and eternity—a schooner sailing gently by, a steamer on the horizon heading for the sunset and the world. Here he thinks of the past, of the continents he visited and the wars he fought, of Greece and the Greek world, Constantinople and the forsaken coast of Asia Minor. Here he holds converse with his cronies over the affairs of the monastery, the elections of the abbot, the elders, or the *epitropoi*. Here, if the community be idiorhythmic, he eats and drinks. The sun, tottering on the rim of the sea, falls. A green pallor overspreads the sky, encroaches on the orange glow, swallows the black outline of Longos. Stars light the sky; a rising moon, the earth. He goes to bed, to rise at three for the church, where the golden points of candles cast only shadows, no light. Slowly the dawn encroaches, bloodless through the windows, bringing shape to the pillars, damping the flames. "*Δόξα πατρὶ καὶ υἱῷ καὶ ἁγίῳ πνεύματι καὶ νῦν καὶ ἀεὶ εἰς τοὺς αἰωνας των αἰώνων. ἀμήν.*—Glory to Father, Son, and Holy Ghost, now and forever, through the æons of the æons." And, sung to God, another day begins.

Finally the balcony forms an integral feature of that remarkable and distinct phenomenon, Athonite architecture. But, marvel that

Dionysiou is, better will follow. Till then it must rest on the laurels of domesticity alone.

Despite its position directly above the water, the climb to the monastery occupied a quarter of an hour, the road leading straight for the heart of the hills in the opposite direction, before it finally curved back in a level stretch to the gate. A portly guest-master, beetle-bearded like an Assyrian king, received us without enthusiasm. And a lesser minion handed the expected tray as we gazed from the windows on to the port and boat-houses immediately beneath, the black conical heaps of charcoal, yellow stacks of wood, spheroid trees of bright green, and vermilion-tiled roofs, all resembling an aerial map. Ignoring our preoccupation, the guest-master hinted that our attendance in the church might be appreciated. Much loth, we descended and stood through the hour, supported on the crutch-like arms of the pews and craning at the frescoes which we hoped to photograph.

The service over, the monks began to assemble before the refectory door in a low cloister adorned with sixteenth century scenes from the Apocalypse. Among them, leaning white and bent upon his staff of office, was the abbot, to whom we bowed our salutations. The monks, however, waved us away. "To the gate," they said, "to the gate." But, wishing to fetch some object from the guest-room, I turned the angle of the church in that direction, to find myself once more admonished, "To the gate, the gate!" So to the gate we went, and sat there beneath a vinery, talking to other monks with us and watching mules eat hay in an open stable on the terrace.

Dinner, a meal of acrid insufficiency, was shared by Father Gabriel, deputed to entertain us—an unusual type, with sad brown eyes and chestnut hair. His voice was soft and deliberative, reluctant of inflexion, as unlike as possible to that of the ordinary Greek. At first, conversation progressed slowly. But a casual remark led us to Byzantine history, in which he was proficient. On learning that David was not only an "Oxford professor," but had lately conducted the excavations at Constantinople, he warmed towards us. We broached the frescoes. He would make enquiries in the morning. He then continued with the history of the monastery, the youngest but one on the Mountain and founded in 1375 by the Emperor Alexius III Comnenus of Trebizond.

"The imperial chrysobul still exists," he said, "in the abbot's keeping. It has pictures of the emperor, the empress, and their children."

The Trapezuntine Empire, negligible in area and void of political achievement, occupies a singular position in the tale of that uncircumscribed world between Europe and Asia whence the West has drawn its soul. It rounds the pattern of history to completion. The fall of Constantinople, the most gorgeous and dramatic funeral act which a nation ever achieved to fire the chroniclers of posterity, has been sung. But shall the epilogue stop short on this crescendo, this blast of pathos, conscious even in the players? Not yet; the minor theme is heard another eight years. Till 1461 the echoes call over the Black Sea from Trebizond. Only then, with the advance of Mahommet's army against the last Christian emperor of the East and the last of Greek independence, opens the silence.

The span of a human life seldom outlasts a century. This imperial diadem, which Constantine completed with a cross, saw the twelfth of its age begin. History shows no parallel in heroism to that of this institution. And those to whom history, like music and the other arts, offers port in the eternal quest, have run to the scrutiny of this ultimate phase; just as others, inspired by the characters of individuals, have searched the records of their deaths for last fragmentary words. But in the case of Trebizond, beyond the recital of battles and the court's intrigues, small evidence has survived. An English embassy to Tamerlane at the end of the fourteenth century wore its shoe-leather to ruin on the cobbled streets. And Bessarion, the Greek cardinal, whose house in Rome was the focus of the refugees, has left a description of his native place: churches, libraries, palaces, and gardens grouped above the sea. But the mosaic portraits of the Trapezuntine sovereigns, that endured till the middle of the nineteenth century, are gone. And the collections of Greek manuscripts are barren. Gabriel's words, therefore, set our minds afire. When might we see this document in the tail-piece of our romance?

See it? This aspect of the question had not, apparently, occurred to Gabriel. It would be difficult. He himself, an elder, had never seen it. The well-known Professor Millet, who stayed in the monastery a month, had begged and begged; but he had never seen it. The Governor had seen it. But he had come in company with the exiled Archbishop of Trebizond, whom it was impossible to refuse. He had also, he afterwards told us, brought a wooden cylinder on which it might be rolled. For hitherto it had been folded, to the detriment of its illuminations. Our excitement was so marked that Gabriel consented to attempt permission for us in the morning.

But we failed. Anxious not to seem too insistent till the main business of the photographing was accomplished, I waited till the last evening before addressing a letter of supplication, in as elegant Greek as I could devise, to his honoured sanctity, the abbot. This had a certain effect, but for the moment not sufficient. Having been shown in the church an *eicon* of the Emperor Alexius III copied from the chrysobul, I returned again to the charge on the last afternoon. It seemed there was still hope. Gabriel left the church, only to return five minutes later with the news that it was impossible.

"Why?" I asked.

"The abbot has read your letter," Gabriel replied, "and he is willing. But the other two are not."

"Who are the other two?"

"A *cenobion* is ruled by an abbot and two *epitropoi*. It is they who have decided that you cannot see it. Why, I do not know. I have never seen it. No one ever has. But I tell you this—as well as the abbot and the *epitropoi*, there is the *synaxis*, a council of ten. Of that council, which meets on Mondays, I am the leading member. And, when it does meet, we can overrule the two *epitropoi*. If you were to return after a week or a fortnight, it would be easy."

"We will," I said, "after a fortnight. We will write to you."

But it was far more than two weeks before we were ready. And we learned, as we were about to start back, that Gabriel had been called on a journey to the mainland.

It is possible, however, that had we known the nature of the document for which we were enquiring, we should not have desisted in our persuasions so easily. We should at least have returned the Monday after. For it was unlikely that we should ever revisit the Mountain with such credentials as we had brought with us on the present occasion from the Œcumenical Patriarch, the Greek Foreign Office, and the Metropolitan of Athens, all of which were set forth in our letter of recommendation from the Synod. And it appears that this charter of Dionysiou—a monastery noted half a century ago for its secretive tendencies—is perhaps the finest later mediæval manuscript in existence. The description given by Finlay, based on that of Fallmerayer, who published the text without illustrations in the Transactions of the Academy of Munich in 1843, justifies the superlative.

The roll itself is "a foot and a half broad and fifteen feet long, surrounded by a rich border of arabesques. The imperial titles are set forth in capitals about three inches high, emblazoned in gold and ultramarine; and the word Majesty, wherever it occurs in the document, is always written like the emperor's signature, with the imperial red ink. . . . At its head, under a half-length figure of our Saviour with hands extended to bless the imperial figures," stand the "two full-length portraits of the Emperor Alexius and the Empress Theodora, sixteen inches high." It is curious that the children, mentioned by Gabriel, are not enumerated. Below the portraits hang the "two golden bullæ, each the size of a crown piece, bearing the respective effigies and titles of the two sovereigns." These are attached with clasps of gold.

Such is the treasure which we failed to record, and which awaits the death of the two *epitropoi* to gladden the sight of future travellers.

The atmosphere during our stay at Dionysiou disclosed a strange mixture of hospitality and severity, the latter resulting from a stricter observance of ascetic practices than is usual on the Mountain. A cigarette lit while working in the refectory cloister was denounced with angry brow. In which there was a certain irony; since, from the time of leaving school, where tobacco was a convention, I had never once smoked till my arrival on the Mountain, when I found it necessary in order to tide the gaps in social intercourse. But any peculiarity in the monks' behaviour was surpassed by the spectacular eccentricity of the monastery's actual appearance. It is here that the mind of the monkish renovator has found its most fantastic outlet. Pressed about by overhanging hills, the quadrilateral of forbidding grey stone walls rises to a roofing of grey stone tiles. And in their midst, occupying, by reason of the smallness of the rocky pedestal, almost the whole of the courtyard, rears a large church painted from roof to pavement a roaring pillar-

box vermilion, which is kept perennially brilliant with fresh coats.
The effect was such, as we looked between our balcony upon these
mottled scarlet walls scarcely four feet away and framed in a sky
of complementary blue, that Reinecker painfully rubbed his eyes
and expressed the opinion that the monks must be colour-blind.
Each morning a fresh shock lay in store, as, emerging unthinking
from the bedroom, there beat upon the retina these leaded scarlet
cylinders, gigantic in their proximity. Round the corner, as if
further to astonish, rose a balconied and gabled clock-tower that
looked as though it had been built in Nuremberg and bodily
exported, with a clock face in Turkish numerals ready attached.

We had worked all the morning in the refectory. And, on
enquiring once more when we might engage upon the church, there
was unloosed a flood of suspicion upon David as the photographer.
One of the obstinate *epitropoi* was ushered to our rooms, accompanied by Father Chrysostom, who spoke German and was the
holder of two diplomas in philosophy at Leipzig University.
Bearing in his hand the letter which Monsieur Lelis had written us,
and which we had delivered, with that of the Synod, to the porter,
the *epitropos* asked David, through Chrysostom:

"How did you get this?"

"The Governor gave it us."

"Did you ask him for it?"

"No."

"Why did he give it you?"

"We had a letter to him from a friend of his in Athens."

"Oh." This seemed to clear the air.

The *epitropos* then turned to me:

"Was it you who visited the monastery in the company of the
Governor last year?"

"No."

"But you came here last year?"

"Yes."

"In what month?"

"August."

"Good. The church will be open in an hour's time."

Thankful to have negotiated in safety this alarming exhibition
of dislike for the civil representative, we decided for the future

to conceal the Governor's letter. The church was very tall and high, the frescoes being the work of a Cretan of Venetian extraction named Zorzi. His attempted infusion of later Italian grace into the strict iconography of the Orthodox Church was not altogether happy. Later the others bathed; while I, health disturbed by the food, picked my way to an isolated rock in the sea and sketched the monastery from immediately below, with an eye to the balconies: not, let it be said, in the expectation of creating a work of art; but in order to restore my peace of mind. I had no sooner folded my legs on this islet than Æolus blew and Poseidon lashed. Drops of rain clattered on the page. Darkness hid the monastery. Triumphing over the inclemency of nature, I persevered till seven o'clock. When, feeling that in this of all monasteries the gates would not be reopened to the delinquent, I stumbled up the hill as the night, which had lifted, fell again.

The day was Friday, observed as a fast by the guest-master with malignant pleasure. Lunch we could not eat. Dinner consisted of a piece of brown bread and a slice of aubergine. Even the water had stopped running in the taps. So that David, to wash the plates, had recourse to the fire hydrant on the floor below. The fire engine lay padlocked in a wooden cage to one side, a strange machine resembling a small gasometer fitted to the chassis of a Roman chariot.

It had been arranged by Gabriel that on the following morning we should visit the library. This contains one of the finest collections of illuminated manuscripts on the Mountain. The books in the majority of Athonite libraries have been catalogued by Lambros, at the expense of the University of Cambridge, which hoped to discover lost classics, but, fortunately for an overstocked world, was foiled in its attempt. Each library possesses a printed copy of its own section, so that those who are interested, yet ignorant, may discover the approximate date and other details of any particular volume. Though conscious of the sacrilege involved in comment on the historic rather than the æsthetic value of a work of art, I could not but note the extraordinary elaboration of Byzantine furnishings exhibited in the traditional portraits of the evangelists in a copy of the Gospels. Each of the writers was seated at a desk of light wood inlaid with dark, after the manner of the seventeenth century; some containing books on shelves; while that of St. Luke was fitted with a series of glass pharmacy jars such as those which advertise a chemist. On each desk, a smaller reading-desk was supporting the manuscript in progress. While below, such was the variety of office fittings that one looked instinctively for the telephone; pens, paper-knives, clasp-knives, compasses, and ink-pots containing red and blue ink, lay neatly to the writer's convenience. One of the evangelists was seated in a huge basket chair with a hood, such as may still be found in the halls of larger London houses.

Another and bigger Gospels, brought reverently from a drawer and laid on a piece of brocade spread for the purpose, was encased in a cover of sixteenth century Rumanian silver gilt, on which much of the enamel surrounding the heads of the martyrs and evangelists in the border was still in place. It would be difficult to discover a more apt illustration of the cultural ruin that overtook the Balkans after the fall of Constantinople in 1453 than the comparison between this and that of Nicephorus Phocas at the Lavra. The latter breathes the splendour, the restraint, and the sophistication of an imperial capital; the former, though in itself beautiful, a poverty of composition and folky incoherence of motives which tells of a people already a century debarred from the source of their incipient civilisation. The book was presented to the monastery by the "Voivode John Mirtchea and the Hospojda Kniejna and his daughter Stana and his son Peter." So runs the inscription between the portraits of the family. John Mirtchea was Voivode of Wallachia between 1541 and 1559. The metal, though not exactly coarse, possesses a texture that can only be described as "frosted."

The librarian, Father Haralambos, then requested our signatures for the visitors' book. It was with shame that we discovered those of last year, attached to a frivolous superscription concerning the excellence of the monastery's jam, ill placed among the poems and laudations of weighty doctors from Munich and Upsala. On this occasion we made amends with a testimony in cursive Greek to the monastery's kindness. Haralambos then descended with us to the guest-room, where Mark conveyed him to paper in terms of black silk and astrakhan.

The guest-master was now genuinely troubled at our inability to touch his food, and, on my becoming dizzy for want of it during the afternoon's work, hurried to my side with restoratives. Later we were conducted to the church to see the holy treasures. A large candle was lit; a board placed upon two stools and covered with a cloth; the priest invested with his stole. And with much ceremony the incomparable reliquary of St. Niphon was placed before the doors of the altar for our inspection. Of all products of the North Balkan, that cultural no-man's-land between east and west Europe, this object is perhaps the most extraordinary and the most beautiful. Niphon was the successor of Gennadius, the first Œcumenical Patriarch after the fall of Constantinople. But at some unknown date, wearying of public life, he had retired incognito to Dionysiou, where he served the rest of his life as a muleteer. On his death in 1515, his identity was discovered. And his bones, with the exception of his head and right hand, which are now said to be in Hungary, were encased in this coffer, sent from Wallachia by the Voivode Neagnoë, whose confessor and godfather the Patriarch had been.

A dedicatory inscription, presumed to be contemporary with the occasion of the Patriarch's consignment to the coffer, describes it as a "venerable and holy urn." If, therefore, it was already in existence before being converted to its present purpose, the discrepancy between its superb craftsmanship and the ill-balanced hammering of the book-cover described above, which hailed from the same region only thirty years later, is explained. Two feet high, one foot eleven inches long, and one broad, it takes the shape of a cruciform church, bearing five typically Byzantine cupolas glittering as of gold, though in reality they are probably of silver gilt. Around all four sides of this edifice, below the roof, runs a double frieze of saints in enamel. It is noticeable how the quality and colouring of the latter has deteriorated from the true Byzantine. But the outstanding and astonishing feature of the whole is the magnificently wrought tracery which, together with the numerous pinnacles of the cornice, is entirely Gothic. Thus it is shown how, with the destruction of the Eastern Empire, western forms began to permeate the strongholds whence all mediæval culture had originally sprung.

The priest also submitted to our curiosity one of St. Christopher's tusks. St. Christopher, it will be remembered, was born with a dog's face, which was only transformed to human after his embracing Christianity. His personal beauty then was such that he converted 48,000 persons, including the courtesans sent to seduce him. But most historically interesting was a small cross engraved with the following words: "Dedicated by Helen Palæologina . Princess of the Romans . wife of King Manuel Palæologus . daughter of the Draga . Lord of Serbia." This inscription refers to Helen, mother of the Emperor Constantine XI Dragases, last of that unbroken succession of sovereigns who ruled the East for 1,123 years—he who fell fighting the Turks on the walls of Constantinople. This cross, we felt, was something in the nature of a personal relic of him. For, beyond a doubtfully accredited sword in the Constantinople museum and the stone eagle marking the site of his coronation at Mistra, there are none. Helen, whose father drew his title from a principality in Macedonia, predeceased her son by three years, dying on March 13th, 1450.

Having pressed upon the priest, whom we had kept nearly an hour, an offering for the church, and on Gabriel an elegant little tome dealing with some province of Anglican ecclesiastics, we sought the guest-master. So poignant was his remorse for his *cuisine* that he could hardly be persuaded to accept our donation. The luggage was taken on mules to the sea. And we unloosed in a small boat dangerously weighted in view of a threatening storm. As we coasted warily along the cliffs, there assailed us a violent smell; and, dropping our eyes to the bottom of the boat, we perceived that our overcoats had descended with a thud on to the matter whence it was exuding. The holy boatman was so convulsed with merriment at this discovery that he was obliged to drop his oars— an alarming action in so rough a sea. But he was induced to resume them by the sudden advent of another boat which threatened to run us down as we passed between the promontory round which it had come and an evil black rock. To warn us, its occupants blew a long blast on a horn, which echoed weirdly over the grey sea and up the cliffs.

Thus we reached Gregoriou.

Chapter IX

SOCIETY

LIKE DIONYSIOU, Gregoriou also stands on a rock above the water, but presents a domestic and less spectacular appearance. The buildings ramble unpretentiously round two courtyards: the outer, large and square, dating from the early nineteenth century; the inner containing an old stone campanile ornamented with double stripes of tiling, and an unassuming church washed primrose yellow. Our guest suite had a classical flavour, each door being surmounted by a broken pediment. But the coloured stencillings on the walls, and the round table transfixed upon a pillar stretching from floor to ceiling of the reception-room, betrayed a later taste. On the table, which was deeply fringed, sat various albums and a small globe.

The guest-master's assistant, whose inordinately tall Byzantine body ended in the face of a girl of seventeen, snub nose and liquid eyes mooning from his beard, eyed us with a drop-jawed contempt that led us to doubt his sanity.

"Is Father Stephen here?" I asked.

In reply he left the room. But returned to demand our credentials. These evoked not Father Stephen, but Father Barlaam, a twinkling monk with an authoritative walk, short ragged beard, and turned-back cuffs. He was interested in our work, and was a man of much intelligence, having catalogued both the history and treasures of his monastery in an illustrated book which he showed us lying on the table. The subject of certain Byzantine professors arose, upon whom he exercised an unholy sarcasm more reminiscent of the *Edinburgh Review* than a "simple monk." In doing so, he echoed the tone of the monastery. Let those who think to leave the conversational graces at home beware when they arrive here.

It was late. And with the darkness, dinner was immediately announced. We were invited, as I had expected, to dine with the abbot and the elders. Having attempted a certain spruceness of appearance, we were lined up for grace in a small refectory, when Father Stephen appeared.

Last year, reaching Gregoriou from the other direction, we had encountered the abbot of Castamonitou, who was returning from conducting a service in the church of the Transfiguration on the summit. A ceremonial banquet was laid in a larger room than the present, to which we were bidden as now. Thanks were given God, calls for cocktails mingling with the repeated *Kyrie eleison*. All were then seated, the guests being so disposed as to separate as far as possible members of the respective parties. Being ignorant at that time of all but the travelling essentials of the language, conversation seemed for me impossible. Nor could the food—cold octopus in an oily salad—be expected wholly to occupy the attention. My only recourse was the decanter, provided, as is customary, one to each person. Gripped by a vinous pentecost, I launched into speech:

"We bathe every day, Father Stephen. Are there sharks here?"

"Sharks? They abound."

"Have you seen them?"

"I? No, I haven't seen them. But there are quantities."

"But if you haven't seen them, how do you know?"

"How do I know? They ate a deacon two hundred and fifty years ago. A lamb was set as a bait; they caught the shark, and there he was inside."

Having long arranged, in case of natural and accessible death, to be buried in a mackintosh and manure the garden, I was appalled by this prospect of leaving my vile body, not even digested, in the stomach of a fish. And resolved, in the contemplative silence that followed, never to bathe again. Next morning, however, we were all swimming about the bay as usual. And would have been, had the teeth of the monsters been snapping at the actual steps of the jetty. It needs more than the prospect of death and hell to forgo the waters of Athos.

Father Stephen was the most remarkable personality we met. His age was expressed in his short, snow-white beard. But he was tall and upright, exhaling as he walked, that conceit, hairsbreadth from a swagger, which marks a peer who has won the Derby. In conversation dry and witty, he was versed in current affairs; historically, his outlook was based on a broad appreciation of national temperaments. In his youth, he had been imprisoned by the Turks in Salonica for maintaining that the Œcumenical Patriarch was the head of all the Greeks. His theories with regard to the Near East were interesting. With Napoleon's expedition to Egypt, he said, the whole Levant had been Gallicised. And after that came the German King Otho and his Bavarians. It was only lately that the Greeks had adopted the English as their model in the West.

On the morning after the banquet, Father Stephen had taken us to the church, helped us to photograph an *eicon*, and also stood for us himself. We had promised to send him copies. But, as neither shot succeeded, we were unable. He was now, as he took his place at the head of the table, reproachful.

"How do you do, Kyrie Vyron? How are you? Well? You never sent me those photographs last year."

"I did not forget, Father Stephen. But they were not successful."

"Ha! Ha!" He was incredulous.

"It is the truth. I knew nothing about a camera then. The light got in. This year I will send you lots."

He appeared to doubt it, and changed the subject.

"I see that the Prince of Wales is doing well in Canada. And the Foreign Minister with him."

"No," I said. "It is the Prime Minister."

"Ah, Mr. Baldwin. And what do people think of Lloyd George now? And the Socialists, Macdonald and Thomas? There are Bolshevists in England, are there not? You really must cut off their heads. Here we have none. If we had, that is how we should treat them."

This singular knowledge of British affairs is common enough on the mainland, where strangers in trains will frequently put the casual Englishman to shame by enquiring the rights of some abstruse incident in the early career of Mr. Clynes. In the monasteries it is not. We met a number of monks who, enquiring tenderly after our political state as though of the health of a friend, were anxious to know if we were engaged in any war. While one and all spoke with vague affection of Lloyd George as "the friend of Greece"—a generous tribute, considering the proportions of the catastrophe

Simopetra

David and Mark with the Guest-master at Docheiariou

The Church of the Transfiguration

Synesius reading

Chilandari: The Courtyard

The Grape Pickers' Lunch

Orthodox lighting

Metropolis

which his policy engendered for them. At the same time, the above extracts of conversation show that, to apply the hackneyed epithets of ignorance and stupidity to the whole of the Athonite community is to deflect their mark only to the writer. Nor is this merely a happy condition of the present. Tozer remarked in the 'sixties upon the monks' solicitude as to "whether the queen had recovered her health; and they were quite ready," he continues, "to talk on such subjects as Victor Emmanuel and the state of Italy, the war in America and the Atlantic telegraph, the Leviathan—as they called the *Great Eastern*—the Suez Canal, and similar topics of the day." This, moreover, was in one of the smaller and poorer monasteries.

Grace completed, we sat down. The abbot took the head of the table opposite Father Stephen. On his left was myself, followed by Mark and David; on his right an *epitropos* and Father Barlaam, between whom were placed a priest from the mainland and a layman, plump and moustached. The assistant guest-master, towering over the table with eyes lifted in eternal protestation, waited. The light was localised by two lamps, one warm and incompetent, the other cold and bright, which cast the farther side of the room into total blackness.

A certain stiffness pervaded the meal. The abbot, though human and pleasantly inclined, was none the less an abbot. Each dish was placed before him first, with a bow. Once in five minutes he addressed a remark to the company. After an attempt to initiate conversation by remarking, in the voice of a practised *raconteur*, that we had been to the top, I thought it better to wait till I was spoken to. The layman attempted to fill the gap. But, having learnt his English in the United States, was troubled by our inability to understand it.

"You pronounce different," he said.

"Yes, we do."

"I ran over Canada once. Friend mine had lill mo'-cycle. Fine place. Now do business here—buy wood from monks. Make no money in Greece"; and he shrugged his shoulders and jerked down the corners of his mouth as Greeks do to denote disgust. He was a pleasant example of a type which, being compounded of the most conceited mentality and the most democratic manners on earth, is as repulsive as anything that humanity has yet achieved.

Though loth to revert to the details of our food, it is impossible to pass in silence the disintegrated and nameless fish with which the meal opened; the cod that followed, salted after it had rotted in the summer sun; the macaroni, embalmed in the juice of goats' udders curdled to a shrill sourness; water-melon, ghastly pink like some spongy segment of a body delved from the intestines of a dog-fish; and accompanying all, like a rasping bassoon in a band of village oboes, thick resinated wine tasting of pine-needles and reducing the human mouth to the texture of a cat's. The abbot continued to heap my plate. And the others ate greedily. Nevertheless, at the end of the meal we were thankful for this profuse hospitality, since having starved at Dionysiou, we were in need of food.

Later, we drank coffee in the reception-room of the guest suite and looked through a book of paintings of the War of Independence by that Teutonic Delacroix, Von Hess, which were reproduced in colour. The monks and priest left early, as it was the eve of the feast of St. John the Prodrome, and there was to be an *agrypnia*— an all-night service.

"This is our work," said Father Stephen, with assumed bitterness. "Good night to you."

On returning to our rooms, we found that all the luggage had arrived from the harbour with the exception of my suit-case. I descended with anxious query to the kitchen. The guest-master looked surprised. But a monk was found who, after much prevarication, admitted that, owing to its weight, they had locked it up in a boathouse.

"But I must have it."

He shook his head.

"I shall stay here till it comes."

He departed. There was a full moon. Framed in the supports of the balcony outside, it lit the olive-grown slopes of the Mountain, casting a small round shadow beneath each evanescent tree. Below, the sea came washing silver-spittled down the jagged black line of cliffs. The clustered domes and chimneys of the monastery stood silhouetted in the foreground. And from a faintly glowing window in the depths beneath came the sour melancholies and sudden halts of chanting: "our work." Then clouds came up, taking the light;

the sea went dull as silver breathed on; the olives lost themselves in the earth.

And the bag arrived.

We had intended, as there were no frescoes of importance, to spend only one night at Gregoriou. But so great was the relief, both of David and myself, at being quit of the photographing, that we consented to the monks' importunities and stayed another. The anxiety of obtaining permission for our labours has been described. To the operator and the interested spectator the actual process was not less harassing. A monk was always with us. Sometimes he was all assistance, an actual hindrance in his wish to be of use; at others, a lynx-eyed religious guarding the Lord's treasures from the heathen; barring the doors of the *eiconostasis*, frowning on the manipulation of the sacred luminaries, lamps, candelabras, and candle-holding crosses which obscured the camera's view; and closing the church at the first possible excuse; all from plainly comprehensible motives, but not the less irritating for the feeling that, in his place, we should probably have acted likewise.

But, even with every facility granted—ladders thrust upon us, feet urged to the very altar—the hair-raising feats of equilibrium demanded, destroyed all peace of mind. Anxious to reassure David in the importance of all the frescoes which, being my choice, he naturally likes least, I enter the church. He has disappeared. Only the monk is asleep in a stall. Suddenly the sacred fane trembles with the oath of a Heliogabalus, and he materialises: clinging ape-like to the ridge of the *eiconostasis*; balancing on a step-ladder four feet across the bottom, four inches at the top; vainly digging the points of the tripod into the marble inlay; hurling psalter and Bible from his path; elbowing concealed sacraments. Crash! Two plates hurtle to the ground; a colour-filter twitters into fragments; or the camera itself collapses like a spread balloon, the tripod becoming more and more, as time went on, a thing of string rather than wood.

At length the first half-dozen plates are used (or broken) and must be changed. This needs darkness. Sometimes a convenient cupboard offers; in which David performs the operation, his ears contorted between his knees, while we, spreadeagled over a counterpane to block the cracks, are entertained by muffled rattles, half paper, half human. When the doors are opened, the blast of a furnace rushes into the room, and David goes to change his clothes. If there is no cupboard, it is necessary to drape a small table with the bed-clothes and form a little house such as used to enliven the nursery on wet afternoons. The merriment of dignified fathers at this shorn and muscular Venus emerging from its linen foam at their feet, was painful to the ear. Ultimately David returns to the church, to find the monk imprinting his own eye upon the plate in the middle of an exposure, by looking down the lens.

Thus freed on this particular Sunday morning, from an onerous duty, we lay idly abed. Till the sun, creeping round the corner of the bay, called us to the water. I had swum across to right beneath the monastery windows, rousing the inmates with cries of "Sharks!"; and, having returned, had wheedled a mug of boiling water from the kitchen; when Reinecker, face blanched and lips incoherent with the pressure of words, rushed upon me to say that the American Greek had told him there was no boat to-morrow night but one to-night which he must catch owing to the connection on Tuesday night at Salonica and his journey at Munich he definitely had to be in Paris by the fifteenth and everything would be all right if it wasn't for his beastly passport which he knew all along we ought to have got out of that man in Caryes all his life he had never liked to be without it now what was he to do?

Frozen by this spate, I covered the mug with a handkerchief and approached Father Stephen, at the end of the balcony outside the window to our room.

"Good morning," he said. "How much did this clock of yours cost? It's a nice thing."

"I don't know. It was a present."

"Who from?"

"My——" The word for aunt escaped me. "My father's sister"; though, in fact, it was my mother's. My father's sisters dislike me too much to speak to me, far from placating me with gifts.

Reinecker's teeth were grinding.

"But tell me," continued Father Stephen, "how much would such a clock cost in England?"

"I suppose about 1,500 drachmas." And, before he could interrupt again, I broached Reinecker's dilemma.

"There's one of our boats leaving for Daphni this moment," said Father Stephen, pointing down to the sea beneath. "He must catch it."

I translated. Demoniac, he rushed to pack, while Father Stephen yelled to the boat to wait and I devised letters to the police. Snatching them up, Reinecker tore from the building with a strangled good-bye. We last saw him rounding a cliff in a tiny cockle, which, for some unexplained reason, was filled with open umbrellas.

It seemed, after a lunch off cold red octopus tasting between rabbit and oil-cloth, our duty to attend vespers. This perpetual church-going on hot afternoons is the least enjoyable incident in the sequence of Athonite life. At first the service interests; for the Orthodox ritual possesses an impersonal beauty lacking in the West, where pomp of priest or humility of parson inevitably obtrudes. Instrumental music is forbidden; and the singing, at first unintelligible to the western ear, is taken up alternately on different sides of the church. The central moment is the opening of the *eiconostasis* doors at the elevation of the sacrament, when the monks remove their veils and the whole congregation and all the *eicons* are censed individually. The Athonite churches too, however modern, are not, with the exception of the Russian, ugly. Those like that of St. Paul's, which, being comparatively modern, are not frescoed, but bare white, provide perhaps the better setting for the holy pictures of an older date that now hang about the walls and pillars. But the majority are covered, and wholly covered, as tradition demands, with scenes from the life of the Virgin and her son, each occasion being divided from its neighbours by narrow bands of red and white. From the fourteenth to the eighteenth centuries, artistically valuable or not, their effect is invariably decorative.

Imprisoned in a narrow stall; fearing for etiquette's sake to rest wholly on the narrow ledge provided by the upturned seat; half stupefied with the heat, the incense, and the midday meal; the beholder develops an unconscious familiarity with the different cycles of iconography that prevail upon the Mountain: the alert ass of the Passion in this arch; the oxen lowing to the new-born Christ in that; in the south transept, geometric rays of Christ transfigured, distorting to the curve of the terminal vault; opposite, in the north, Christ treading delicately the grave-tops of purgatory; over the entrance-door, the Virgin stretched in the rigid pallor of her assumption, Christ gathering to himself her soul in the guise of a little child; behind the painted wooden crucifix that surmounts the *eiconostasis*, itself so deeply and minutely carved as to resemble some giant creepered wall petrified to gold, glimpses of Pentecost and the Ascension; they all become imprinted on the mind; till, with any change, the attention, hitherto subconscious, is suddenly aroused. Wearily the seconds join the minutes, and the minutes form an hour. At last the monks, kissing and prostrating at their chosen *eicons*, file out. And we are left to ask if we may see the treasures, while the priest—for only a few of the monks are priests—is here to show them.

In the present church of Gregoriou our interest centred round the paintings. The first was a head of St. Nicolas, a piece of fresco saved from the old church and converted into an *eicon* by an inharmonious casing of modern silver. Only the face was visible, a fine example of Byzantine formalism; though of what date, no record of the previous buildings has survived to tell. The other was a seventeenth or early eighteenth century picture of the Virgin, a life-size head and shoulders, set in an original carved gilt frame and designated the *Panaghia Galactotrophousa*—the Milk-Feeding All-Holy. This must be one of the most notable of later Greek paintings in existence. While departing in some degree from the austerity of the earlier Byzantine, it has nevertheless kept clear of the Italian influence that was gradually permeating such flickers of culture as the Balkans still could boast. The face, more rounded, more gently shadowed, more filled with sympathy than is familiar, has yet lost none of that abstraction and detachment that characterised Byzantine art in its heyday before the Latin conquest and in the later Renaissance under the Palæologi. The drapery of head and mantle are of flowered scarlet silk. The child sucks a pear-shaped breast, dark in tone as the face. And punctured and engraved on the gilded jesso background is a halo, interrupted by a high painted crown.

But as we looked, our admiration was tempered with horror. For, in addition to the ancient silver hands, there had been superimposed upon the old crown since my previous view a new one of

shining silver, set with glass jewels. Here at least it is impossible
not to wish that the Greek Government had not renounced the
power to forbid the desecration of recognised works of art with
these metal sheathings. Yet the history of this actual *eicon*, together
with a large company of others that adorn the church, renders the
Hellenic authorities forfeit of sympathy. The pictures had, until
1916, formed part of the church furnishings of a farm near Salonica
belonging to the monastery. In that year the monk overseeing the
estate had delivered them, persuaded by the possibility of invasion,
into the custody of the newly founded Byzantine Museum. And
it was not until 1921 that the monastery was able to regain possession of them by the ultimate despatch of Barlaam to Athens, where
his tongue no doubt caused consternation among those on whom
it was loosed. Items in the correspondence with which the incident
began and ended were quoted in Barlaam's book; a copy of which,
accompanied by a fine plate of the *Panaghia*, which is here reproduced, he gave me next morning as a farewell present.

In preparation for arrival at Daphni and its post-office next day,
we wrote letters during the evening, amongst others one to the
Œcumenical Patriarch to thank him for his recommendations. This
was an illiterate screed, in no way comparable to the flower of
prose penned several months before with the aid of a tutor in the
yellow attic off the Marylebone Road.

At dinner Father Barlaam alone entertained us, referring once
more to the original orientation of modern Greece towards things
French.

"Now we follow England alone!"

This remark was succeeded by a series of compliments so
embarrassing in their sincerity that I pretended not to understand
them.

"I should like to be an English subject," he said.

"When I am an old man," I replied, "we will exchange. You
shall become one; and I will be a monk on Mount Athos."

"Why not now?"

"I have things to do first.

"What do you think," I continued, "of the new constitution
and the new governor?"

"We shall see how it works in a few years."

"There always used to be a Turkish *kaimakam* in Caryes, did there not?"

"Yes. But he had no work to do."

"Has this one?"

"No, but he thinks he has. Another time, Kyrie Vyron, when you know Greek better, we will discuss many things."

Exhausted after his last night's vigil in the church, Father Barlaam forsook us immediately after dinner.

Seated round the albums, the conversation turned on national dress.

"Everyone knows," said David and I, "that Prince Albert invented the kilt."

Whereat Mark also retired, embittered.

Chapter X

REJECTION OF GRAVITY

IT IS POSSIBLE, for those who are old or young enough to have escaped the latter age of rationalism, to define the human itinerary as the quest of Reality; and by the assertion that the infant conceived in the twentieth century is nearer that goal than his ancestors the anthropoid and the lung-fish, to suggest, despite the flavour of moribund Liberalism that attaches, a theory of progress. To the attainment of this Reality, frequently termed, with the perversion of common speech, Abstract, all sincere self-expression is directed. Thus it might seem that those who have moved farthest up the line are the religious. But theirs is only a pavement, and one on which, in the present state of human mentality, the majority is not content to walk. It is the road, laborious with traffic, that carries the race—the road to which every province of human activity contributes the laying. The real motive-power derives not from the transient soaring of individuals, but the daily toil of millions.

This fact the Middle Ages, when religion was paramount, recognised, seeking to inculcate the Christian precept into the smallest details of existence. And in the degree of their attempt lies the fundamental distinction between the Byzantine and his contemporary of the Latin West. For in the West the ways of men were divided. Either they sought the cloister, there to focus every particle of their beings on the significance of religion. Or else, bearing the heat of those hard days when people scarcely outlived their forties, they were free to leave the business of salvation to that enormous and efficient proxy, the Roman Church. In the East, on the contrary, there was no such machinery. The world and the Church were one, dovetailed with each others' capacities, moving level. Men and women gave themselves to God as to-day they sign hotel registers. The world was a monastery, and its convents

therefore not isolated, but of that world. It was a great experiment:
to reconcile in human life the opposing aims of spiritual and
material welfare for the individualist—that Greek individualist
who can be loyal, but not led. If a thousand years, a greater span
than any European polity achieved before or since, be success,
it succeeded. When it failed, it was in face of odds before which
middle Europe also crumpled as a rotten tree. But the psychological
difference remains. In the mediæval West there were two means:
there was the path to be followed; or else there was its postman,
the Church. In the East every man was his own postman. And the
way, lighted by neither ethic nor logic, was shrouded in mystery.
To the understanding of all they both created this distinction holds
the key.

Enter a Gothic cathedral. The eye is swept to heaven with a
brute impetus, magnificent in purpose and aspiration, like the
Catholic hierarchy that built it. Turn, in contrast, to St. Sophia.
Here is no definition of journey. The lines of construction and
means of support are invisible. The shadowless, misty interior
seems not to rise from the earth, but to swim, poised above it.
Gothic reaches to the firmament. This has recreated it.

But it was not alone into their temples of the spirit that the
Byzantine infused the element of great inspiration. When Gothic
turned utilitarian, it was mean: witness Oxford and Cambridge.
Little of Byzantine domestic building has survived. But it is possible
on the Holy Mountain to study almost the exact counterparts, both
in date and plan, of the English university colleges. Fortress
through the centuries of a vanished temperament, Athos has
achieved that which the architects of our new industrial world
are also seeking: the impregnation of the utilitarian, of the walls
that house life's chores, with a sense of something other than the
present. Such, too, was the function of Byzantine religion. While
it was these, the Sunday and the week-day, that the Latin Church
strove to separate.

In analysing the architecture of the twentieth century, the new
architecture which is assailing cycle upon cycle of imitative pedan-
try, it is possible to term its underlying motive "movement in
mass." This has been achieved hitherto by neither the Gothic
nor the classical; the former being mean, or degenerating, as in

the case of the Houses of Parliament, into lifeless textural ornament; the latter being wholly stationary. To-day the new spirit may be observed in such diverse buildings as the later skyscrapers of New York, Liverpool Cathedral, the town hall at Stockholm, and the large block known as Adelaide House at the north end of London Bridge. To this companionship may be added St. Sophia, the outside of which, viewed dispassionately and without the minarets that do not belong to it, resembles some modern German laboratory characterised in the daily Press as the "last word in the revolutionary construction of the steel age." What, then, have all these in common? By what means is this movement in mass attained? The secret lies in uninterrupted stretches of flat perpendicular surface; in the avoidance of cornice, architrave, or any ornament that can disturb the sweep of the walls; and in the manipulation of perpendicular lines so that in fact or in appearance they are made to converge.

Hence, therefore, the novelty of twentieth century building. But there exist, none the less, two localities where a precedent style of architecture has developed and where the same abstract vigour informs buildings other than places of worship. These are contained, as if to confirm the other-worldliness of modern dynamics, within the two monastic dominions that the earth still possesses: the Byzantine community of Athos; and that little explored and little understood tableland above the Himalayas, Thibet. Here in post-mediæval times have the holy men in their seclusion erected buildings to which only the London and New York of the last ten years can offer parallel.

But the affinity between these two monastic republics is more than one of mere distinction politically from the rest of the world. The actual similarity in the form and colour of their buildings is due to more than coincidence. And, though one is Christian and the other Buddhist, it is plain that the contemplative life, untrammelled by the western doctrine of justification by works, is productive, no matter what its religion, of grand conception and grand execution when its devotees are engaged on material creation. None but the most inspired genius could have produced the two buildings which in each stand out above all others—the monastery of Simopetra on Athos and the Potala at Lhassa. And none but the same genius could have produced buildings so similar. Further, it must be remembered that these two, the tableland and the mountain, are not merely isolated communities of a few hundred such as we know in the West, but worlds within a world, capable of individual cultural development.

How far early Christian and early Buddhist monasticism were related is a question that has not been satisfactorily determined. There is no doubt that while the Buddhist theocracy in Thibet was actually taking shape, Nestorian Christianity, which had spread even to Pekin, had many flourishing communities adjacent. Some influence, it is supposed, must have been exercised by the already established religion in the formulating of a rule of life for those of the neighbouring creed who wished to give themselves to the eternal mysteries.

Apart, however, from the historical consanguinity—if such, indeed, exists—of the two systems, a more important common factor has contributed to the moulding of their supporters' temperaments. The psychological relation between landscape and art is admitted: what country but that which contains Kent, could have produced Reynolds? And how much more must the eternal panorama cast its spell over the soul of a monk who day in, day out, contemplates nothing else? In these God-governed states, the grandeur of the earth is unique. Of Thibet, even from photographs, it is possible to conceive the gigantic scale on which the land is cast, the enormous valleys stretching deeper and farther than the eye has ever seen, and the hills rising in vast sweeping tiers, one after the other, in the distance. While to anyone who has sojourned beneath the Holy Mountain; who has watched its peak, 6,000 feet sheer from the sea, white against the blue summer sky or magnet of fierce winter storms; has travelled the wooded ridges and sailed beneath the marble cliffs; who has gazed on the dim shapes of the horizon, Lemnos, Longos, and Thasos, colouring and paling to the time of day; and who has lived in sight of that inexorable sea: gleaming smooth all colours of a pearl, or silvery blue roughed by some haphazard puff of air; green turquoise, spitting up white horses in the clear windy air; leaden grey, pouring over its own troughs, clanging the shore in ear-filling monotony—to anyone who has experienced this whole combination of man-made and

God-made individuality, there cannot but have come an intensification of his impulse to indefinable, unanalysable emotion.

The quality of "movement in mass" is exhibited in some part or other by most Athonite monasteries, usually on that side facing the sea where they are buttressed from a falling face of rock. St. Paul's and Dionysiou we have seen. There are others. But preeminent stands Simopetra.

.   .   .   .   .

The journey from Gregoriou to Simopetra's arsenal occupied twenty minutes, the boatman boasting his knowledge of Africa, where he had peddled unspecified wares also in Bulawayo. He told us that the Greek for prickly pear, which we saw growing on the shore, was "Frankish fig"—a poor compliment to the other side of our continent. Arrived, we disembarked at a little quay, to be greeted by a monk of immeasurable girth, who ushered us to his house and fed us with grapes taut and sweet as himself. These we ate upon the verandah over which they grew, perched on struts above the water like a Samoan village in an instructional film. The heat was intense. Anxious to forget the climb that lay ahead, we sat in motionless content beneath the vine. And our host was enquiring after the others in whose company I had first met him, when a fleet of mules clattered past a door visible at the other end of the passage. He hailed them. And, loth to lose this chance or a ride, we gained the muleteer's approval with a present of cigarettes, and mounted. Our luggage remained below.

To portray a building whose dissimilarity from its fellows on this globe robs metaphor of its natural function is best left to other means than words. Yet, in the case of this building, the action of its changing aspects is invisible to the stationary beholder. A film might suffice. Unfortunately, this is a book.

Approaching, hypothetically winged, from the southern point of Longos, there is disclosed, as the promontory resolves into detail, a plain white mark high upon the ridge. Other patches, scattered along the shore, proclaim by their innumerable roofs and walls other monasteries: Gregoriou, Russico, Docheiariou. This, on proximity, consists, unlike them, of three tall blocks, towering backward on a crag, white against a mountain slope half

[139]

as high again as the distance beneath. Their brilliance is accented by a deep shadow, cast westwards in the morning light from wall and rock alike. Far below, at the water's edge, a tower and house, white specks, denote the monastery's port.

The hills close round, shutting out the summit, and the other valleys and other monasteries, till they form a shallow bay. The tower at the edge reveals a new dignity in reflection. Above, the building, risen, now that we are underneath, to the skyline, thrusts its triple clump aloft, each incredible façade exaggerating its own perspective to the call of some invisible scene-shifter behind the imminent cærulian canvas. Trenched inward from the contour of the bay and the spreading hills, a wooded ravine of perpetual shadow rises perpendicular some 900 feet. Until, from its womb, leaps to the light a pedestal of twisted, golden rock; and from it, gathering to itself the shadowed, shrub-grown ledges, Simopetra, the monastery, "Rock of Simon."

The path, topping the tower, twists up one side of the indentation, among precarious olive-groves. At first the building is invisible; until, upon a corner, it reappears, expanded, astounding. With every zigzag of the road it swells: new planes revealed, new lines composed. For the three blocks, each built back one behind the other as the rock demands, are not set square. The middle meets the foremost at a greater than a right-angle, the hinder the middle at a lesser. From no two positions, therefore, is the building consistent with its former self. As the blocks rise, unadorned save for the encircling stripes of wooden balconies, they narrow. Or, more accurately, the foundations diverge, that of the most prominent resting on a gigantic buttress sloping down the rock to a terraced foothold. And below it, from the curving beds of beans and tomatoes hanging nervously fifteen feet above each other, dark cypresses also engage in the festivity of line, urge up and on, till the human eye, unused to these dynamic harmonies, must slip its socket. With their perpetual variation and impatience of gravity, the three striped torsos resemble a group of footballers in that instant before the ball descends. Thus, petrified in colour, feet hidden in the cleft, knees of golden rock, white linen shorts and striped jerseys, they stand everlasting.

And the ball does not descend.

We dismounted at the long, upward-sloping tunnel that gives entrance to the monastery. And, reaching a courtyard, picked our way to the guest quarters along a balcony disclosing broad fissures of eternity between its creaking boards. The guest-master said that lunch would be ready in an hour. David lay down to read. Mark and I launched into the heat.

He walked up to the back to sketch. I, casting about for a vantage-point that might admit a level camera, noticed a platform of rock forty feet immediately above my head. Descending to a small chapel on the left of the path, which contained in its crypt the skulls of deceased fathers disinterred after three years and neatly docketed on shelves, I leapt down a bank of marrows; and, rounding a corner, came upon a gully that seemed to lead whither I had hoped. The ascent at first was easy: a mere creeping underneath the roots of bushes. But suddenly it took a right-angle—not to one side or the other, but in point of gradient. Perpendicular, it was not a gully, but a pipe. The sun was at its highest; the shaft in which I was imprisoned airless. All the view was the sea, awaiting the corpse that should come hurtling to its bosom. The stream, dry since May, trickled again, but red from lacerated flesh. Movement became fainter and fainter. Had not the sky reappeared, I should have remembered no more. Writhing like an Iroquois after a scalp upon the pinnacle of my desire, I poised the camera. Behold the result. And weep my life's blood.

Lunch, despite a protracted benediction, was welcome. Finished, we set out again, walking this time in the other direction, where the monastery is joined to the hill by a double-tiered aqueduct. From here its aspect changes. The pedestal of rock rises at the back of the monastery to within three stories of the roof, instead of, if the foundation walls of the front were windowed, approximately twenty. The domes of the church within the courtyard are visible. And the whole assumes an air of fantasy, like a Rhineland castle perched at the brink of an unscaleable crag, but made safe by the net of stone that hooks it to the hill behind. Below the scenic-railway entrance, the shadowy outline of ironbound double doors was visible, leading into the bowels of the rock. Our curiosity was aroused. But their objective remained an enigma. It was presumably an older entrance, dating from before that ghastly fire, still recorded, when the entrapped monks could only hurl themselves down the precipices of the front to escape the flames. This was in 1625. A sketch of the building as it later appeared was appended by Robert Curzon to his *Monasteries of the Levant*, published in 1849. But, as the foreground of this is entirely imaginary, it is impossible to rely on the accuracy of his depiction. He makes it more whimsical in form than appears to-day, like a windmill on the scale of the Eiffel Tower. The present group dates from another fire of 1893, thus carrying the climax of Byzantine domestic architecture to the birthday of the twentieth century. For the monks built and designed unaided.

Those who have lived in Athens, and lunched, as Athens does, at Costi's, will recall the lovely Madame Kogevinas. Her husband, an artist, is the author of an etching which shows Simopetra from a peculiar angle, rising its most precipitous into the sky. This view I also had in mind to see. Searching the landscape for whence it might be possible, I espied a small brown patch among the trees on the farther side of the ravine. It was necessary to approach from the back. On a bridge over which the path was carried stood a number of mules, who double their near hind-legs in readiness for my ribs. But, alarmed at the unfamiliar imprecations which greeted this movement, they thought better and galloped off into the mountains. Their master, hearing the noise, emerged upon a balcony to vent his anger upon both them and me.

By means of a track scarcely a foot wide, coated with dry slippery leaves and tunnelling among the undergrowth at an angle that necessitated sitting, the brown patch was reached. And perseverance was rewarded. Far above, a huge tilted box, creamy gold, and striped with the shadowed silver of oaken struts and planks, was rocketed into the blazing turquoise sky. It lived; like the flowers of the mystic, it sang; insensate; irresistible; inexplicable.

Seated on a rock, I sketched. My pencil, prone to be romantic, fled over the page in ecstasy, exaggerating the tone of the sky to the ferocity of a thunderstorm. But the others were waiting. The progress of the ascent, owing to my sandals slipping two paces for every one they took, was dependent on the arms. The heat was insupportable; the handkerchief that might have solaced, plucked from its pocket by the barbed vegetation; and the last thorn added to my crown when I was confronted, after twenty minutes' climb, by an impregnable cliff. Returning to the bottom, I found another track. My mouth was so parched that, on entering the guest-room, it would not utter, and the others feared for my reason.

Bidding the guest-master good-bye, we started the descent to the sea. It was my misfortune, when at school, to suffer from weakness of the ankles: a welcome safeguard against compulsory athletics; but one which jeopardised the hopes entertained by my house of my winning cups for its dining-room table—which I never did. Massage, therefore, was the remedy, applied by the Misses Dempster, ladies of frightening intelligence, who would invite me to consider the claim of a landscape "permeated," as they said, "with spires," to superiority over one which was not; or to analyse the composition of the uneasiest of Sargent's charcoal portraits, reproduced and presented them by Lord Spencer. Their house, indeed, was an illustrated Debrett, comparable only to the portraits of the *Almanach de Gotha* displayed on the walls of Madame Sacher's bar in Vienna. Massage finished, the ankles were tightly bound, and, thus reinforced, would gradually regain their strength. The morning of our visit to Simopetra, the muscles, long quiescent, had uttered a minatory twinge. Unwinding from a chintz bag some lengths of bandage provided by a parent who had envisaged the dangers of glacier and crevasse, I performed the remembered operations. But in vain. And now, emerging from the monastery, I could scarcely walk. Nor were there mules.

The debility arising, as in the case of running-shoes, from my sandals having no heels, relief was only gained by remaining poised on the toes. Thus I set off, hopping from rock to rock like an inebriate ballerina. But the pace, in such heat, was not to be borne. And, the feet being comfortable in any position but their natural, I turned and went backward. Physically this was perfection; but the mental strain, owing to the precipitous twists of the path, was insupportable. Eventually I fell on David's arm and dragged behind him like a rag doll. We reached the shore; and, despite the presence of a small sword-fish, flung ourselves from the jetty. To tired, hot, and aching bodies never was bathe so delicious. Eyes shut; rocking on the ripples of a breeze, shaking the water to drink the fullness of its cold; eardrums vibrating to its tinny throbbing; we lay entranced, almost asleep; confronted, when the eyes opened, by the wide doors of the boat-house at the head of a causeway of logs; the monk's house, balconied and vine-shaded; the white arsenal tower; the hills around, full of large shadows; the black gulch; and at the top, alight with the sun, the great building, falling back into the sky, ready to kick its foundations down the trees and crush us in the water at the foot.

The fat monk opened his spare room to our toilet—a sunny apartment, and for that purpose chosen to contain a string of drying haddocks in the smell of which, festooned with blue-bottles, lay the secret of many of our meals. After an hour's journey in a boat, during which we slept, we arrived at Daphni.

There, while the boatman waited, we hurried ashore, excited at regaining this Sybaris of luxury. But our feelings were damped by the discovery that we could obtain neither a glass of beer nor a clean pocket handkerchief. A box of plates, and a kit-bag hitherto filled with food and unused films, were deposited with the shop-keeper. With a dozen fresh tins of sardines in our saddle-bags, we again set sail—this time literally, as a breeze had risen.

The sun was setting, striking hidden fire in the purple hills. While the water, as if in protest, turned a shivering glass-green. Schooners, vermilion and orange, lay at anchor. Another in full sail rode by, with a red gold on its bellying canvas. Then the wind dropped, and we took to the oars again. The sun was gone, and the twilight deepening, before the barracks of the Russian monastery of St. Panteleimon loomed above us.

Chapter XI

WHITE RUSSIANS

THE JETTY was desolate, the night imminent, and the monastery gate a quarter of a mile away. Leaving Mark, David, boatman, and luggage a black heap on the farther side of the large artificial harbour, I set off to find it. Coarse, booted figures, rolling downward, stared. At the entrance was a group who spoke Greek. One of them led me over a tree-dotted space to a large detached block. Here we descended to a passage below ground, stone-flagged, without end. And hither, in response to calls delivered down yet deeper stairs, came the guest-master.

The environment was now as Slav as it had formerly been Greek. The fineness, the delicacy of Hellenism had given place to something more remote, less coherent. Flat-nosed Mongols and giant blonds passed by, "*shck*" and "*kck*" issuing from their lips in place of the familiar liquids. The figures, high wrinkled boots creaking beneath their cassocks, seemed either to lurch, hurling their bodies in movement above legs astride; or else to drag themselves along with a kind of abysmal inertia, each step falling deeper into the slough of their own inactivity. Of the latter was the guest-master, tall and bent as a poplar in the wind, with soft white moustaches floating from his nostrils above a spreading beard. His eyes gazed beadily into another universe. His hands, hanging as though on strings from the forward arch of his shoulders, could not cease their wringing.

Our luggage? On the quay? At this hour? Out of a boat? In the dark? Characters of Chekhov, Turgeniev, Dostoievsky! the whole gamut of their joint procrastination, the indecision that has wrecked half two continents, fought my appeals. We argued. When down the passage came a crowd of boys, sailors and scouts on a visit from Salonica; and, surging round, must needs put in practice the English lessons of their schoolrooms. My knowledge of Greek is by no means complete. But to be assisted in conversation by persons who know neither my language nor that of him addressed, reduces me to a mental disorder which precludes even sound, far from words, leaving my mouth. It was now quite dark. Bending with the volume of noise, eyes ahead of time itself, the monk maintained a despairing obstinacy. But the ring of boys suddenly parted; and there appeared Mark, David, and the boatman, bearing the first instalment of the luggage.

So vast a problem settled, the weight of Atlas suspended from his shoulders, the guest-master brightened, his eyes came to earth, and to the question of food he affirmed hope. David, meanwhile, having lately affianced himself to a lovely refugee whose tales of escape have long whitened the roots of all our hairs, bethought himself of her tongue.

"*Me otchen golodny ee oustali Otietz. Skoro li boudet obied?*"

An ecstasy lit the dim departing face.

"*On seitchass boudet gotov.*"

"*Ato horoscho. A gdie nam mojno spat?*"

Of his best we should have, rooms and food. Keys jangled, doors flew open. And David, wheedling his three dozen words into choking permutations, obtained for us three separate rooms, large and airy, supplied each with a green-shaded reading-lamp, and hung with a variety of pictures: oleographs of bloom-spattered grapes surrounding apples peeled to the waist; ghastly scenes of wolves tushing at sledge-borne damsels, snowflakes flying, moons caught up in firs behind, drivers peppering their horses' hindquarters with blunderbusses; and everywhere the interminable Russian royalties; the Empress Marie, chignon and throat dripping pearls; Alexander II saved from an exploded train, surrounded by small daughters in buttoned boots against a background of telescoped rolling-stock, Cossacks foraging in the wreckage for the malefactors, the Virgin and other celestial beings making their bow in the sky to the invisible public, grateful for their timely intervention; and finally, last victims of a throne that from time immemorial has crushed "average men," the sad-lipped Alexandra Feodorovna, radiant even through these crude colours, and her husband Nicolas II. Chekhov, Turgeniev, Dostoievsky: their characters have made history as well as novels. Russia . . . a cherry orchard.

White Russians

We went to bed early. I was too tired to sleep. The Elinor Glyns, Cupid's Bædekers of the Edwardian errant, were finished. And I had perforce to blow out the light and lie awake, ankles throbbing; the white faces and mountain paths of Simopetra stabbing out of the darkness; from the passage the noise of boy-scout good nights like the faint echo of a swimming-bath; and outside the windows the sea, arriving and receding with that just sufficient effort to whisper in the shingle of days and nights ahead, unbroken in the calm that now possessed it.

Next morning, in prospect of a day of idleness, we slept long and late. It was nine o'clock, and we were drinking tea in pyjamas, when the door opened with a jerk, to disclose the jovial bowing form of Father Mitrophanes, the abbot's secretary.

Last year, having arrived at a more reasonable hour, we had slept within the actual precincts of the monastery. Our dinner had consisted mainly of bortsch and tea. But what it lacked in substance was compensated in spirit by the company of Father Mitrophanes. Speaking fluent and witty French; an old stuff cap squashed like an inverted castle pudding on one ear; the fine strands of his beard falling to a paunch as broad as his smile; cheeks like door-knobs; his whole sparkling being cried query to his vocation. But, despite the evident joy of life, there were clouds.

"We get letters and newspapers from Russia. But there are no visitors, no pilgrims. We cannot return to our own country. Everywhere are financial difficulties. Our property in Russia is confiscated. Similarly our estates in Greece. On that point we appealed to Lord Curzon in 1923.[1] But it had no effect."

Had Mitrophanes read what that acute political observer wrote of the Russian monastery after a visit to the Mountain in 1891 he would not have been surprised.

"Not even the dainties . . . with which we were regaled could blind our eyes to the character of the whole institution; and, in taking leave of it, I could not help wondering whether the Russian monastery might not be heard of again in the drama of European statecraft." As usual, Lord Curzon was right.

[1] A second appeal was forwarded to the League of Nations in 1928, to which the Greek Government replied with a definite promise of compensation. The appeal also contained a claim for war damages to the value of £285,626 4s. on account of the billeting of Greek troops and the requisitions of both German and Allied forces.

"To think," Mitrophanes continued, "what has happened in the last ten years. Rasputin, you know, stayed here in 1913."

"He was remarkable to look at, was he not?"

"On the contrary, a man of very ordinary appearance!"

He entertained us till ten o'clock, when he rose and rolled vigorously from the room.

And now here he was again. Leaping from my bed, I introduced Mark and David. After much conversation, he departed in a whirlwind of bows. And we had resumed our breakfast when there entered Father Valentine.

A greater contrast to his precursor could not be imagined. Still young, his face remains indelible in the memory of one who has seen it. Of a waxen, ivory complexion; moulded in unearthly perfection, nose and mouth Praxitelean in their straight drop and double curve; framed, chin and cheeks, in silken chestnut ringlets; surmounted by a black cap set sideways in jaunty reminiscence of the past; emitting gentle faultless English, soft and musical, yet inhumanly devoid of either expression or cadence—his whole demeanour was so interwoven with tragedy that his presence was an event, a phenomenon. There was a wall between him and other human beings; the ordinary pleasantries of intercourse were too petty. His manner was that of a servant; his personality of one born to rule. Faint terror consumed me at this second meeting. But it seemed to me that Father Valentine had become, with this his second year in the monastery, in the faintest degree more reconciled to his lot.

He had arrived, he said, to show us round. We attracted his notice to our pyjamas. He therefore sat down on a bench outside. And we, knowing that no more nails could be added to his cross, shaved out of the tea-pot.

The buildings of Russico, as the Russian monastery is known, are enormous, modern, and wholly out of harmony with their environment. Tier upon tier of windows rise at the back of the courtyard above the church, with its green domes surmounted by gold balls and wired crosses lit with chunks of stained glass. To one side is the campanile, where gigantic bells, taller than a man, are seen hanging from its lower stages. And behind it is the refectory, big as Westminster Hall and slavered with the frescoings of a nineteenth century Perugino. By the entrance-porch the buildings are smaller, covered with wistaria and corniced with traditionally Athonite balconies. But it is outside that the horror is revealed. Block after block of huge tenements that would disfigure a Clydeside slum, balconies rusting, windows broken, stretch down to the sea, six or seven stories high. There, a harbour, formed by an L-shaped mole for the reception of steamers, embraces two fishing-boats. Over all, more squalid than romantic, broods an air of disuse. For the monastery once contained close on 1,500 monks. Now there are 600. There used to come yearly, ship-loads of pilgrims on their way to or from Jerusalem. Now there come none.

There is pathos, almost tragedy, in this deflation, in this remnant of a once overflowing community debarred from country and traditions—an outpost of old Russia in the Ægean. And there is also history, wherein the fate of the Holy Mountain, sanctuary inviolate of Byzantinism, wavered in the balance as it had not since the Latin conquest of the thirteenth century. It was computed in 1903 that the aggregate of Slav monks on the Mountain, Russian, Rumanian, Bulgar, Serb, and Georgian, already numbered 4,156, as opposed to 3,276 counted by the Greeks. This showed a preponderance of nearly 1,000. And even earlier, in 1901, Professor Charles Diehl, experienced student of the Near East, committed himself to the following prophecy:[1]

"The Hellenic element resists these encroachments with all the strength of its acquired rights, its ancient traditions, and the numerical superiority which it still possesses. None the less, it is possible to foresee what must henceforth be the outcome of this unequal contest. On their side the Russians have industry, energy, money, and perhaps, also, intellectual superiority; in the end they will have numbers. Thus, in the long run, despite the resistance of despair, the defeat of the Greeks is inevitable. And the day will come when to them also shall be said, as in Molière: '*La maison est à moi; c'est à vous d'en sortir.*'"

These prognostics of the days when Russia was an active participant in the concert of the Powers, and a Turkish deputy-governor dreamed of his harem in Caryes, have not been fulfilled. Nor will they be. But the whole latter history of the Mountain, and the whole

[1] *En Méditerranée.*

tenor of its present status, have been so largely the result of the Russian *Drang nach Süden* in the Levant, that the tale is worth telling.

From the twelfth century there has always existed on Athos a monastery ascribed either in fact or politeness to the Russians. After various vicissitudes, its numbers, at the beginning of the eighteenth century, were reduced to four. Re-endowed a century later by a family of Greek Phanariots, it was inhabited, after a period of abandonment during the Revolution, by Greeks alone. But in 1834, being heavily in debt, it accepted the entrance-fees of fifteen Russian probationers, who, wishing to enter the Athonite community, not unnaturally chose the convent which tradition assigned their nation. These attracted others; the whole of the outstanding debts were paid by them; and large new buildings erected for the reception of yet further compatriots. At length they found themselves in a numerical majority, and claimed on that ground the rights, first of reading the services on alternate days in Russian, then of electing their own abbot. The latter demand gave rise to bitter dissensions, in which the Holy Synod in Caryes supported the Greeks. But they were overborne by the Patriarch Joachim II, who, in return for substantial presents from St. Petersburg, threatened them with eternal flames unless they acceded to the Russian wishes.

Then followed the Russo-Turkish War. The Treaty of St. Stefano, concluded in 1878 behind the backs of the Powers, contained the following passage: "The monks of Mount Athos of Russian origin shall be maintained in their former possessions and hermitages, and shall continue to enjoy . . . the same rights and prerogatives as those assured to the other religious establishments and convents of Mount Athos." Thus the Sultan, the lay suzerain of the Mountain, recognised the existence of exclusively Russian communities. But the suspicions of the Powers had been aroused by the closing of the Black Sea, and a general war was only averted by the conference and Treaty of Berlin at the end of the year. Article 62 ran as follows: "The monks of Mount Athos, *whatever* their country of origin, shall be maintained in their former possessions and advantages, and shall enjoy, *without any exception*, complete equality of rights and privileges." The guarantee of the Russian status, with modified emphasis, was retained. But, infinitely more far-reaching, there resulted from the jealousy of the Powers the recognition in the most important international treaty since that of Vienna, of the autonomy of the entire Mountain. "Former possessions and advantages." By these vague words, ratifying at one sealing the heterogeneous precedents of nine centuries, the preservation of Athos as a theocracy, an independent political organism on the face of Europe, was assured.

Encouraged by their foothold on what now was virtually—and, in Russian hands, would be actually—an Ægean government immune from Ottoman interference, the Russians purchased the leases of two *skitai* and twenty *kellia*, separate communities, but fortunately the inalienable property of the Ruling Monasteries. The buildings that existed were replaced by new ones, which disfigure the Mountain with their garish semi-oriental domes, and have often been enlarged to twice or three times the size of the parent monastery. Thus at the beginning of the century, out of the 548 monks attached to the poor Greek monastery of Pantocrator, 435 were Russian, resident for the most part in the *skiti* of the Prophet Elias, one of the two which they had purchased. In every case, the rules which limited the enlargement of these dependencies were circumvented. And matters were complicated by the inevitable willingness of the poorer monasteries to raise such money as they could by the sale of deserted religious sites.

The Russians now hoped, by argument of numbers, to promote these inflated offspring to the status of Ruling Monasteries, and thus to add other representatives to swell their meagre vote in the Synod at Caryes. Thus eventually might they obtain a majority and a ruling voice in an Ægean Government whose integrity was guaranteed by international treaty. But in place of the venal Patriarch Joachim II was now Joachim III the Magnificent, whose purpose it was to combat the foreign menace. Not only did he resist all advances of the Russians; but addressed himself to the work of tabulating and revising the confused unwritten tradition of Athonite law. From the constitution which finally took shape, and which has been examined in Chapter III, one clause emerges with significant clarity. Any addition to the twenty Ruling Monasteries, seventeen Greek and three foreign, which already exist, is absolutely and ultimately forbidden.

But events of even greater moment were at hand. Two years after the original draft of the present constitution was published, the Balkan War broke out. Constantine occupied Salonica. And on November 2nd, 1912, after an interval of more than four and a half centuries, the Holy Mountain was delivered of the Moslem thrall. A Frenchman who arrived at Caryes to present his credentials towards the end of October, has left us an account of these incomparable days:[1]

"This evening a feverish impatience stirs this chorus of old men. The Greek army is at Salonica! The naval squadron here in the neighbourhood! Did I notice in coming the battleships of Condouriotis? Will they call soon at Athos? Is it to-day, to-morrow, that the imprisoned Mountain shall at last be delivered?"

Leaving the Synod, he proceeds to the Turkish *Kaimakam*, who states the opposite case. "Look around you," he says. "Look at these thousands of monks; visit their monasteries, question them yourself. Of what, in reality, can they complain? Have we touched their rules? Have we violated their property? Have we forbidden their pilgramages? Have we altered even a tittle of their secular constitution? . . . Always the West is talking of Turkish fanaticism. But what race, I ask you, what conqueror could have treated these people with greater humanity, greater moderation, greater religious tolerance? Under our law they have remained as free, even freer, than under the Byzantine emperors. And . . . they have not had to endure under our domination a hundredth part of the vexations that you have imposed on your monks in France. . . . They will regret us, monsieur."

The moment of liberation overtakes the writer at the Lavra. He is "brutally awakened by an unexpected uproar of shouts, explosions, and hurrying feet. In the courtyard crowds of monks are running about between the cypresses . . . dragging ladders which they lean against the walls. Many are already on top, upright between the battlements, as though in the days when pirates were visible on the horizon.

". . . It is nine in the morning. Down below, on the glittering sea, four battleships, four black dots, advance: the fleet of the Condouriotis! The monks embrace one another, cry for joy, intone

[1] Jerome et Jean Tharaud: *La bataille à Scutari.*

chants, discharge old guns into the air. The Greek flag, white and blue . . . flies from the top of the highest tower. All is radiant, magnificent; the cupolas, the golden crosses, sparkle as though to make welcome these harbingers of victory.

"The events of that day," continues the traveller, recounting them as told him immediately afterwards, ". . . must have constituted the simplest military operation of the whole war. The cruiser *Averof*, the flagship, and the three torpedo-boats who accompanied her, cast anchor at Daphni. In sight of the Greek battleships, the five or six Ottoman officials employed in the customs and the post-office fled precipitately for refuge to the Russian monastery of St. Panteleimon. A torpedo-boat, stationed in front of the monastery, sent a request to the abbot to surrender the fugitives. This, after some discussion, was done. Meanwhile 70 men had disembarked, and, having hoisted the blue and white flag over the customs-house and the post-office, set off for Caryes. . . . The unfortunate *kaimakam* was arrested on his divan."

The narrative proceeds at length: tells of the arrival of the soldiers and the banquets given in their honour; of the whole Mountain enveloped in the distant echoing of bells; of the news of fresh successes on the part of the Balkan allies; and then of the dissensions that were springing up between them. On Athos these are reflected: "Everywhere . . . a great inquietude has given place to joy. The bells have ceased to peal. . . . What will happen to the Mountain, now that it is free? Will it be reunited to Greece, as the Greek monasteries demand? Or, in accordance with the wishes of the Slavs, will it remain independent under the control of the Orthodox peoples?"

Thus in jubilation and anxiety the Turkish rule was ended. The Holy Mountain was once more under Christian governance. But the question was now: under which?

On February 6th, 1913, it was reported in *The Times* that the Russian Foreign Office had requested "that Greece should not proceed with the substitution of Hellenic authorities for the pre-existing administration." It proposed, alternatively, that Athos should be governed by an international commission, composed of the representatives of all the Orthodox states—among which Russia must inevitably preponderate. The scheme was countered by the claim of Austria-Hungary to inclusion, as ruling over the Serbian Orthodox Patriarchate of Carlovitz. And was further complicated by the insistence of the Greeks themselves, voiced by Meletios Metaxarchis, the present Patriarch of Alexandria, that Great Britain should be represented, as possessing jurisdiction over the autocephalous Church of Cyprus. A wholly negative agreement was reached at the Treaty of London in 1913, Article 5 of which confided "*le soin de statuer sur le sort . . . de la peninsule de Mont Athos*" to the five Powers; as though, with every other point of dispute in that diminutive pre-war world, it were not already in their keeping. Thus the issues were skilfully avoided; save that, temporarily at least, the threatened domination of the Russians was averted.

This was in May. The second Balkan War was to come. Meanwhile the interest still evinced by Russia in this, the most holy place after Jerusalem within the confines of the Eastern Church, was further aroused by a heresy which threatened to deprive the Russians of their strongest claim to predominance on the Mountain —that of Orthodoxy. A monk named Antony Boulatovitch, formerly a Hussars officer, and now in the *skiti* of St. Andrew at Caryes, had experienced a religious ecstasy on discovering that, on the authority of many of the fathers, "the name of God, being part of God, is in itself divine." His joy was communicated to his companions. And, on hearing that the Archbishop Antony of Volinsk had denounced the doctrine which entranced their souls, they appealed for justification to their abbots and *epitropoi*. These refusing to support them, they elected others. But the first resisted, and in both monastery and *skiti* the Russian monks came to blows. The heretics, at first besieged and deprived of food, were eventually victorious. And the Russian Government, with the approval of the Holy Synod of Moscow, sought leave of the Patriarch of Constantinople to quell the infringement of dogma by force. This was granted. Troops were landed on June 24th, 1913.

There came also a special delegate of the Moscow Synod, the Archbishop Nikon. Unannounced, he disembarked at Russico, and, hurrying to the church, delivered a sermon which the monks disdained by walking out in the middle. To the *skiti* of St. Andrew he was refused admission altogether.

On July 15th matters came to a head. The Archbishop, wishing to conduct the liturgy, was refused the keys to the monastery's vestments. The doors, therefore, were broken open by the troops. The fathers, retiring into the woods, stoned them. And they, in reply, opened fire in the dark. As a sequel, 616 heretical monks were deported, the majority seeking voluntary exile on the shores of the Yellow Sea. The Holy Synod of Moscow admitted officially that 24 had been wounded in the disturbances, and threw a curious light on the ranks whence the Russian monks on the Mountain were recruited by stating that "40 with criminal pasts had been imprisoned at Odessa." The abbot of Russico telegraphed his thanks to the Tsar, who replied wishing the monastery "peace, prosperity, and piety." And the Greeks, having heard the gun-fire, now considered the Russians not only overweening, but disturbers of peace and suspect of faith into the bargain. Grisly rumours, harking back to the embarkation of monastic reservists in the Russo-Japanese War—an incident which in itself gave colour to them—continued to encircle the Near East. The buildings were barracks, the monks an army. Munitions lay hid. And all the newly transformed *skitai* and *kellia* commanded the strategic points of the Mountain.

A year passed. And then these petty convulsions were engulfed in a larger. The intended dispositions of the five Powers lapsed into oblivion. And the Mountain remained to all intents and purposes identified with Greece. Four years later that beneficent comity deputed to assign its fate was reduced to two. And by one of the clauses of the Treaty of Sèvres, which was afterwards ratified at Lausanne in 1923, the sovereignty of the Hellenic state was recognised, and the following assurance given:

"*La Grèce s'engage à reconnaître et maintenir les droits traditionels et les libertés dont jouissent les communautés monastiques non grecques du Mont Athos d'après les dispositions de l'article 62 du Traité de Berlin du Juillet 13, 1878*"—Article 62 of the Treaty of Berlin, which invokes unspecified the precedents of nine centuries. Thus the inviolability of the foreign monasteries is guaranteed. But in view of the assertions that have persisted in the English Press that the Greek Government has decided to close the Mountain to monastic recruits of Greek nationality, and thus presumably resign it to the Slavs whose position is impregnable, the student of political

curiosities may refer to Articles 106 to 109 of the Hellenic constitution. There, with rigid emphasis, locked in the keystone of the
state, the autonomy of the Mountain and the inalienability of its soil
from the twenty Ruling Monasteries are ensured for all time on as
firm a basis as words can build. In reply to the suggestion that it
would be an act of friendship on the part of the Greek Government
to promote the Rumanian *skiti* to the rank of a Ruling Monastery,
it was stated that:

"Greece is unable to modify the *status quo* of Mount Athos either to
her own advantage or to that of any other Power. She is prevented by:

"1. The law of custom hallowed by the centuries.

"2. Her treaty obligations.

"3. Her own legislation."

The position is settled. And future generations, when Christianity
has passed into history, may still enjoy the spectacle of a solitary
survival secure within the political barriers. History has been
paradoxical. The autonomy of the Mountain was conserved, while
the rest of Europe was robbing the monks of the last vestiges of
temporal power, by the inertia of an infidel government. And it
was brought to the notice of international guarantee, and thus saved
from summary incorporation in the Hellenic state, by Russian
ambition. It has dictated its constitution to the sovereignty which
it admits. And it now remains the preserve of that splendid yet
unearthly beauty which Byzantine civilisation once carried over all
the coasts of the Levant.

But how near and how odious the Russian domination might
have been, was recalled to us by prints of the Mountain upon our
bedroom walls: high roads with carriages, Cossacks marching,
bands playing. The menace is past. Let us return, forgiving, to the
chastened remnant of its contrivers.

Last year, sated with the clattering magnificence of the church,
we had turned with relief to a small chapel beside it, and discovered
therein an old Greek *eicon* of the Assumption of the Virgin. Thither
now Valentine led us again, and promised to ask permission for us to
photograph it. We then ascended to another church enclosed high
up in the main building among the cells; a species of enormous
room, divided by a row of pillars and still more ablaze with nineteenth century gilt and lustres than the one below. On emerging,

we encountered a monk six and a half feet high, with the figure of a
drill-sergeant, a cruel, tight-lipped face, broader in jowl than forehead, and sprouting in opposite directions two grey, compact
points of beard. At the feet of this colossus Valentine knelt till his
head touched the ground. Then asked permission for the photographing of the *eicon*. The deputy-abbot, as this proved, disappeared
into a room where, like the twinkle of a star, we caught a glimpse of
Mitrophanes. He returned with the abbot's assent.

Unfortunately, the feast of the Assumption was not long past,
and tucked within the framing of the picture was an edging of linen
apple-blossom—a pretty ornament in itself, with its tinted buds, but
disastrously encroaching. The sacristan of the chapel was called;
hammer and pincers produced; and the whole construction torn
from its pedestal and delivered of the actual panel. The painting,
dating from the seventeenth century, exhibited a richness and
warmth of colour unlike most of its fellows on the Mountain;
where, being on chestnut wood, we presumed it to have been
painted. There was an unfamiliar sympathy also in the figures. But,
like that of Gregoriou, it was entirely devoid of contemporary
Italian facility, and lacked none of the decorative Byzantine formalism: the sky patterned with gold florescent asterisks; Christ
erect in an aura of elliptical refulgence; and the inevitable insistence
on detailed light rather than shadow.

The exposures completed, we lunched with Valentine in a
miniature guest-refectory. Desperate with the hammerings of
Mark's curiosity, he vouchsafed a word of information. In this
monastery, he said, the abbot, though advised by the deputy-abbot
and a council of elders, ruled with the power of an autocrat. On
arrival each monk was apportioned certain work; at first something unsuited to his abilities, which should act as a test of character.
Valentine, we felt sure from his more content demeanour, was
engaged on something less uncongenial than formerly. It seemed silly
that a man of his education should perform menial offices. One day
perhaps he will be abbot. And one day we shall return to discover
the story of his life. We were told at one of the other monasteries
that he had escaped from the Crimea with Wrangel's army.

In the afternoon we visited the monastery shop, where a confused array of pre-war souvenirs for pilgrims lay ranged on long

[157]

counters: *eicons*, Bibles, spoons, postcards, strings of beads, and every blend of sacred oleograph. We discovered some quires of writing-paper, damp with age, and bearing, in lieu of an address, a representation of the Mountain rising like an emerald cone from the sea, with all the monasteries depicted as red-roofed German villas. With these we eventually succeeded in so astonishing the importunate tradesmen of the mother country, that many, believing we had forsaken both home and sanity for ever, ceased their clamour for months to come.

At four o'clock we climbed to the upper church for the afternoon service. The air was hot and sleepy; sheets of sunlight struck the polished wooden floor and glittered over the jungles of golden ornament. The singing, full of tragic harmonies unmodified to the western ear like those of the choir in the Buckingham Palace Road, played on the emotions as nothing can. Last year it had been more impressive still. We had risen in the dark. The gloom of the shadowy, candle-lit church was accentuated by the livid tapping of the dawn without. Four men sang. Unaccompanied, in tones of unfathomable sadness, they seemed to echo in exile the memory of a life always sad, now extinguished.

During dinner, at which the guest-master descended from the twilight of his imaginings to exhale a gentle mirth at our request for more soup, the last night's boatman, hired for the purpose, arrived with letters. Several of the batch were addressed to others than ourselves. But as they had been rotting in the post-office for most of the century, they were included on chance. One bore the superscription of a Turkish lady. What ghastly clue it held to the Mountain's previous violation we could only guess.

There is something grotesque, almost alarming, in the combinations of letters that find their way to remote places. There transpired now a night-club circular; a bill for writing-paper stamped with Mrs. Byrne's address; a telegram from friends in Venice addressed to "Cairo" instead of Caryes and requesting me to answer to "Vienna"; an invitation to a wedding in Westminster Cathedral, enclosing ticket admitting "to railed enclosure"; and a request to attend the Navarino banquet, to be held in London at the nominal fee of £1 12s. 6d. a head. To this last I replied that I should, I hoped, be celebrating the occasion in its native bay.

[158]

Events, as it turned out, took us to Crete instead. But we returned to Athens on the day following the anniversary, to find the streets gay with bunting and uniformed Codringtons; the English colony fluttered, because the Minister had left the British Government's wreath behind; the Minister himself stamping over an impending dinner-table arranged by an inadvertent secretary to seat all the guests but those very Codringtons for whom it was being given; the Legation hushed beneath the noise of stitching medals on and off dress coats for every new reception; several new issues of stamps; and the whole diplomatic corps, the Press, the intellectual leaders, the financial magnates, the Foreign Office, the Ministry of Marine, and the Parliament, all recovering from the effects of unwonted celebration on two successive nights. For the Greek Government had chartered two ships to convey its guests; and with a hospitality, a largeness of heart, which deserves immortality in some Treasury of Golden Actions, had ordered all drinks to be served free at its expense.

"I assure you," old men rumbled at me later, "I haven't touched more than a single glass of claret for dinner for the last thirty years. But these naval fellers are so generous, there's no getting out of it. I thought I'd try a cocktail. And I don't mind admitting after about five I felt damned odd. It was all I could do to crawl to a coil of rope. . . ."

One of our friends, who was an attaché at the Legation, had purchased, before leaving on this expedition, a game of snakes and ladders, and one which had been expanded into a landscape beset with witches and deadly nightshade. A distinguished professor of theology, the greatest living exponent of the Orthodox view of the *Filioque*, had also been of the party. And it was, we were informed, piteous to behold him, in the guise of Little Snowdrop, counting up his dice and crashing the life's edifice of his intellectual prestige upon an encounter with an ogre or a swallowing of poisoned berries. Obliged to return to the beginning again, he felt it as though Eastern Christendom had renounced the Patriarch in favour of the Pope. In our opinion, it would have been more fitting if in place of these floating gin-palaces and gambling-hells the occasion had been observed in the spirit of REMEMBRANCE. But that is because we were not there.

Chapter XII

GARDENIAS AND SWEETPEAS

M ARK AND I, anxious to hear the singing again before we left, were called at four o'clock. We dressed in haste, and were urged by the guest-master with clucks of agitation across the starlit courtyard; till we trotted one on either side of him into the upper church. Each of us put his hat upon the floor. Whereupon from each side of the nave a venerable father darted forward and placed it in a stall to itself. Unfortunately the service was almost finished, and it was plain that the guest-master's flurry had been due to a sense of guilt in not having wakened us earlier. As we descended after only twenty minutes, he tried to rectify his mistake by propelling us toward another candle-lighted doorway. We declined, and went back to bed.

After a fitful two hours, we rose again, this time at the instance of David, who, having slept oblivious of his vaunted love of music, now bounced into the room like a Brobdingnagian lark and said that he wished to make an early start. While we breakfasted in pyjamas, off the Daphni sardines, we were conscious of a droning boom such as a 64-foot organ pipe sends vibrating over a cathedral. Throbbing and fading, sometimes broken by long intervals, it resolved at length into a human voice. But by the time David and I had reached the passage sink to shave, it had ceased. Semi-nude, we had just balanced the mirror on a nail, when a sound like a funeral march arranged for Chaliapine began again at our very elbow. Framed in a doorway stood a monk of indescribable proportions, eyes almost closed with the good humour of his cheeks, beard tangled as pre-Raphaelite brambles; and from his shoulders, broken at an angle on the apex of his paunch, a green and gold brocade stole. In one hand he carried a cross, in the other a receptacle of holy water and a bunch of basil. Espying us in the moment that our eyes lighted on him, he moved upon us with mammoth gait, chanting the while. He sprinkled our defenceless chests with holy water from the little green broom. And then, regardless of soap or skin, he enveloped us each in an overpowering embrace, his whole form garlanded with Christian love. The sudden horror of his oncoming was mitigated by the exquisite spectacle of David's shrinking soapy torso engorged in his black folds. After learning our nationality, he took his way, voice uplifted. It appeared, upon subsequent enquiry, that on the first of every month it is the custom in Orthodox countries for the priest to go the round of the monastery or village, as the case may be, blessing the cells or houses and their inmates. To-day, being the fourteenth by our calendar, was the first by theirs.

At length we were clothed, our homeward letters delivered to Mitrophanes, the guest-master's hand shaken and rewarded, and ourselves ensconced in a boat at the quayside. In half an hour we were moored against the jetty of Xenophontos, a monastery almost on the water's edge and hidden from Russico by the great inward twist, three miles across, with which the promontory is here indented.

Willowing over the rough cobbles of the little pier stepped a thin, bent figure, adorned with a silver nannygoat's beard and bobbling eyes interrupted by the rim of a pair of pince-nez. This was Father Damascene, who had been expediting his monastery's merchandise in a schooner that set sail as we arrived. Eyeing us with curiosity not unmixed with contempt, he ushered us to the guest-house, the Russian boatmen following with the luggage. As when, after a night journey to some outlying part of Greater Britain, the house of a friend is reached at breakfast-time, so here we felt something of embarrassment in our morning arrival. But this was immediately dispelled by the welcome of the guest-master, a small, untidy monk in an apron, and speaking a little German which he had learnt as a prisoner of war. As we sat balancing our coffee-cups, there entered the abbot, the Archimandrite Akakios—as a visiting card later informed us was his name and style. Though of middle height, he was of most distinguished appearance, having a high forehead and long aquiline nose of clear white skin ; below which was a bold black beard, curling and silken, where played a smile of that exceptional charm which is only as a rule found in little children.

The pronounced variation in atmosphere exhaled by each individual monastery contributes, more than anything else, to the enchantment of the hospitality which the Holy Mountain extends to visitors. It is as though, in the days of horse-transport, a round of great country-houses were in progress, each conducted on the tradition of centuries. For our impressions were confirmed, not only by those of last year, but of long previous travellers. Thus the Lavra resembles a huge rambling palace, enlarged generation by generation, ill-kempt, but still capable of great splendour; St. Paul's, on the cleanliness of which Robert Curzon remarked exactly ninety years ago, a Georgian mansion where the amenities of life are fully understood; and Dionysiou, the castle of some Draconian great-aunt, widowed and religious, where meals are punctual and smoking forbidden in the drawing-room. At this latter, our experiences have been more than corroborated. Riley speaks of "a churlish reception"; though this we do not wholly endorse. While Tozer, who made two visits in the 'sixties, describes the monks on both occasions as "singularly suspicious and unwilling to show their treasures," phrases very applicable to their attitude toward our letters from the Government and our request to see the Trapezuntine chrysobul. To leave Dionysiou for Gregoriou was to exchange the great-aunt for her nieces and nephews, with Father Stephen the centre of their mischief. At Simopatra we did not stay the night, and Russico lies outside the category. But arrived at Xenophontos, the charm of environment was accentuated beyond any we had met. At last we had reached the one house that exists in everyone's life—that of an intimate friend and perfect ease.

This side of Daphni—that is to say, north-west, since we have been moving up from the south-east—the character of the promontory has changed, the spine of the ridge sunk, and a more benign air overspread the landscape. Beach, hitherto rare, has become the general rule; cliff the exception. Separated from the shingle by terraced vegetable-beds cultivated with that economy and neatness which connotes the monkish gardener, the bottom wall of Xenophontos stands an unpretentious creamy yellow, surmounted by the usual projecting rooms of painted wood. But, from the side whence we had approached, the crenellated walls of the enclosure ramble far up the hill to the back, with cypresses and cupolas,

almost Tuscan in their dark and light, projecting from within. Near
the water on that side stands the boat-house, to which huge barred
doors fasten an entrance so shaped that it might, one feels, give
sudden vent to the frescoed and cross-bedizened coaches of the
Athonite tube. Between this building and the foundations of the
garden rises the path to the entrance, embowered with wistaria
and oleanders, the latter a startling pink when viewed against the
blue sea on descent. Once within the gate, the way twists up
between walls of great antiquity, supporting what appear to be,
outside Mistra, some of the very few Byzantine domestic buildings
still in existence. They possess the original windows, double-
arched and supported by a single pillar up the middle.

The air of the courtyard, even though deserted in the midday
heat, was that of an industrious farmyard. Here was revealed to its
fullest that idyllic mode of co-operative living which flourishes on
the Mountain and which Communism seeks to introduce on a larger
scale elsewhere. Repugnant, for personal reasons, as Communism
may be, its idealism is the more easily comprehended after a visit
to Athos. For in the East, unlike the West, the monasteries were
primarily not seats of learning, but exponents of an ideal social
system. Comment on this aspect of Orthodox monasticism has
usually been confined among western writers to negative abuse of
the monks' ignorance. But there is a hint of deeper perception
in the extract from Buondelmonti, at the beginning of the fifteenth
century, with which this book opens. And Belon, writing in 1553,
before western monasticism had received the full onslaught of the
Reformation, pictures the Athonite commonwealth in words as
relevant now as then:

"*Des six mille religieux que i'ay nommez caloieres, viuants en la
susdicte montaigne, ne pensez pas qu'il en y ait un oyseux, car s'ilz sortent
de leurs monasteres de grand matin, chascun avec son oustil en la main,
portants du biscuit et quelques oignons en un bissac dessus l'espaulle, l'un
une houe, l'autre un pic, l'autre une serpe. Chascun travaille pour le
mesnaige de son monastere. Les uns beischent les vignes, les autres buschent
le bois, les autres fabriquent les navires. Et ne scauroye en faire meilleure
comparaison que à la famille d'un prince, mettant une economie en
commun: Car les uns sont cousturiers, les autres massons, les autres
charpentiers, les autres d'autres mestiers, travaillants tous en commun. . . .*

C'est une œconomie, concernante le proffit du monastere: laquelle estant ainsi gouvernée, est grandement differente tant des mœurs que de façon de vivre aux monasteres des Latins.''

"Excuse us," said the abbot Akakios, as we descended into the courtyard to see the church, "that there were no men to fetch your luggage. But everyone is out picking grapes." Other evidences of the common husbandry lay about us. At our feet was spread a dust-sheet of figs drying in the sun, purple and brown, and so delicious in their fragrant heat that the monks were soon wondering if there would be any left for the winter. Beyond lay other piles—figs again, or walnuts—on which we also fastened. Upon a kind of wooden staging, erected over a fearsome pool that trickled beneath arches into the very heart of the buildings, stood rows of circular pewter trays supported on trestles, and each covered with a paste of beaten tomatoes. Fleets of mules, each bearing a pair of tall, conical vats piled with grapes, clattered in and out beneath the wooden galleries with which the whole of one face of the building was covered, like some old London inn. Clothes—calico underwear and socks of coarse white wool—were hanging out to dry, almost to scorch. Odd corners were stacked with wood—faggots here, logs there. Against them leaned other pewter trays not in use. Beyond the big cream-coloured church a carpenter was working in a recess in the old wall beneath its upper pathway, covering the ground with his shavings. Later Mark and I went down to bathe. In the shade of a trellis of vines, among its own ploughs, sat a grey ox, the ferocity of its pitchfork horns belied by the blinking suavity of its face. And as we lay in the water, there arrived upon the beach a herd of long-haired swine of a dark piebald brown, which gobbled up a pottage thrown them by a black-robed herdsman with a cough. These, which are peculiar to the northern monasteries, we supposed to be the progeny of the wild boars which inhabit the Mountain's forests. Wild we never saw them. But now and then upon our rides we came upon a solitary monk carrying a gun.

The morning was young, and David itching to be at his work. First, however, the abbot must show us the treasures of the new church, the one we had noticed, a large early nineteenth century building of the traditional plan. Fortunately it was never frescoed; and it now presents a cold, dignified interior, unornamented save for a number of *eicons*, none more than two feet square, which form one of the finest single collections on the Mountain. To attempt their description is useless: for even the broadest generalisations will convey nothing to those who are not familiar with these paintings of the Orthodox Church, their rigid symbolism, extraordinary mastery of composition, and brilliance of colour and light. One larger than the rest, a *Panaghia* behind the altar, stood pre-eminent, not only for its uncommon depiction of the Virgin and Child in the act of kissing, but for a treatment of flesh and drapery so savage in its contempt for the naturalistic that, were it exhibited in a London *salon*, it might be criticised as the culminating blasphemy of the mechanical environment. The identity of vision displayed by industrial and contemplative artists, however explicable, never ceases to astonish me.

There hang in this church, besides the paintings, two works of art of universal significance. These are two panels in mosaic, about 40 inches by 18, representing St. George and St. Demetrius, and dating back from the eleventh or twelfth century. The absence of any comprehensive work on Christian mosaic is one of the gaps in the artistic literature of the world that remains to be filled. Christian mosaic; for to the ancients, despite their facility, mosaic was never more than an opaque medium of architectural decoration.

For the first ten centuries of Christianity, the mediæval Greeks were almost the exclusive keepers of its culture and its art; that art which, deriving primarily from Constantinople, gradually took root throughout Europe, and upon the advent of Giotto, its immediate child, flowered to perfection in the early Renaissance. Fostered by the necessity of instructing the illiterate, more attention than hitherto was devoted, under the Church, to coloured representation on a flat plane. This clumsy definition implies, for us, painting. But, for those who moved within the sphere of that fabulous wealth guarded by the queen of cities, painting was a cheap and secondary craft. Mosaic—by which it meant, not the marble cubes of antiquity, but those of glass coloured in a layer at the top—was the medium commanded by the well-to-do, who rightly considered it to surpass paint, both in richness of colour and of general texture. And it was not therefore surprising that the artistry of inlaid squares in the Levant should have reached a standard far beyond the conceptions

of those who have only explored the semi-Roman friezes of Ravenna
or the Italianised imitations of St. Mark's. The initial masterpieces
of this forgotten art are at Daphni, near Athens, at the monastery
of St. Luke of Stiris in Phocis, and at the Kahrié at Constantinople.
But these are all mural; and, as such, subordinated to the architectural necessities of the buildings which contain them.

For purposes of classification, mosaic falls, like painting, into
three categories. These are: wall decoration; miniatures; and pictures proper. The first demands exaggerated breadth of treatment,
equally disposed throughout; the second a corresponding attention
to detail; and the third, the picture, a combination of both those
characteristics with an intermediate technique of its own. Thus,
in a portrait, the background is broad; the face of delicate construction; and the drapery must bridge the two. While the mark
of a fine portrait is the unity of the three: achieved partly by the
texture of the paint, partly by the relation of each to the other, the
background lending importance to the figure and the figure to the
face. Nor is it different in a mosaic picture: the coarser mural
blocks are employed upon the background; the raspberry-pip
minutiæ of the portative panel for the hands, face, and such other
incidents of the composition that may need accentuation; and a
middle size of glazed cube, about one-seventh of an inch square,
for the intermediate provinces.

To most people, even those who have pilgrimaged over the Near
East, mosaic is familiar only as a wall-covering. The existence of
the tiny panels whose dimensions can only be counted in inches is
recognised; such is that of St. Nicolas, damaged by an oyster during
a marine sojourn, which we had seen last year at the monastery
of Stavronikita. But of mosaic pictures, such as fall within the
definition suggested above, hardly any are known. There is a
Panaghia in the Byzantine Museum at Athens which was brought
from Asia Minor by the refugees; although few visitors to that city
think it worth their while to inspect its incomparable delicacy of
colour, varying on face and hands from coral pink to olive green,
and its interplay of cubes, coarse and fine. This is fourteenth
century. And there are also the two at Xenophontos.

The figures are standing three-quarter face and full length, St.
George facing the beholder's right, St. Demetrius his left. St.

Gardenias and Sweetpeas

George is clothed in dark chocolate clasped with lapis and varied with another drapery the colour of deep eighteenth century brick; the whole powdered with broad arrows, circles, diamonds, and trellises of gold. The robe of St. Demetrius, similarly ornamented, is of dark sapphire, lighted with turquoise; while, underneath, the same dark brown alternating with weathered vermilion appears above boots of brilliant faience blue and green. But it is in the rendering of heads and hands that the marvel of technique is achieved. Placed in lines of tiny blocks, firm and regular, the colours range from shadow of deepest sepia, through olive green, to scarlet, pink, and at last, on the face, lines of pure white miraculously worked down the outline of the nose and round the corners of the eyes. While in places, to express not a depression, but a quality of the skin, minute patches of brilliant blue are introduced. And all within a compass of three inches radius. Nor is this fineness confined to flesh alone. Facing the forehead of each saint is a small truncated Christ, whose attitude of admonition is expressed with a strength and precision exactly opposed to the delicate merging of the colours elsewhere. The haloes of the saints are of blue, and the backgrounds of gold. Round St. Demetrius runs a border—three single lines of large cubes in red, white, and blue.

From the new church the abbot then led us to the old. This building lies nearer the gate, presenting from below an extraordinary picture in the brilliant sunlight, its walls and cupolas of clear spring yellow outlined in white and reducing the brazen blue of the sky to a colourless dark. The interior, paved with eleventh century *opus Alexandrinum*, is unusually small, having for this reason been abandoned; and it is consequently free of that load of ornament —corona, chandeliers, candlesticks, thrones, and reading-stands— with which the churches of the Orthodox rite are always obscured. It was possible at last to gain an idea of the true decorative value of one of the older Athonite churches, where no inch had been left unpainted. And the livid, angry lights and ruthless impressionism of these frescoes in particular were lent an extraordinary intensity by the emptiness of the building. Here, moreover, is vouchsafed the ultimate corroboration of our thesis that El Greco was a Byzantine artist of the strongest conviction, who, having dispensed with the iconographic formulæ of his native church, spent his whole life in reverting to its spirit, technique, and colour; and who alone of all his nation, and of all the Slavs, Russians, Serbs, Bulgars, and Rumanians over whom its influence extended, brought Byzantine art to its logical fruition. Nowhere exists a link one half, one quarter so strong with this great painter of all time, and direct forebear of modern art, as in this small church decorated by an unknown hand in 1544, three years after El Greco was born. Here is displayed all the maladroitness and crudity which the separation from the cultural fertility of a capital necessarily entails. But the troubled spirit of the artist has clamoured through his limitations. Not great painting, his work is none the less great expression.

The abbot Akakios overwhelmed us with help. No trouble was too great for our convenience. David began focusing with the aid of some small steps. On requesting larger, ladders that would have scaled the walls of Babylon—such, of course, as any well-conducted farm would naturally possess—were brought to our assistance, the abbot directing operations in person. This friendliness was not, as is sometimes the case, the result of poverty. All the buildings were well kept, the monks neither few nor squalid, and the abbot was arrayed, after the custom of his kind, in a rustling silken gown.

Athonite ladders are peculiar. That part which contains the steps goes to a point, from which depends, not, as with us, a similar construction without steps, but a single hinged pole. Owing to this pyramidical tendency, the higher the ladder, the larger its base. Two such erections and the whole floor-space of this small church was filled. What, therefore, was David's surprise when, on looking out from behind the *eiconostasis* where he had just released the shutter for a twenty-minutes' exposure, he found himself imprisoned by the initial gabble of a service, conducted in and out the ladders. This was that same rite which had so assisted our toilet earlier in the day, numerous old monks and labourers coming forward at intervals to be sprinkled with holy water from the bunch of basil.

"Don't," said the officiating father, "interrupt your work for us."

David did not. And the office was brightened by an orchestra of splintering plates and maledictory hisses. Mark and I had escaped, meanwhile, to the sea.

After lunch, served in a small refectory furnished with a table covered in green American cloth, a cruet, and a Greek map of Europe, Father Damascene arrived for his portrait. The time was past when Mark expected me to make these appointments for him. He had learnt the sentence, "May I do your *eicon*, my father?" by heart. And the types that he picked now prowled upon our slumbers unheralded. Damascene, whose acquaintance, it will be remembered, we had made upon the quay, sat himself in a chair, at his feet my suit-case, by his shoulder a lamp of pink glaze decorated with forget-me-nots. His pinched face, with its wispish silver growths, bent pince-nez, cap crushed slightly on one side, and air of portentous, almost lunatic solemnity, lent itself to more than portraiture. After an hour he inspected the result. He was speechless; and, dismissing it with a gesture, tottered furiously out of the door. Thus, as always, while David and I laboured in our joint rebirth of the history of European painting, its delivery altogether dependent on the goodwill of our hosts, Mark must needs undo the tact of days, and the construction of sentences calculated to fracture our cranial bones, in the practice of a frivolous and unmoral art. . . . We dined off red mullet, delicious as trout, and aubergines fried in slivers. David then developed. But the water in the sink had ceased to run; and we perforce sat near the courtyard fountain till nearly midnight, looking at the stars, turning our faces to the velvet cold of the breeze and listening to the distant presence of the sea.

It occurred to us on the following afternoon to walk up the hill and help the grape-pickers. First, however, I was obliged to take some notes in the church. When these were completed, David, panting on the apex of a wooden Eiffel Tower, found himself without a colour filter. This I went to fetch. But, before I could return, the guest-master was blocking the doorway with our afternoon coffee. At his heels came the abbot, lighting the room with his smile, and bearing two waxen, full-blown gardenias, which reminded me, as I put one in my buttonhole, of cricket matches at Lord's, and the triumph over the despicable majority who only wore carnations.

"These flowers," said the abbot, "are very difficult to grow. We must go and see the monk who gave them to me. He has a little tree."

I was about to excuse myself, on the plea of David's necessity, when the monk in question stepped into the room, burly and benign. We thanked him, shook his hand, and said that in England such flowers were worn only with ceremonial clothes at weddings. Both then caught sight of Damascene's portrait, to which Mark was putting last touches. Now, I thought, grasping the colour filter for an exit . . . when Damascene himself trailed his boat-like feet over the threshold. Once more he inspected the drawing, and, fixing his eyes on space, marched from the room. Whereat the abbot and his friend of the gardenias resolved into a paroxysm of laughter, and, snatching the picture from Mark, held it up between them, shaking as they sat. The noise attracted the guest-master, the guest-master others, till half the monastery was heaving and chuckling over this unholy likeness of its worthy, but evidently not respected, brother. Again I moved to the door.

This time fate took flesh in an elderly professor, Edwardian tweeded, who paused in alarm at the brink of this unedifying mirth. Was I Mr. Byron? Evlogios of the Lavra had told him in Caryes that he would find me. He could not stay the night here, being obliged to return to Russico. But perhaps we should meet later at Vatopedi.

"Do you," I said, "know Father Adrian of Vatopedi?"

"Adrian! He is my greatest friend in the world."

"Tell him," I begged, "that we are arriving on such and such a date."

The professor then forced his way to the abbot, who, we were glad to see, disdained him. His visit, however, had the advantage of gaining us an extra round of *ouzo*.

And so at last I reached the church. David had disappeared.

We set off then, as originally intended, up the hill. But the walk was marred by Mark's arrogance in the field of natural history. Delivering himself, over the smallest flies, of rhapsodies in which I felt bound to join for fear of hurting his feelings, he had the habit, whenever I espied a butterfly recorded hitherto only in Patagonia, of quickening his pace in the opposite direction with an air of assumed boredom. This odious jealousy, combined with the heat, led us, instead of up the hill, to the beach, where we found David already in the water. The bathe was enlivened by our imitation of Queen Victoria—had she ever swum—in propelling her rigid bust through the waves with that peculiar bustle motion which she would doubtless have employed. This pastime may seem unusual; but not unnatural, in view of the goodness of Providence, who has reincarnated the face of the monarch upon the person of the author. Her motions were the cause of some astonishment to the professor, who was taking his departure in a small boat.

We returned now to draw the abbot. Fetching his tall black staff, his black rosary, and his veil from the "abbotry," he unlocked the door of a private room, of which the wallpaper bore the impress of the Byzantine eagles and the likeness of a servant's bedroom. There he arrayed himself, and we drew till the light failed. Upon my showing the result to the guest-master as we sat upon a balcony drinking cocktails, he asserted that the staff was too big. I defended it with heat; till at length we were shaking our fists at each other's noses. I then perpetrated a caricature of him of such malice as to leave him quite bewildered.

"The beard, oh, the beard—it *is* bad," he cried.

Morning broke with the arrival of the abbot, bearing a bunch of sweetpeas, mauve and fleshy, which pervaded the whole room with their smell. It was complicated, later, by the descent of Mark's sponge and shaving-brush into a vegetable-bed. The gate was locked; but the gardener was found, and, on recovering Mark's property, presented him with a tremendous citron, four inches long, which he plucked from a tree near by. After packing, we visited the library, where such manuscripts as survived Robert Curzon had perished in a fire. The only volume of entertainment was *Great Britain's Coasting Pilot*, written in 1744 by "Captain Greenville Collins, hydrographer in ordinary to the King's most excellent Majesty." On a table stood a ghastly corset, fitting over the shoulders and round the chest and waist, which was composed of jointed iron plates, each one about three inches long, one broad, and a quarter thick. This had formerly been an instrument of mortification. Here of all monasteries it seemed out of keeping.

At last, with honest grief, we said good-bye, presenting the abbot with a volume on church needlework. In return he showed us the abbot's official treasures, more *eicons*, and a bellying silver jug presented a few years ago by an English *lordos* who had arrived in a yacht. We pictured the latter's relief at its departure from the dining-room table. The abbot then posed himself on some steps for a photograph; I, myself, on a pile of logs, to take it. The latter collapsed, and, with a crash that deranged the whole courtyard, I descended into the mouth of an adjacent cooking-pot.

Chapter XIII

FRANKFORT

OUR BOATMAN was a native of Gytheion. On hearing of our intention to visit the churches of Mistra near by, his pride of birthplace surged up within him and he harangued us till the boat swayed. To me also the amenities of the district were not unknown. And his words threw my thoughts into a train of reflection on the circumstances that first led me to those parts.

My early days in Athens were spent in an exiguous basement flat one quarter the size of Howe's, and giving access, like his, to a vine-covered courtyard. A small but genuine bath—that is to say, not a tub—had been placed in a hen-house at the farther end. Here, such water as had not been stolen by the neighbours was heated in a witches' cauldron suspended over a bonfire, whence the flames came ravening into the bath upon the unwary body. Directly opposite, five feet across the yard, lived an old woman in a miserable plaster hutch, who sat all day long at her threshold knitting. Though even the hen-hole of our bathroom door had been boarded, her sense of propriety was appalled at the splashings within. And no sooner had the first saunter of a dressing-gown signalled from the entrance of the flat, than she let down a curtain of thick white lace over her own and retired within. Since there were no windows, she was obliged by our ablutions to spend the whole of every morning in darkness.

Atop the daily remorse thus inflicted came the Greek Easter. The landlady had a lamb. Arachne, the ancient knitter, had a lamb. We had a lamb. And none ceased, day or night, to bleat the terror of its impending doom. Ours broke loose on Good Friday. With the agility of an ibex, it leaped through the window upon my host and curveted from room to room, lent wings by the resilience of the beds. Next night was Easter eve. With the whole city, we waited outside the cathedral; watched at midnight the Metropolitan emerge from the lighted doors, bearing the holy fire that had descended on his candle as the Easter morning broke; surged with the crowd towards him; lit our candles as soon as we might from the first within reach; and, carefully guarding the sacred flame, set off to our Passover. This consisted of eggs dyed red and blazoned "Christ is risen," accompanied by the lamb, now turning whole upon a spit over a bed of wood ashes. The party was a large one, containing, besides ourselves and Phyllis, a former colonel of the Coldstream Guards, his wife, his brother, and the latter's wife.

Overwhelmed, therefore, by this mounting burden of domestic and social stress, we left early in the following week for the south.

The train to Tripolitza, owing to that astonishing conformation of sea and mountains which is Greece, takes thirteen hours to cover eighty crow-flown miles. This allows ten minutes for lunch off macaroni offal and hot beer at Corinth. Corinth! Corinth: with the shunt of goods trains ever in the ear and the slag-heaps gaunt and black against the faience blue of the gulf. Corinth is the Reading of Greece, and the S.P.A.P., its railway, the Hellenic Great Western. To one whom the Great Western has borne to home, school, and university, Reading stands apart from all places, rusted in the heart. What hours have I paced those platforms, endlessly, hopelessly, where the draughts of Siberia and the solstice heats of Ecuador focus their unscrupling rigours on the eructated passenger. I have swallowed the chocolate of automatic machines, I have smoked their cigarettes, I have snivelled at their unguents. I have written novels like Roman inscriptions on their rose-labels, that have stretched across the platform and on to the lines. I know each waiting-room as a home, each waitress as a mother, each porter as a brother. Reading, my Reading! Be I thy Brooke, thy Tennyson, thy Sitwell! Shall biscuit fade and railroad wane, faithful I will e'er remain. And second only to this, my incomparable amour, second in body though one in soul, is Corinth.

Nor, for me, has Corinth lacked the weaving of human romance. Returning on a June evening from the monastery of Megaspilion, with the sun setting over the mountains across the gulf and the purple spikes of buddleias stroking honeyed kisses on my boots as I sat on the dashboard of the train, I came to conversation with a Mademoiselle Vlasto, who was breaking a sojourn in the country to visit her Athenian dentist, owing to a tooth which was causing her insupportable pain. There was no restaurant-car. It was sultry to the point of suffocation. And the journey was four hours more. As we drew in to Corinth station, I forced my way through the numerous crowd that gathers in these parts to see trains on their way, and fetched her a bottle of lemonade. In the twilight of the carriage I caught a gleam of velvet-brown eyes, heard a murmur of thanks. But closer I never probed, since her face was entirely hidden in the veils and bandages of her affliction. Picture, then, my chagrin when, a few days later, she reported to a mutual friend that she had "found a new admirer, a young Englishman." The vision of that unseen face has not ceased to haunt me.

Thus ran my thoughts. And they must have continued to Gytheion, whither we were bound when the journey began; where the dark-leaved oaks spring singly from the ploughed red earth; and where, it will be remembered, the boatman was born; when that holy man, switching from the cradle to the hemispheres, enquired whether London was in England and what lived in Australia. Jerked into the present, I tried to ease his curiosity. On arrival at Docheiariou, he carried our luggage up from the sea, and, seating himself in the guest-room, launched further periods of speech upon us. Lunch was on the table before he was gone.

The room in which we sat was the prettiest we had occupied, and instanced, as at the Lavra, the similarity between monastic ideas on decoration and those dictated by the fashion of the 1920's. The walls were of white, broken only by blue folding doors panelled in green lozenges, which were outlined in red. Though the tones of these colours were in themselves dull, their juxtaposition produced an intensity that made them difficult to look at. Round the top of the room ran a curved vaulting about two feet deep, spottily marbled in gentian blue, and adorned, in the middle of each wall, with a floresque design in the same blue. On this was supported the ceiling, where a circular pattern of carved wood consisted of a series of radiating baroque spokes in hot brick-red on a background of green. Since the room, in the manner of Athonite rooms, was built out over the lower courtyard, its windows ran the whole length of two walls. In a third was an open fireplace enclosed by a thick stone mantelpiece above a raised hearth. Sir George Bowen, who visited the Mountain in 1849 during colder weather, talks of fires that blazed in every room. To-day, except at Kerasia, this was the only fireplace that we saw. Elsewhere was always the tall, organ-like blue and white stove. Above this mantelpiece rose two tiny pillars of twisted black and lilac, curving over into a miniature baroque arch. The room was erected in 1753, and was described by Walpole in 1818 as "elegant." Even previous to its existence the Jesuit Braconnier, at the beginning of the eighteenth century, found the guest-rooms of Docheiariou the most comfortable on the Mountain.

Externally also the monastery possesses an individual and rather intimate charm. The hills here slope sharply from the sea, and the buildings are arranged on a series of terraces. Almost the whole of the main courtyard is occupied by the church—the largest on Athos, and dating from 1568. This building is surmounted by a series of tall, fluted cupolas washed a dull chocolate. From the uppermost terrace, whither gave the guest-house porch, it was almost possible to touch their leaded, shell-like domes.

We had arrived this year a month later than last. And the profusion of flowers which had completed the scene was less. Then I wrote: "Above, hung an arbour of wistaria in flower against the rusty plaster and grey stone of the buildings. In a corner, the delicate light green leaves and scarlet flowers of pomegranate-trees showed in contrast against the larger, deeper mulberry"—to-day there were pomegranates instead. "Beyond appeared the pink and grey of an oleander. On the low wall in front, hung with the virulent purple-blue trumpets of morning glory, stood rows of bright green pincushions—basil, the sweet herb. Surrounding the church stretched stone roofs covered with yellow lichen and sprouting armies of tall white chimneys like ninepins. While below all lay the silver blue of the sea, with the off-shore currents trailing away to further wooded promontories. And at last the summit, caught in the sun above a wreath of cloud, reared its white point against the deep blue sky."

Synesius of last year was guest-master no longer. His place was taken by a rubicund old monk whose cottonwool beard grew at right angles from his chin, and ended, at some distance, in a final upward flourish towards his nose. Of him, during lunch, we enquired for our long expected Frankfort.

"Frankfort?" he replied. "What is Frankfort?"

Later we bathed. But, conscience-stricken by the gusts of singing that were wafted on us from above, we returned in time to see the end of the service and the relics afterwards. The first of them was the head of St. Friday, or, if the name of the last day but one be translated from the Greek, of St. Preparation, a lady, and not, as some may have supposed, the factotum of Robinson Crusoe. This was followed by that of St. Denys the Areopagite: "CUT OFF IN ENGLAND!" shouted the keeper of the treasures in a sudden fury, as if, in his estimation, our whole nation were still blood-guilty of this blackest infamy. Then came an ancient gold cross, set with a profusion of small diamonds and emeralds, which had been presented to the monastery by one of the Voivodes of Moldo-Wallachia. A traveller had once tried to buy it. And he was a member, we were given to understand, of a nation not apparently content with the single crime of St. Denys' execution. Last and most prized of all the treasures, however, was a shapeless piece of white marble. A young monk, discovering a buried horde, reported it to the abbot, who despatched two others to help him bring it to the monastery. These, thinking to keep it for themselves, tied this piece of marble round his neck and threw him into the sea. Next morning he was found in the church, having been delivered by the archangels Gabriel and Michael. He forgave his assailants, and the stone, which was to have been the instrument of his death, is preserved. But the interest of this rather tedious and not improbable story, to which the archangels have been attached, lies in the fact that for not less than four and a half centuries, and who knows how many more, this stone has been shown and this story told to the monastery's visitors. The marvel is related in 1489 by Paisios, a Russian monk of Chilandari, in exactly those words with which the priest now held our attention.

Many early Russian accounts of the Mountain are extant. And the first of them, from the pen of Ignatius of Smolensk in 1389, confirms the fact that the Athonite community has not changed in substantial outline since. The rest are uniformly dull. Such, indeed, is the outstanding quality of most of the accounts of the Mountain that have survived, the exceptions in our own language being those of Tozer, Curzon, and Dr. Covel. The attentions of the majority seem to have focused solely on the collection of statistics, the discovery of classical inscriptions, and the inspection of fishes' viscera and plants' bowels. In particular, the sententious moralisings of the nineteenth century, humorous as we have grown to regard them, still exhale a nauseous reek when applied to those who had the good fortune (though bad taste) to be dwelling outside the British Isles at the time. Thus, for instance, writes Lieutenant Webber-Smith in 1837: "Dokhiariu, a small monastery containing 30 caloyers: nothing worth notice. Near this spot is the cave of a noted recluse who has lived here in a cell for fifty years apart from all mankind; yet his feelings would seem not to be blunted, as he bestows the care and attention on a favourite rose-tree which, if well directed toward the good of his fellow creatures, might have made him a useful member of the community." But the words of this inflated naval cub pale before those of Mr. Athelstan Riley, who is still amongst us. He, a religious of the 'eighties—those years which threatened to precipitate the Anglican Church from a comfortable evening of desuetude to a painful and despised end—Mr. Riley has bequeathed posterity the following eulogium of his hosts: ". . . those poor folk whom the world despises and condemns, the humble and illiterate peasant monks." Such is the Christian understanding which simultaneously avows its hope for the union of the Anglican and Orthodox Churches. Comment fails. Save that, in this despising and contemning world of which Mr. Riley forms a part, if not a whole, Christianity, which the monks have kept, has been lost.

After the relics, we examined the church, admiring the numerous slabs and lintels of late Byzantine carving with which it is decorated. In keeping with its spacious proportions, the pillars are unusually tall and thick, their capitals being freshly gilded. The frescoes, by the same Zorzi as worked at Dionysiou, have been repainted out of recognition. But their decorative value remains, enhanced by the size and lightness of the building.

As we were sitting over our wine after dinner, Synesius arrived. He had heard that three Englishmen were asking for Frankfort, and knew that I must be one of them.

"You see," he said, "I am no longer guest-master. I have become an elder." And he rustled a new and elaborate gown. We were surprised, seeing that, despite his intelligence, he could not have been more than 30.

"There are ten elders and three *epitropoi*," he continued. This is usual; however a monastery is governed, its superiors habitually number thirteen, in imitation of the first Christian corporation.

"And how is everything on the Mountain?"

"Better. Now that the Government's policy is settled, our affairs will continue to improve. How big is London? Seven millions; really. And New York? Oh, two. Where are your friends of last year? Here is Hamid. Frankfort I can't find. But you shall see him in the morning. Hamid! Hamid!" And Hamid, a grey and yellow tortoiseshell, jumped obediently in and out of Synesius' outstretched arms.

The morrow dawned with Mark in a cheerful mood. This may be spared the reader. It was only damped by the re-entry of Synesius, begging us to visit him. I excused myself that I was busy. But, as his house was so placed on the farther side of the terrace that all its windows looked directly into ours, and as he did not cease to wave, I found concentration impossible. Opening the "red door," as directed, Mark and I entered a small flat, the living-room of which was decorated with Synesius' treasures. Above the divan on which he sat hung numerous prints and enlarged photographs: King Constantine and his family; Venizelos; Clémenceau; Plastiras; besides a wealth of snapshots. He also possessed, he said, a portrait of Lloyd George; but it was too big to fit into the room. Upon the fringed table lay lumps of golden-coloured quartz—a frequent refinement, we noticed, of Athonite taste. But our attention was diverted from these details by the arrival of Frankfort.

Frankfort is a black and white cat, who, when bidden, reluctantly places his head between his paws and turns a somersault. He is apt, however, when lazy, simply to roll over on one side. This he did to-day. But Synesius was firm, and the whole turn was eventually completed. Then, disturbed by our approbation, he vouchsafed us one look of unutterable hatred and rushed from the room.

From his pantry Synesius now fetched brandy in a decanter,

glyco made of quinces, grapes, and peaches; to which he added, from a drawer, cigarettes. A white dove in a wicker cage such as wizards' ravens inhabit, was dangled for our entertainment. Finally, having eaten and drunk, we stepped on to the balcony. The view was one of radiant beauty in the clean morning sun. Below us glittered a rocking line of roof, tiled in slabs of shimmering silver stone, and bursting up into the high white chimneys. And instead of earth, there were only olives, profuse as soda-water bubbles, with a high-light to each tree. They fell to the blue sea, a deeper tone than any tree save the cypresses in a group at its edge. Land showed again on the horizon: Longos, the middle of the three fingers.

Synesius, not content with being photographed himself reading a book upside down, asked us to do the same favour for an old man who lived next door. Wishing to please, we were ushered into a small dark room impregnated with the unsupportable odour of human mortification. Propped on a divan sat a very old man, helpless and immobile, in whose eyes was only the beyond. Replacing his cap by a new and stiffer one, Synesius roared in his ear to be still. As the shutter waited, Mark and I sat tremblingly forbidding the senses of sight and smell to record the ghastly evidences of extreme debility which the room afforded. Startled by shouts for assistance from David in the refectory below, we left as soon as we could. Synesius gave us each a parting gift—Mark a topaz, "old and Byzantine"; myself a wooden chalice, containing two wooden rings and a wooden hand holding a purple wooden egg. The mystic significance of these I never discovered.

David we found in a temper. He considered the particular paintings in the refectory upon which I had picked, to be ridiculous. Our altercation was interrupted by a monk who knew ten words of American and chose this moment to ask David his name.

"Holdjertonguedamnyou," was the reply, which puzzled the monk and sent Mark and me fleeing into the sea. On the way we passed an old *epitropos* standing in a rampart of faggots before a weighing-machine, by which he was measuring the barrels of the monastery's wine. These were then borne off on the shoulders of labourers for export, to a schooner lying at anchor beyond the jetty.

Lunch of monkey-nut soup and salad was marred by a number of rotting sprats. Maddened by the stench, we threw one into the fireplace and one out of the window. The former could be replaced in its garniture of parsley, and, when our tempers had subsided, was. But the other, to our discomfiture, landed on the roof of the church, and remained casting looks of reproachful intensity through the open windows. Fortunately this hypnotic glance proved without effect on the guest-master.

In the afternoon we were fetched to see the library. It was hot. And David refused to come. But Mark and I, equally loth though more polite, triumphed. For we discovered a miniature of a Byzantine emperor seated in the royal box of the Constantinople hippodrome, watching the dismemberment of St. James of Persia, which David was incensed to have missed, since it might have proved a valuable clue in the excavations at Constantinople. But our departure was fixed and his opportunity lost. Shaking once more the hand of Synesius, we rode down to the beach, and along it for an hour, to where the arsenal of Zographou was visible across the bay.

We had approached Docheiariou on a former occasion from the other side of the promontory altogether. And had stopped for lunch at Castamonitou. This monastery, one of the four that are situated right away from the sea, is so lacking in architectural feature as to be remarkable. Its austere grey walls rising among the sunlit green of planes and chestnuts seemed such as might enclose a Yorkshire farmhouse. Unlike their environment, the inmates who entertained us were the most genial and expansive old men. I had thought we might call on them during our present journey. But the muleteer informed us that it was an hour out of the way. It was therefore upsetting to learn later that they had known of my presence, and had expressed themselves deeply hurt that I had passed their very door without coming in.

My progress on the ride was somewhat retarded. The pony—for such was its genus—was disposed to lag behind. My coat dropped, and no sooner had I with infinite difficulty remounted—for Greek saddles, being girthed with a single cord, usually slip under the animal's belly unless there is somebody to hold the other side—than I was again on my feet to retrieve a pair of spectacles dropped by a passing monk. A ruined tower then demanded a photograph. By this time the pony was out of temper, and the others half a mile ahead. From the tower to the arsenal—the latter flanked by a row of Lombardy poplars, a marsh of bamboo, and a light railway for carrying wood down from the hills above—I walked, the pony following. The path led me to a peculiar building shaped like a beehive and resembling a Kentish oast-house. Anxious to obtain another photograph of it, I started out to sea along the pier. This had subsided in the middle, and, as I was walking backwards, it was with a shock that I felt one foot suddenly descend into a watery crater. At last, however, I obtained a reasonable perspective; when the pony, who had been cynically watching, now pirouetted off home to Docheiariou. Leaping the crater, the sea, and the beach, I pursued it. But the faster I walked, the faster it trotted. I ran. It cantered. I leapt from olive terrace to olive terrace in the effort to cut off the hairpin bends of the path. It galloped. And when at last it had flung my coat, my despatch-case, and the monastery's new Turkey rug to the ground, I left it.

Twilight was falling. It was extremely hot. I did not know the way, and was exhausted with my steeplechase. Laden like a carpet-vendor, I stumbled wearily back to the pier again, where I found a monk, who regarded my purple face with horror, till we simultaneously broke into devilish mirth.

"How long," I said, "is it to the monastery?"

"An hour."

"An hour? What am I to do? I won't walk for an hour. I am tired. I have these things to carry. I don't know the way, and it is getting dark."

He shrugged.

"Is there a telephone?"

He negatived.

Then, catching me by the arm, he tiptoed up the causeway, over the beach, to a shed at the back of the arsenal. Therein glimmered the hindquarters of a mule, ready saddled. This animal he coaxed without, sat me upon it, disposed my property on the saddle, and with a fierce thwack, sent it clattering up the cobbled road. No sooner did hoof touch stone than the yell of a Goliath reverberated from the shore. Looking back, I saw a man, arms uplifted in commination, moving upon the monk. Chivalry called me back. But the mule, whose home was above, had no such feeling. A corner intervened as the two closed.

David, meanwhile, had come back to meet me. He did not notice that I had a new mount. Nor did the muleteer responsible for the old, till I told him. His concern for the pony was negligible. But his astonishment at my having conjured a second beast from the pebbles of the beach knew no bounds.

The landscape had now become entirely unlike that of the southern end of the peninsula. Those broken hills to which we were accustomed, half shrubs, half rock, pierced by gullies and made savage with naked crags; those, with all their lines leading to the ridge, and the ridge to the peak, now gave place to a great sweeping country, densely forested and cast in tremendous dales so deep that, with the sun in decline, all the bottoms were in shadow. The road was broad, and the bridges built on a grand scale. In the river-beds the light leaves of the plane-trees, trunks gnarled with the rushing of winter torrents, contrasted with the darker tones of the rest. And again, as we had found on the summit, there was autumn in the air. Half the leaves were already fallen.

Chapter XIV

THE PURSUIT OF CULTURE

ZOGRAPHOU, the monastery "of the painter," for which we were bound, has been consistently occupied by Slavs and Macedonians since the tenth century, and is now entirely Bulgarian. It was formerly very rich, owning lands in Bessarabia, whence the Russian Government, being anxious to foster the Slav element on the Mountain, did not hinder the revenues. Hence the fine road and broad bridges up which we had ridden. The present late nineteenth century buildings are built on an immense plan, of plain squared stone, four or five stories high. As we approached, it seemed as though here were some huge eighteenth century palace —a mixture, if such a thing can be imagined, of Windsor and Blenheim. The impression was confirmed by the entrance, where a porch like a railway terminus sheltered a coarse, bloated porter whose obesity was such that he could scarcely speak or move. When our letters had been examined, we were conducted to the guest-house, where passages as broad as main roads gave access to the rooms. David was installed single, that he might develop; Mark and I found ourselves in a kind of college hall, where we were also to dine.

Two monks, one an *epitropos*, the other named Joseph, came to visit us. The latter possessed cameras of his own, one of which was stereoscopic. We discussed the League of Nations, for, on the confiscation of property by the Greek Government, the Bulgars of Zographou had appealed to Geneva under the treaties. They had been no more successful than the sufferers of other nationalities. But Joseph said there was still hope.

At dinner the guest-master, an elderly man who had been an Ottoman subject, sat down with us, and he and David discoursed in Turkish and Russian, which latter language hardly differs from Bulgarian. Amid this babel of savage sounds, broken from time to time by the schoolroom aspirates of Mark's now profuse Greek—

hho and *hhe* the definite article will always remain for him—I was glad to forgo the everlasting necessity of leading the conversation. Being very tired, I fell gradually asleep over my plate of cold broad beans in iced gravy. And on my drowsing drums played the echo of the guest-master's ceaseless talk.

"Have you a father? Any sisters? Perhaps you are married? You aren't drinking. Do women drink in England? Do they smoke too? What's your occupation? What work do you do? What's your name? Mind you shut that window at night. You'll get rheumatism if you don't." The room had smelt like a deed-box before we opened it. "Well, I see the little boy (me!) wants to go to bed. Your health! Your health! Your health!"—and with bows all round he left.

So completely had we lapsed from the sequence of days and dates with which life is ordinarily regulated, that a Sunday came upon us with surprise. The church, dating from 1801, whither we suffered ourselves to be led at seven the next morning, presents an exterior emphatically striped in red and white and flanked by two gigantic cypresses, considerably older than any of the existing buildings. The service, which differed somewhat from the Greek, was reaching its climax as we arrived. And it was with a sense of embarrassment that we were conducted, in view of the whole congregation, to pay our respects to the famous *eicons* of St. George. Of these, one was painted supernaturally. The other came of its own volition over the sea from Arabia. It arrived at Vatopedi. But the other monasteries, learning of this monstrous good fortune, insisted that it should be placed on the back of a mule and allowed to go whither it pleased. This was done. The mule made straight for Zographou. And the picture has remained there ever since. Our guest-master, having prostrated before it and kissed it, recounted this history as we stood upright and ridiculous in the middle of the church. Eventually we were placed among the choir, which on our side was led by a little monk who, when not singing, quacked disconcertingly into a red beard.

When the service was over, we visited a smaller church, similarly striped. The tradition of the abominable persecutions inflicted on the Holy Mountain at the time of the Latin conquest, when the whole of Byzantine Europe was in the hands of the Franks and a papal legate installed at Salonica, has gained rather than lost at

[185]

Zographou during recent years. In one corner of the courtyard is a nineteenth century cenotaph commemorating the 26 martyrs "burnt by the Pope of Rome"; a legend which is thought to have arisen from the conflict between the Athonite monks and Michael I Palæologus, the Emperor who retook Constantinople; and who, knowing that only with the support of the West could his nation hope to defend it, applied himself to the reconciliation of the Churches. To this project the opposition of the Athonites was unflinching. And, the Bulgarian Church being already spasmodically schismatic, Zographou was perhaps singled out for the Emperor's punishment. In commemoration of the appalling outrages that resulted, the smaller church is frescoed with graphic representations of the arrival of the Pope in person; his incarceration of 26 monks and 2 laymen in a tower; and the subsequent pyre that he made of buildings and bodies. To complete the accuracy of the spectacle, the date 1873 is attached. As the Pope at this time was Pio Nono, he who remarked to the Anglican Bishop of Gibraltar and Southern Europe that he had "the honour to reside in your lordship's diocese," it is sad to think that he never beheld the portraits that would so have pleased his sense of humour.

The food at lunch, though plentiful, was of a nastiness without precedent. Seeing me unable to swallow, Mark asked me why I did not eat the cheese.

"Because I don't like it."

"But it's delicious—just the same as we have in Scotland, called Crowdy."

Thus the barbarians always reason. The veneer which they have acquired in the centres of the world falls off. Without a tremor they conjure up some filthy habit of their native fastnesses. And, not content with the very shame of the revelation, must needs elevate it to a standard for the universe. "Crowdy!" It has always been apparent to thinking people that some frightful custom, some orgiastic rite that would discredit the aborigines of Papua, has attended the childhood of those grim tribes among whom Albert and Victoria, in the guise of "Lord and Lady Churchill," were the Rosita Forbeses of their day. And now it is plain. "Crowdy!" These rancid, foetid curdles that I needs must eat "because we do in Scotland." Scotland? Where is Scotland?

The Pursuit of Culture

Later Joseph arrived to show us his cameras and the library. In the latter a selection of English literature proved more interesting than the few early Slav manuscripts on paper. We noticed with envy: *Second Love, or Beauty and Intellect*, 1851; *Pocket Companion to Oxford*, 1802; and *Poppleton: Conversation en anglais et français*, 1812.

As it was growing late, we departed immediately afterwards, pleasantly rested by a day at a monastery where there was nothing to photograph.

This labour on our part to record, pictorially and otherwise, the works of the Athonite painters, may seem strange to those who have read reports of their restoration and comparative novelty. It was originally supposed, on the word of the monks, that the majority dated from the eleventh or twelfth century. When it was discovered that they were mainly of the fifteenth and sixteenth, there arose a reaction among the great intelligent, the antiquarians for the sake of age alone. But there are, nevertheless, other works of the Byzantine Renaissance that have remained untouched since the day they were painted. These are at Mistra. And to Mistra, later in the year, we continued. Then, to seek the psychological inspiration of the "Cretan school" and its luminary, El Greco, we went to Crete as well. Our journey to the southernmost point of the Greek dominion, contained in the following interlude, was the complement to our long stay on the Mountain in the north.

.   .   .   .   .

Those for whom Athens is but a city of broiling dust and broiling sun will find it difficult to imagine our start for Sparta at five o'clock in the dark of a drenching October morning. As the train drew out, the familiar country was changed; the glaring putty-coloured earth was now a deep red brown, almost Irish in its softness; the greens of trees and shrubs were richer; the hills and rocks a cold grey; and the sky a scene of billowing clouds, decapitating the hills and allowing occasional searchlights of sun to bathe a patch of plough or an olive-dotted slope in pale but startling radiance.

Arrived at Tripolitza after the thirteen miserable hours, myself racked with the shivers and heats of a feverish cold, we chartered an ancient but powerful Lancia. This motor, being painted entirely white, resembled a ghostly landau rushing through the rain behind some invisible Pegasus. The drive was interrupted by numerous requests for lifts and petrol. Until our patience was exhausted; and, wishing to die in a bed, I informed the chauffeur that if, not only did he stop, but even freewheeled again, his money would not be forthcoming. Immediately afterwards we topped the mountains that the road was climbing. And, with darkness almost upon us, there was revealed that incomparable view of the valley of the Eurotas, watered with the river and its tributaries, and rich with mulberries, olives, and cypresses; in the centre Sparta, white and modern; at the back Mistra, climbing indistinguishably brown to the castle at the apex of its conical foothill; and, above it, the towering, blue-black range of Taygetus, hump upon hump, with the clouds thick on the top sending torn white wreaths down its clefts and valleys. Then it became dark. The rain, lashing in upon us with increasing fury, blinded the windscreen from the lights. But the driver, obedient to his admonition, descended the 4,000 feet that lay before us with his foot pressed to the accelerator. I recalled that previously, being only two, we had shared a car designed by God for five, with the luggage and persons of eleven others. These were so disposed that the driver was obliged to trust the use of the hand- and only brake to our discretion, since he himself could not reach it. At length on the present occasion, conscious of nothing but the cold, we drew up outside the Pan-hellenion Hotel. I chartered my death-bed; and was removing my clothes for the last time, when the Great Summons was averted by a lesser, which announced that the mayor and prefect were awaiting us in the Commercial Club across the square.

Our ears had been filled, while on the Holy Mountain, with tales of the resentment aroused throughout Greece, and particularly in the neighbourhood of Sparta, by the action of a distinguished professor who was supposed, though unjustifiably, to have injured the frescoes by treating them with chemicals. I had been at pains, therefore, while in Athens, to ensure that we should not be identified with similar roguery. But it was with grateful surprise that we learned that a telegram had been sent by Monsieur Zaimis, the Prime Minister, advising the civic authorities of our coming. An interpreter whose English was acquired in the Sudan led us to their presence. Seldom, perhaps never, has shattered frame made so great an effort. But life and merriment were restored by brandy. And we were treated to a civic banquet beside which one I had previously eaten at the Guildhall was a mere snack. *Hors d'œuvre*, *pilaf*, chicken, pork, *gâteau*, grapes, and melon followed one another in a series of stupendous helpings; each of which was washed down with yet another glass of that resin-tasting wine which has brought the Greeks into national disrepute, ever since its first denunciation by Liutprand, Otto I's ambassador to Constantinople in the tenth century. The mayor, exerting the whole strength of a forceful personality, insisted we should drink. And drink we did. Till the aged prefect sank altogether beneath the gastronomic battery of his colleague. The meal ended with *Mavrodaphni*, a kind of Marsala, served in champagne glasses. Next day David's interior was so deranged that he could not eat. And the prefect was in bed. To the latter the interpreter invariably referred as the "perfect," and, when called on to denote his place of office, would say, "The perfect, Mr. Byron, is at the perfection."

Mistra, situated three miles from Sparta, is the only purely Byzantine city in existence. And its houses, bearing the famous royal names of the despots, Lascaris, Cantacuzene, and Palæologus, remained inhabited up till the time of the Revolution. The site is a steep and narrow cone, reaching a thousand feet above the valley and falling from its summit, still fortified by the gigantic walls of Villehardouin's Castle, down a sheer precipice behind. Here, huge cliffs of black shale rise to the lower contours of Taygetus, dotted with conifers. In front, the ruined city drops down, house above house, enclosed in massive double walls; intersected by tiny streets in which two mules may barely pass; and displaying in panorama the centres of a capital: to the left the great trisected shell of the palace of the despots, its many-windowed banqueting-hall on the first story still visible; and everywhere churches, many of them roofless, the chief being the Metropolitan at the bottom, where a priest is still attached and services held. It was here that Constantine XI Dragases, last of the 88 emperors of Constantinople, was crowned. The spot is commemorated by a slab carved with the royal eagles.

These churches contain the whole clue to the semi-Oriental paternity of European painting. Their importance is not to be exaggerated. And it arouses a feeling of despair to see them, in this age when the lesser monuments of other pasts are treated with wasteful and absurd reverence, either roofless or fitted with doors and windows that would discredit an Irish pigsty. With one exception all are being rotted with the damp, are covered with a coating of nobbly blue mould, which, though still possible to remove, is eating through the paint to the plaster. This exception, the church of the Convent of the Pantanassa, has had the cracks of walls and ceiling so coarsely mended that many of the paintings, otherwise as brilliant and delicate in colour as when the artist left them, are barely intelligible. And in the nave are two layers of frescoes on different coatings of plaster, both of value, one of which needs removing and setting up elsewhere. There is the work of years to occupy an expert. And the employment of such a man might prove, in the end, a profitable investment. For the Greek Government must realise that, with the world's advance towards the appreciation of the dynamic in art, broken pillars and black and orange pottery will not attract the rich tourist for ever. But with the refugees, the country is harassed for lack of money. Is there no institution endowed for the preservation of the world's cultural monuments that will override the enforced inaction of the Athenian Byzantinists? It is heating that is primarily needed. Cannot five art-loving continents afford as many stoves?

Every day from Sparta we came and went. Every day we ate a chicken at the Marmora, the café at the bottom, where a young man and his aged mother tend the needs of infrequent visitors; a delicious chicken, accompanied by fried potatoes, tomato salad, and afterwards large green grapes, plucked from the arbour above our table. Water we drank, cold and deep-tasting, from the antique trough which catches a stream and gives the place its name. It was curious, and somehow satisfying, to see the beasts of such few residents as remain in the lower houses of the town watered at this richly carved museum piece.

Our second centre was the Pantanassa half-way up the hill, where Sister Eusebia and her sister by blood, the abbess, treated us as their children. Coffee and *ouzo* they insisted we should have when we came in and out to fetch our cameras and note-books; and a black-robed maiden used to follow us about the courtyard and up the terraces at the back with these little trays of welcome. Finally, one day David decided not to come down to the Marmora to lunch, but remain at his work without food till the evening. Sister Eusebia would have none of it. And he was arranging the camera in the gallery of the church when his eyes were suddenly blinded by the exquisite symmetry of two poached eggs, set out between knife and fork, salt and pepper, on the balustrading. The hospitality of this tiny community of seven women was different from, though not less than, that of their male counterparts. Theirs was that pleasure in motherliness that only women possess. And there is a gallant spirit in their pertinacity—clinging to the hill which all have deserted, but they will not. They know all the ruins, the inscriptions, and the history of the despots. And it is to their efforts in repair that posterity owes such of the frescoes as still survive. They were jolly old ladies, with a welcome for everyone. Men and maidens from below used to make their gate a rendezvous. Though this may have been temporarily due to the posse of policemen who acted as our permanent guard of honour, and lounged about the courtyard as we worked.

Whatever the nuns' isolation, the natural beauty of their situation must fortify the weakest soul. For those epicures in landscape who demand not only form but colour, for whom central Europe is but a chromatic photograph and an Alp in a sunset comparable only to the asbestos in a gas-stove, the Levant is without peer. And in all the Levant, in Europe or Asia, pagan or Christian, there is no place where the divine soul of the earth can so fill the heart, so suffocate the eyes with tears, so make man proud, as the Eurotas valley. Last year, as this, we had come every morning from Sparta. And at the end of each day we had plodded home along the dusty road through the olive groves, bidding the peasants good evening and good night. Never in life will the memory of those May nights escape; of the air enveloping, dark and real, the breathing human kiss of the earth; of the bells of the birds dropping round and full from the trees, with a red vein to their silver curves; of space lit with the scattered mercury of the stars; of one star balanced on the black brow of Taygetus and suddenly, as by a hand, snatched off; and last, of the meticulous scholastics from under the bridge: Brekekekex Coax Coax.

Now it is on rainy October days that we sit up in the Pantanassa, drinking coffee in the Byzantine white-pillared cloister beneath the egg-topped tower. Below us, the stone of the ruined houses, brown and grey, merges into the hill. Then the walls stop. And the last roots of the great mountain behind slide out into the valley, where the rich red earth is dotted grey with olives or striped with the spring-green of vines. Over all hangs the odour of fresh rain. With distance the trees lose their detail in patches of colour, Sparta hiding a white toy town in their thickest. Each way the valley stretches, till on the east, as we look north, a soft glint of the sea parts the rival ranges for ever. All along above the twining silver river floats a veridian haze. Far away rise the parallel hills, deepest sapphire, sweeping high and regular as far as the eye can see, with the black and white clouds rolling up, and their shadows like foreign armies traversing the plain. In all lurks the colour of light, of the fire of the earth, burning in watered leaf and sodden plough, catching even the sounds as they run hazard through the air: this colour which Greece knows and other lands do not; and which Greeks have brought to rest, not in stone, but paint.

Leaving Mistra one drizzling evening, our hearts wrung with David's good-byes, we journeyed on mules to Trypi. At the entrance to the village stood the president, the chief of police, and other leading men, grouped upon a rock in the rain to await our coming. They conducted us to the inn, where they gave us drinks and talked American, a language which we did our best to recall, as they did not understand English. A vase of marigolds had been placed upon the table of our room. But, beyond that, luxuries were few. Being high up on the side of the mountain, it was extremely cold. The beds, of straw, had a surface like their native land, and were filled with hungry animals. The sanitary arrangements overhung a pigsty at the end of an open gallery, along which it was necessary to creep shielding a lighted candle from the howling storm. These were tenanted by a Glamis monster, a livid rat big as a fox, which rushed madly from side to side, to the terror of the bare feet. At seven next morning we mounted the same mules for the thirty-mile ride over the Langada pass to Calamata.

The path twisted at first up such precipices that it was more comfortable to walk. Then we reached the gorge, where walls of rock on either side reared above us into the clouds, grey and lowering as a November sea. Here we kept to the river-bed, winding among boulders and plane-trees; till at last the hills opened out and we climbed among plantations of walnuts. The cold was bitter. Two cabins on the path were already shuttered and forsaken for the winter. And snowdrops and crocuses, purple, yellow, and white, were flowering on the banks. At the top of the pass, where the trees parted as though on purpose to reveal the view and the ground was brown with pine-needles, we looked down over range after range to the faint blue of the sea and the most southerly coast-line of Europe. Turning whence we had come, the fir-covered hills fell steeply back to the dark entrance to the gorge. And then above all, even ourselves, rose the extended mass of Taygetus, its three flat peaks naked and glistening in a single patch of sun.

At Lada, a mountain village, we lunched with difficulty, pigs, dogs, cats, and mules, none of whom had tasted food since the day they were weaned, thrusting their nozzles into our sardine tins. For four hours more we rode, up and down the grey inland cliffs, smeared and scarred with dirty pink. Then we stood above the bay, the port with ships at anchor, and, a little way inland, the town. Unearthly colours, the prototype of the Byzantine painter's landscape and as unlike nature, filled the countryside. The earth was of deep claret, and the road along which we now galloped, of a paler tone. The rocks, in Giottesque formation, such as attend St. Francis' more adventurous moments, blared orange rust. And the vegetation—aloes, thick-leaved bamboos, and even bananas—was not more improbable than that of Van Gogh.

We arrived, trotting along the tram-lines, at five o'clock, and hurried to remove a week's filth in the public baths, where a portion of loofah was included in the shilling ticket. Returning to the hotel, where, as at all Greek hotels outside Athens, clean and properly appointed bedrooms were to be had for one and sixpence a night, we encountered a flabby Italian who turned out to be the Lloyd Triestino agent.

"Go from here to Crete?" he said. "Quite impossible."

It was impossible. Of that we were aware. For there is an international convention which forbids steamers of one country to carry passengers between the ports of another. But the Lloyds, one of which we knew to be already in the harbour, are the only boats which connect the south coast of Greece with the neighbouring island. Once at Sparta, we were loth to return to Athens; we wished to ride over the Langada; and we looked forward to a single night's comfort among the Austrian traditions that the line still maintains. Was there no solution to our dilemma? Could we not book third class to Constantinople, the first foreign port of call? Mr. Triadaphilopopoulos, the harbour-master, thought not. Fortunately telegrams were cheap. And by dint of importunity over the wires to Athens, combined with a torrential mastery of Greek on the spot, we eventually persuaded ourselves on board, to the chagrin of the Lloyd agent. Next morning we found ourselves at anchor in a rough sea outside Canea. Arrival was as difficult as departure. The governor of the island was in bed. But he was awakened and our letter of introduction read him over the telephone. At last we were safe. Though the mental strain and the prospect of travelling round and round the Mediterranean on that Lloyd, visaless and penniless, till she was broken up and our bones discovered, had left us exhausted.

To portray here the individuality of Crete, this island which, till the beginning of the twentieth century, had been "700 years in perpetual revolt," is scarcely possible. Our visit was a reconnoitre, a prelude, perhaps, to further exploration. At first we remained in the capital, Canea. The buildings of this town epitomise the whole history of the Levant. Across the mouth of the harbour, as the rowing-boat enters, runs a mole ending in a Turkish lighthouse, a truncated minaret delicately embroidered with stone ornament. Nearer in, on the east, stands the earliest mosque on the island, a tiny building with a dome that resembles three-quarters of a doughnut and is supported by flying buttresses that might have been borrowed from St. George's, Windsor. Look now across to the west. It is Venice. High, multi-coloured houses, each black window reflected in the sunlit water, jumble along the quay; and reveal, on closer view, that it was Venice, and that the lions of St. Mark still cry a weatherbeaten echo from the bellying walls. Behind, up the slope from the sea, it is the same. Twisting narrow streets, the houses so tall as to exclude all sun, display Renaissance porticoes, escutcheons of the Venetian nobility, and even basrelievo portraits of the generals of the Republic in plumed helmets. On one such there appeared also the stone fez of a later tenant. And above, as if to complete the tale, the cornice had been furnished with a row of Greek *acroteria*. Adjacent lies the old Turkish quarter, to-day the centre of commerce, where lanes of windowless shops are piled with the importations of the West, side by side with the traditional clothing and commodities of the island.

It was October. The weather was clearing. And the sun shone with golden warmth in the squares, upon the tall swinging men in their dress of top-boots, black Turkish trousers falling in a huge bag behind, and black cross-stitched shirts, to which were sometimes added blue cloaks embroidered and hooded. At all the street corners chestnuts were cooking on braziers. Fruit and game were piled high in the market. We lunched as a rule in a disused mosque, where we were always invited to choose our own partridge in the kitchen. This building was also the theatre; and, since a different performance was given nightly, there were frequent rehearsals. Our meals were protracted by the tunes of operettas such as *The Contessa Maritza*, and the declamations of love-stories advertised on the posters as "ΣO'KIN 'EPΩTIKA—Shocking Erotics"—delivered by unshaven men and down-at-heel ladies, savagely painted. These, when not upon the stage, lounged around us in basket chairs, looking strangely irrelevant in the dim green light of this Mahommedan temple.

In the afternoons we bathed; or sometimes went driving with Madame Venizelos, who was now leading a not altogether diverting existence in the new house which she and her husband have built at Haleppa, Canea's residential suburb. He, unfortunately, was ill with phlebitis. On one occasion we visited Mournies, the place of his birth, and saw the house of that event, subsequently burnt in a rebellion and now overgrown with creepers and morning glory. Thence we continued to a monastery, where the monks showed us the Venetian deeds of their foundation, gorgeously illuminated with the badges of the Republic.

But our visit to Crete had a definite purpose. We had heard the White Mountains described in a passing sentence as resembling "whitewash on coal." And we were determined to explore this landscape, whence the Cretan painters, as all schools of painting do, must have drawn their light and colour. Early one morning we left the town in a motor, accompanied by three saddle-bags containing a few clothes and one enormous sausage, on which we lived for three days.

Sphakia, whither we were bound, is the most savage and inaccessible province of the island, being inhabited largely by outlaws. These are not brigands, but simply those who have not seen eye to eye with the police over some such trifle as a missing sheep. The White Mountains, haunt of the human vampire, here fall with cataclysmic suddenness to a sea as deep as the middle of the Pacific. Cleaving these walls of hell, leafless and arid, where the rippling contours reflect the oblique morning sun in a succession of strange lights—"whitewash on coal"—come titanic cracks, deep shadow-black, to the very lapping of the water, where reflection confirms their sinister reality. Down one of them, slit by some prehistoric tantrum, we travelled by mule; slept that night in the office of a police-station upon policemen's beds; and rowed all next day along the devilish ramparts of the sea, till we reached a tiny church, a mere crumb among the boulders of the beach and the cliffs above. Here the remnant of a fresco bespoke a primitive art such as flourished in the churches of Cappadocia. Some way off-shore at this point a fresh spring bubbles to the surface. But, though we lapped as we swam, till the Mediterranean was lowered, we could not find it.

In the afternoon we arrived at Aghia Roumeli. The only inhabitants were the police, who welcomed us particularly for a basket of new bread that we brought, their only provisions for the rest of time being a single tin of sardines and half a loaf, green with mould, which hung in a net from the ceiling. A ruined Turkish castle, spattered with bullet-marks, dominated a hill up which we climbed. The police, excited beyond bounds by fresh faces, could not leave us. And, for our diversion, first destroyed the path by rolling the boulders of which it was built on top of Mark, who was beneath; and then, as it grew dark, setting the whole hill on fire. From the castle we could look down to the Samaria gorge, with the blue smoke of a tiny village rising at its entrance, and its interminable walls of rock towering up to the peaks of the range. That night we slept bedded in the shingle, the waves at our feet, a cold moon overhead and a threatening whisper in the air. At four, the hour when men die, we woke. Between the livid sea and the half-lit cliffs it seemed as though the chill, angry breeze was bearing the angel of death upon us. Tearing green oranges, and filling our water-bottle with the burning red wine of the island, we set off before it was light, accompanied by four policemen, their dog, and one mule which they had been able to find, despite the fact that "people round here don't like us."

As dawn broke, the gates of the gorge loomed above us—enormous faces of rock scarred in diagonal strata; so that by looking from side to side it was possible to see how accurately they would fit together again should a second upheaval ever heal the wound of the first. Then followed the little valley into which we had looked the night before, and the village of low brown cabins shaded with oranges and walnuts. This brought us to the actual neck of the gorge, a mile long and a thousand feet deep, walls sheer and in places no more than ten yards apart. In winter the water from the snows makes this cloven route impassable. To-day its volume had already swollen to necessitate the use of stepping-stones.

All the time the path was slowly climbing. At length the walls and the line of sky above them widened, and we found ourselves at the foot of fresh peaks. Everywhere grew cypresses of all shapes but their own, disguised as cedars and pines. Surrounding the church of St. Nicolas, where we rested, are said to be the largest in the world. And, by comparison with the lesser giants of Athos, the date of whose planting is known, it seemed not impossible that these first saw light, as the tale goes, in pre-Christian times. Here we met a caravan of mules, whose attendants fortunately directed us off what appeared to be the main path, to the left. Even the police had never attempted this journey before.

For we were now insinuated by gorge and valley into the heart of the mountains, at the foot of the Xyloscala. We had risen 2,500 feet; 1,500 more remained to the lowest gap over which we could return to the north of the island. And the path, discarding compromise, attacked the escarpment zigzag. The sun beat upon us. The policemen took frequent rests. And the others waited in turn for the mule. Feeling that if I stopped it would be for ever, I reached the top alone. Turning, the view had attained proportions to which only the Grand Canyon can offer parallel. On the west towered a sponge-like cliff, the moving mountain, which is always falling, and where lives the rare Cretan ibex. Below lay the valley, soft with distant trees, winding in and out the feet of the hills till, with the beginning of the gorge, they closed in to form an arena deeper, higher than the eye could compass. Over all the peaks poured the powdery light of the sun, filling the interior with a dull, warm haze. Some grouse whirred from my feet. And then suddenly, as if to emphasise the sheer magnitude, there shot into the circle of the sky an aeroplane, a purring flea at which the mountains seemed to shrug and laugh. The British battleships were in Suda Bay.

Five minutes later I had twisted up between two peaks as close together as the banks of a road-cutting, and was walking on the grass of the square mile plateau of Omalo. I fell in with an old peasant more than six feet high, who asked, as he strode along in his tall boots with gun and dog, how long a crossing separated England from France. He gave me rotten crab-apples to eat, which were sweet and tasted of medlars. As we walked we came on others sowing their last seeds before the winter; for snow was expected daily. It was high as Ben Nevis. And from behind a mild hillock, out of a perfectly clear sky, there suddenly floated a puffy white cloud, which proceeded to walk sedately across a patch of plough, wholly obscuring its cultivators from our view.

It was midday. Not till six o'clock did we reach Lakkoi, whither came a road, and where we rested to eat and drink on a terrace. Around us chatted the male inhabitants, each sheltered from the wind in a white woolly capote with a peaked hood; so that the effect was that of a party of ghostly witches. From here we were able to telephone for a car. As I sat at the instrument I said to the police officer:

"We are very tired."

"So," he replied, "am I."

"We've come 40 kilometres from Aghia Roumeli."

"I've been out shooting."

"Shooting what?" I asked. "Wild ibex?"

"No; bad men."

Chapter XV

BUILT IN THE FOREST

WE WERE riding, if the moment of our digress be recalled,
between Zographou and Chilandari. It was late in the day,
and a golden glory lapped the feathery canary green of the incense-
pines which lined the path. We were crossing now to the side of the
promontory whither we had originally descended on the first
evening, from Caryes to Iviron. And, as we reached the highest
point of the hills, the whole purple finger of land lay revealed,
floating in a pale sea; the clear-cut capes receding in different tones
like the wings of a theatre; and all leading to the lilac spire of Athos
at the end. Then we descended again to ilexes and oaks. And the
light deepened.

The mules of Zographou, insensitive to the palette of Nature,
were misbehaving. That which bore the luggage, loth to take the
left-hand path rather than the right, dragged the muleteer on his
stomach through the dust, to the ruin of his red beard and national
dress. Rising, he planted himself in mid-road and denounced the
animal with the tones of a Gladstone on the subject of his Disraeli.
Chastened by the moral fervour of this rhetoric, the cavalcade
continued. When David's mule, not to be excelled in unseemliness,
delivered itself of a succession of piercing belches. That the curious
properties of Athonite food should react even on the lower creations
was new to us. Hitherto we had studied their outcome only at
meals and in church. It is to be regretted, in a questioning age,
that the digestive reminiscence as a historic factor has never been
scientifically examined. In Arabian society it is still the compliment
which the host expects from his guest after a meal. While among
the Georgians, reported Busbecq, the imperial ambassador to
Constantinople in the sixteenth century, it was the method of
respectful greeting. St. Simon, when French ambassador in Spain,
had perhaps the classic experience of it, when, on taking leave

of the Infanta whom he had conducted to her marriage, and asking if she had not any messages for her parents, she replied from her daïs with sounds that completely deranged the proverbial gravity of the Spanish court. What catastrophic upheavals may not have hinged, unknown to history, on similar incidents?

As the darkness drew on, and then settled, we were obliged to hurry. A light twinkled. But it was twenty minutes more before the walls and tower of the monastery showed black above us. The gate was shut. Only silence answered our shouts and hammerings. At last, however, a wicket opened; and after much expostulation, which on our side we left to the muleteer, knowing ourselves to be in the wrong, we were allowed to enter. There was no light. Simply voices uttered from the stars, whither our possessions were hoisted on a rope. Finding an entrance in the wall, we followed as we might. And ultimately reached the lounge-hall of the top flat in an exceedingly high building. This was comfortably furnished with a round table, dozens of Windsor chairs, and two to three hundred engravings of the heroes and heroines of Slav independence in the Balkans. For Chilandari is a Serbian monastery.

In one corner was a glass-partitioned pantry. Hence emerged a youthful guest-master carrying refreshments, his tray and its fittings being of lavishly ornamented silver. Everything bespoke the care of a competent butler; a pleasurable surprise, for the ridiculous Czech whom we had met at St. Paul's had curled our toes with his tales of Chilandari's squalor and inhospitality. Could it be that Bohemia owed Serbia a political grudge? Our knowledge of the new Balkans was not sufficient to say whether the two countries shared a common boundary. But it may have been that his remarks were inspired by the truth of his experiences; for his was not the only complaint that reached us.

At dinner, which was not ready, owing to the lateness of our arrival, till ten o'clock—eleven and a half hours after we had last tasted food—we were joined by another guest, a German. The first course was a delicious soup which, when the actual substance of the rank fish from which it was distilled was avoided, tasted as though of hare. Towards this David gave free rein to the greed which was now the property of all of us. And Mark and I, stung to fury, heaped upon him the epithets of corpulence, ending, as he scraped the tureen, by likening him to Diana of Ephesus. Whereat the German, hitherto puzzled at the uproar, understood.

"I see," he interpolated, "you talk of women: *he he he Ha Ha Ha HE HE HE HA! HA! HA!*" and launched himself upon our mirth with the vigour of a Babbitt.

Alone of the Slav, and alone of the inland monasteries, Chilandari has preserved buildings of antiquity, the majority of which, if not wholly mediæval—for many were damaged in a fire of 1722—have been plainly reconstructed on the same foundations as the older. David, who shares the sea's worries and was now quit of them, felt his happiest here, and resumed, as became the surroundings, the life and manner of an English country gentleman. Work in the church was followed, when Vespers put an end to it, by a walk round the place before dinner. Game-birds were plentiful. And the forests in this part contain, besides wild boar, jackal and deer. Another year we shall borrow the dog pack of our local hounds for the summer, and bring them out; thus completing, since there will be pig-sticking and stalking as well, those amenities of sport on which the sun never sets. We look forward, in fact, to the day when the Holy Mountain is transformed from the desultory haunt of artist and penman to a kind of Highland Melton, resort of English sportsmen, who take the shooting regularly from the Synod and are glad to run down to Salonica for a week or two among these decent old dagoes without any damned womenkind fussing about.

The buildings of Chilandari reflect the woods in which they stand. Alone on Athos there is found here the mellowness and harmony of weathered age which we in the North estimate above pearls, and which is entirely opposed to the Byzantine code of æsthetics. Throughout prevails the tint and texture of dead leaves, property of small russet bricks concealed by neither plaster nor colour-wash. The courtyard is enclosed by a diamond-shaped perimeter of tall, thin buildings, the ground so lying that the obtuse angles fall one below the other. At the higher of these stands the tower, a twelfth century structure of dignified simplicity, finished with a convex roof instead of the usual crenellations. To the south, perched up on the foundation walls, rises the octagonal smoke-stack of the old kitchen, exactly resembling those mediæval survivals of the same office at Eton and Glastonbury. Below this runs a stream where the sun, filtering through the leaves of overhanging trees, casts yet further spots on the hairy backs of domesticated boars. At the end, a miniature aqueduct, supporting like a military headdress an impertinent little cypress, carries water across the ravine to the monastery. Thither Mark and I were picking our way, he in pursuit of a swallow-tail butterfly, I of an art view, when the warning patter of sewage on plane-leaves obliged us to return. In the evening we went for another walk, and discovered a colony of tortoises.

Within the courtyard the eye is caught by four cypresses, one of an immense height, surrounding a Turkish baroque phiale. Behind these stands the thirteenth century church, much decorated with brick patterns and sculptured plaques. The whole is Slav rather than Greek in character, the reliefs being flat and lacking that mastery of design for which Byzantines were conspicuous; and the ornament, though pleasant in itself, detracting from the architectural lines. Inside, the frescoes follow the "Macedonian" iconography, and, dating from the beginning of the fourteenth century, are earlier than most of those on the Mountain. But, having been ruthlessly restored a hundred years ago, their artistic value is almost negligible. None the less, it is extraordinary how even now, beneath the colours of a Victorian birthday book, the old spirit has survived in the force of the compositions.

Behind the altar is a remarkable painting of the infant Jesus recumbent in the paten, the chalice upright at his side. Since this uncouth vindication of transubstantiation is without inscription, it may be presumed to record the experience of the ancient monk of Scetis who was unable to accept this novel doctrine of the fourth century. His companions having prayed for him, both he and they repaired to the church. "And when the bread," wrote Palladius not long after, "was placed on the holy table it appeared to the three only as a child, and . . . an angel of the Lord came down from heaven with a sword and slew the child as a sacrifice, and emptied its blood into the cup. . . . And as they drew near to partake of the holy things, there was given to the old man alone, bleeding flesh."[1] Here is theophagy at its grimmest. Such, no doubt, would Gregory of Nyssa, the originator of transubstantiation, also

[1] W. F. Adeney: *The Greek and Eastern Churches.*

have approved, since in his opinion "it is not possible for anything to come to be in the body except it be well mixed with the bowels by being eaten and drunk. Surely, then, it is requisite to receive, in the way possible to our nature, the power of the Spirit that is to quicken us." So a large proportion of Christians appear to have thought ever since. Here, however, was an unwitting memorial to the first Protestant. A thousand years more were needed before Wycliffe and Luther should succeed. But even they must have been restored to faith by such measures.

The floor of the church is a century older than the rest of the building. It was laid in 1197, and is a superb example of *opus Alexandrinum*, marbles of every colour being inlaid round large figured slabs of greyish green. Contemporary with it was the foundation of the monastery itself by SS. Symeon and Sabbas. The former of these was in lay life Stephen Nemanja, King of Serbia. His second son, Sabbas, called by secret voices to religion, set off unknown to Athos. Soldiers were sent to retrieve him. But, taking refuge in Russico, he divested himself of both his hair and his royal robes, and bade these be returned in his stead. The result was that King Stephen followed him, and they both settled at Vatopedi. But Stephen—or Symeon, as he was now called—being the son-in-law of the Byzantine Emperor Alexius III Angelus, obtained permission to found an independent monastery for the Serbians. These incidents are depicted on the walls of the refectory, where they were painted in 1621. In a corner of the church, behind the stalls, is a magnificent panel under glass, representing St. Symeon recumbent in his monastic robes. The black folds are lit with wine-coloured planes and formal lines of gold. Near his feet stands a group of monks. And the background is formed by a row of buildings diverse as a city street, and grouped solely for pictorial purposes, as in a Carpaccio. The inscription is in both Slav and Greek; and each version states clearly that it dates from 1780. Its excellence of condition corroborates this. But there is not a gallery in the world that would not be glad to possess it, and would not at the same time, but for its inscription, hang it as contemporary with the earlier Italians. St. Symeon's tomb, though his body is now elsewhere, lies at the back of the church. Here grows the famous vine whose grapes bring milk to suckling mothers. When ripe they are put in the empty sarcophagus to dry, and are afterwards entrusted to certain Serbian bishops to distribute. The monks hold them very precious.

The sacristan was a strange little creature, with a pinched Mongolian face and only a few wartish hairs blossoming on his chin. He was at much pains to make us feel at home in the church, and showed us the treasures. Among them the only object of importance was a portative mosaic of the Virgin about 21 inches by 14; but it was a crude piece of work, and lacked the genius of colouring and technique apparent in the others described above.

"Do you come from London?" he asked as we were working.

"Yes."

"How far is that from Jerusalem?"

"A week's journey."

"I must go to Jerusalem. How much would it cost from here?"

"£3 10s.," said David, to whom the transport facilities of Joppa are as familiar as those of Piccadilly Circus.

We, too, decided to visit Jerusalem, though the opportunity has not yet arisen. There is something that tickles the humour in the materialisation of cities which have haunted childhood. That of Pericles is sufficiently entertaining on first sight. But to sip the night-life of the heavenly city or rattle up the Jericho road in a 'bus must arouse a delirium of mirth.

Mark, meanwhile, was sketching. To him also came the inevitable question from a passing father: "Are you from London?"

"Yes."

"London, London, aaah"; and, with a dream in his eye and romance in his voice, he whispered, "Seven millions."

The meals, to our now coarsened palates, were periods of un-clouded enjoyment. The younger guest-master, who had received us and who spoke only Serbian, presented a character which will one day carry him to the top of his profession. After a single year on the Mountain, he already spent his spare time sitting on a stool in the corner and practising chants that would enable him to sing in the choir. His hair and beard were red, and his sad and staring eyes, of watery pastel blue, were vividly contrasted thereby. These facial characteristics were so accentuated by Mark's pencil and paint that he exclaimed: "Have I really become like this in a year?" and begged that he might be allowed to sit again with the added dignity of gown and veil. His efficiency was remarkable. Automatically he came to fill that intricate receptacle, the syphon, and place it on the table before each meal. We were saying, in fact, as we picked our red mullet, that life in England would plainly be no longer tolerable without a monkish butler, when the edge was taken from our appetite by a resounding snort, followed by the opening of a window and a sound of prolonged extrusion.

There sat at dinner with us on this occasion a Salonican photographer, born, he hastened to say, near Sparta, who was making an album. The album has retained its prestige in the Levant; for it is the photographs that are taken to fill the album, not the album bought to contain the photographs. The guest-master having, on the close of his operations, left the window open, we enquired, knowing the sensitiveness of those who live in hot countries, if the photographer would like it shut.

"I?" he said. "Mind the cold? I was nine years in the army. Soldiers don't mind the cold.

"I am a captain," he added suddenly.

Mark, understanding the words "I am," for some reason took it into his head that the honourable designation of rank "$\lambda o\chi\alpha\gamma\dot{o}\varsigma$," meant "tipsy." And there followed the disgusting exhibition of his tapping nose and forehead at the insulted officer, accompanying his gestures with assurances of sympathetic comprehension of his state and a gleeful leer as he passed him the decanter. The unfortunate man was not slow to demonstrate that he could at least rid himself of our company with unfaltering motion.

It seemed, in such spare time as offered, that this of all monasteries must lend itself to my inept but persevering pencil. As I was setting off up the hill, an old monk called from an upper window and begged me to put out my cigarette. I did. And found, on ascent, that the whole of the farther side was a tangle of blackened roots. It was easy to imagine the danger from fire to a monastery set among the trees as this one was. The path, as I continued, disappeared. And I perforce went on all fours up a perpendicular stream-bed. At the top, surrounded by trees, it was impossible to obtain even a glimpse of the monastery. The sloping ground was slippery with dead leaves, and every strand of vegetation to which I clung shot barbed spines into my hands. At length I reached a gap torn by three fallen pine-trees. And here I sat a whole happy afternoon and evening, kept company by a sociable though pugnacious wasp.

On our last night, David and I lounged on the steps of the guest-house discussing the future and the possibilities of the pen. For the public at large David expressed a profound contempt. It was his aim, he said, to produce books of such expense and erudition that they should actually repel it. I, on the contrary, suggested that even contemporary public opinion was probably a better judge of lasting value than those artificial cliques which, sensibly enough from the point of view of their own finance, were strangling British intellect. This led us to the novel, an ulterior goal. And we agreed that if ever a great novel, to rank with Shakespeare, Velasquez, and Beethoven, could be written, it is now. Only now are we learning to probe the unreasoning machinery of the human mind. And now, for the first time, man holds the world in his palm, placed there by mechanised transport. It remains for an artist to leave posterity a picture, not of dialects or tribes, countries or continents, but of the globe of the twentieth century. For the longer the opportunity lasts, the less worth while will it be. Western civilisation is becoming universal, the race a homogeneous one. And before we die, half the variety of the picture will be gone; as if a showman had sold his swing-boats, his hoop-las, his fat woman, and even his merry-go-round, and invested the proceeds in one superlative chairoplane. The view is enlarged, the motion more poignant. And then: all is dull.

The night itself was peaceless. Dinner was interrupted by Mark's discovering, on returning to fetch the chutney, an unfamiliar layman examining our tooth-cleansers and poking in our shaving-creams. David later developed; and, as usual, left the plates in the sink beneath a running tap. I was sitting at a book in the lounge-hall when, unexpectedly as a ghost, a very old monk picked away the oil lamp. I seized it from him. But he looked so piteous that I returned it and sat in the dark. To my unspeakable rage, he tottered slowly down the passage to the sink and turned off the tap. Luckily David at that moment returned to his guard.

Outside blew a great wind. At two o'clock we were awakened by the sound of David's window, opened for the first time since construction, bursting into fragments on the courtyard below. Nor did we sleep thereafter. For the grunts and whistles of the storm were broken by a carillon of bells pealed in mysterious semi-oriental conjunctions, the rhythm slackening and quickening, till, fortified by a new gong-like note, they reached a climax reminiscent of Prokoviev's industrial ballet, the *Pas d'Acier*. Combined with the wind and the rattle of casements high up in this lovely, tree-girt monastery, the sound caught the emotions in the waking dark with the force of tragedy.

It appeared in the morning that so great was the distance to Vatopedi, our day's objective, that we must start at ten o'clock. At eleven we reached Esphigmenou, a monastery actually lapped, when the sea is rough, by the waves. Here we were more or less expected, as one of the monks had visited Chilandari during our stay there and begged us to choose to-day for our visit, since it was a feast and there would be fish. The guest-master was the most winning and fatherly of old men, and implored us to stay the night.

"Anyhow," he cried, "you will be punctual for lunch in an hour's time, won't you? Yes, you can bathe now . . . everyone is asleep"(!)

The buildings, though almost entirely modern, formed a pleasant group, and were fringed with a profusion of bright flowers such as we did not see elsewhere. Dr. Covel tells of a font that he saw in 1677, fourteen feet across and hewn from a single block of porphyry. Of this magnificent object we discovered no trace. The chief treasure is a piece of cloth of gold, once the property of Napoleon, and variously described as either from the tent that he used on the Moscow campaign or from one of his coronation robes. The latter seems the more likely. One account states that it was stolen by pirates and presented by them to the monastery; another, that it was bought by a member of the community in Vienna. Of the many and diverse objects held in veneration on the Mountain, this perhaps is the most curious. It is only exhibited on the most important feast-days. Unfortunately, the abbot was asleep, and as he keeps its key, and we were unable to stay the night, we could not attempt to identify it.

Our bathe—the first since we left Docheiariou nearly a week ago—was ecstatic. After lunch we were put to rest in a large and grandly furnished room. Seeing a number of beds newly made, we feared to disturb them, and lay on the divans instead. Upon which the guest-master, entering with drinking-water, asked us if we thought the beds were not clean. "Too clean," we replied, "for our dirty clothes." Indeed, his kindness made us wish we could stay. But if the mules were to be back by dark, it was already time to start.

The ride lasted three hours. We had now reached the north-east coast, and were moving directly down the peninsula in the direction we had originally gone. In the distance rose the summit. And from it came wave on wave of wooded land towards us. High above great cliffs, we threaded through the tree-heather. Until across a bay was visible the clustering group of Vatopedi, largest and richest of all the monasteries, domes, towers, roofs and turrets climbing, within their walls from the water's edge like one of those imaginary cities on an old map compressed to suit the requirements of the cartographer. A man on a pony, galloping like a Delacroix warrior up and down the cobbles, overtook us. Thus we rode throughout the hot afternoon, the last lap in our circuit of the Mountain.

Chapter XVI

THE BEAUTY OF WEALTH

A̲t Vatopedi we have arrived as it were in Rome from the hill towns, in London from the provinces, in Europe—or, as the case may be, America—from the other continents. No longer the perpetual welcome and good-bye, the clatter of hoofs and the thud of the oars to pen the days in twos and threes; no longer the echo of our planet silenced by the crags and trees and the self-sung sea. We have stepped into pomp and leisure, where reminders of the world and age that bore us are not absent, where the contact of mortals is again upon us. This is the temporality of Athos. And the joyousness of life is twice incarnate.

The *salon* of the guest-suite immediately gives indication of the change. But for the stove, it is an ordinary room. Couches of brocade upholstery lie along the walls beneath pleasant and sometimes ancient prints. Above the centre table hangs a grandiose ormolu lamp for paraffin, to which has been attached the less decorative white glass shades of electric light. The floor is covered with strips of thick garter-blue carpet, on which are blazoned in continuous recurrence the crown and eagles of the Orthodox Church, together with the cipher of the monastery, "ιmb," for "*Ἱερὰ Μονὴ Βατοπαιδίου.*" This was originally woven for the reception of a visiting Tsar, and is said to have sheltered his august feet the whole way from the sea to the entrance. Prince Alfred, Duke of Edinburgh, also on one occasion accepted the monastery's hospitality, though tradition has it to have been Edward, Prince of Wales. Other than Daphni, Vatopedi possesses the only natural harbour on the Mountain; and, before the steamers called regularly, travellers often landed here. One and all have borne witness to the numerous cannon with which the walls were defended, those at the entrance being mounted. These weapons, however, were removed at the time of the Revolution. And to this day may be seen the door-knocker into which the Virgin of the time shrivelled the pet bitch of a Turkish officer, brought hither to challenge her supremacy.

Having drunk our drinks, swallowed our *glyco*, and discovered that my devoted Adrian is away at Salonica, we descend to bathe. As we lie sleepily on the fine shingle of the extended, curving beach, we are conscious first that the sun is setting, and then that it has never set in quite this manner before. Sunsets are, often as not, as ugly as the paintings which represent them. To-night the very achievement of colour, gems, birds' breasts, the Pala d'oro, Holman Hunt's bubbles, makes irrelevant the verdict of æsthetics. Drawn out of the west come flaring, ragged arcs of cloud, a wild, luminous pink against a sky of bonfire flames. On the horizon lies Thasos, violet; in front, the sea, hot red-purple of cinerarias, bounces polka-wise a ship in gilded sail. Near at hand the ridges of the promontory take the colour of indelible ink. And over them, falling down to the hills in the east, the sky is a bluey-green writhing with glass-gold clouds. Bluey-green refracts on the cineraria sea, catching each unnumbered ripple like the shooting of a petticoat. The pink in the west goes dark, the clouds black. Then all fades, to reveal the stars. And we are left in the night, literally short of breath.

As we return to the monastery the electric lights are in full glow, and the buildings resound to the clang of the plant. To us, seated at the top of the upward-sloping courtyard, window upon window reveals the unending blocks, in truth as well as metaphor a walled town, one of those great composite institutions with which the Byzantines endowed their poor, their sick, and their religious. An old monk, passing, fetches us a plate of grapes from his cell. The lights glitter. Clang and clang, the engine rivets the scene on senses other than the sight. At dinner, still it throbs. Till at ten o'clock comes a fading of lights, a softening of noise, and then suddenly a definite good night. Next evening the engineer got drunk and broke his leg. We lit the ormolu lamp instead.

On our first morning we sent as usual to the monastery council to ask permission to begin our work in the church. They replied that unfortunately it was the last day of the grape-harvest. And that though to-morrow no pains should be spared to assist us, to-day the sacristan and all his fellows were needed in the fields. The guest-master, who had taken our message, had two assistants. The lesser of these was a layman named Haralambos, pudding-faced but mystic.

"I don't like 'outside,'" he said. "I was in the army thirteen years. I fought with the English at Doïran and received an English medal. Later, I shall probably become a monk."

The other was Father Aristarchus, of a very different temperament: a thickly built, athletic young man with a curly brown beard. He suggested, as there was an idle day in front of us, that I should accompany him up to the vineyards.

I fetched my cigarettes. He donned a white linen sandboy's hat, and was joined by a friend wearing a broad straw, which, surmounting as it did, a tied bunch of chestnut hair reaching to his waist and a tight-fitting cassock, produced the effect of a Victorian schoolgirl in a crocodile. Each carried a basket and a miniature sickle; I suggested I might do likewise, but, being the honoured visitor, was not allowed.

On the way up we inspected the press. This took the form of a long stone warehouse, dark within, and filled with enormous vats, twelve feet in diameter, sunk in the floor. In these the grapes, brought down by mule, are delivered to the triple-knived poles of white ghouls who stand at the edge and prod. They are then trodden with gum-boots and the wine run off. From the residue of pips and skins is boiled the life-giving *ouzo*.

Continuing up shady paths, we came within sound and then sight of the harvesters. Harvesters was indeed the word. But for the lines of green bushes, scarcely different from the currant, it might have been an August day on a large English farm. A crowd of workers, mostly boys, had come from the mainland to assist. With them the monks, every shade of beard emerging from every variety of hat, swayed among the leaves in a doubled mass, shouting and singing to the beating of barrels by the waiting muleteers. We had halted at the lunch rendezvous. In the spotted shadow cast by a fairy ring of cypresses stood a stupendous pan, big as a table-top, above a pyramid of white embers. Into this a tall greybeard was heaping beans and garlic as fast as his hands could throw them. Around lounged other monks. I sat down on a bank, while Aristarchus

disappeared into a small stone house. From this he bore cere-
moniously upon a plate *ouzo* and a glass of water.

"A drink, sir," he said, in those actual words. He then proceeded to outline his life. From this and subsequent conversations
resulted a tale of the modern Levant from the unexpected view-
point of the practical man.

English he had learnt as a sailor, in which capacity he had sojourned some weeks in Cardiff. But, in a land where many people
speak American, it was the manner, not the language, that counted.
This he had acquired on a yacht belonging to an English colonel
resident in Constantinople.

"Good morning, sir," was now his daily greeting to us, with a
touch of his holy black hat. He knew, too, that no Englishman could
begin the day without breakfast, and a table fully laid with napkins,
knives, forks, slices of bread, and that precious preserve jam, was
always set ready to greet our demure sardines. Nor, when some
early appointment demanded, would he allow us to forgo the meal.
It happened later, on return from the vineyards, that David was
discovered to have set off to Caryes for letters.

"Well, sir," said Father Aristarchus, "I'm sure I don't know
what Mr. Rice is going to do about his lunch."

Aristarchus' manners were, without exception, the most
impressive monument to British civilisation that I have met.

Born in the island of Samos, he was one of fourteen children.
His mother, not content with this feat, adopted yet a fifteenth, a
bastard in a blanket which she discovered on the church doorstep.
To-day all his sisters were dead. (Mark interrupted at this point
with a bright, "I've got two sisters too!") And only five of the
brothers were left, one having been killed in the war, near Angora.
Of the survivors, one had become a monk at Docheiariou. And it
was he who had persuaded Aristarchus to adopt his present vocation
when all else failed. All else had failed. During the war his father,
once rich, was reduced to poverty. Further, he had remarried an
unsympathetic stepmother. Aristarchus himself had previously
saved enough money to open a shop of his own in Constantinople.
Then, being an exchangeable Greek, everything was confiscated by
the Turks. The girl to whom he was engaged had thrown him
over. And he had gone to fight in Asia Minor. There he had lost

the few possessions—camera and watch—that still remained to him, and finally, as a last cruelty, the book containing the addresses of his English friends. Homeless, owing to the stepmother, and aghast at his misfortune, he had sought his brother. But now, after two years on the Mountain, hope had revived.

"I want to get away from here," he said.

His plan was to save 7,000 drachmas—about £18. This would take him across the Atlantic. Could he find work in England? I thought not. He earned now 3,000 drachmas a year—2,000 for his work as assistant guest-master, 1,000 for tending and ringing the bells in the campanile. Vatopedi, being idiorhythmic, pays these not extensive wages to those whose labours maintain the life of the monastery.

"I don't care for monks," he continued. "They say I oughtn't to have pyjamas and mosquito-nets, because proper monks don't. Every morning I wash my face; but I never can feel clean with this beard. I don't want to cook and sew for myself. I want to go outside and find a wife to do those things, and make me a family. In Canada I shall go to night schools and learn to write English. I can't do that well enough yet. I want two or three pounds a week, so's I can go to the cinema once a month.

"If I did stay here," he added, "I should like to be porter. Then I could sell what I like and make a little money."

The porter's lodge at most monasteries dispenses necessities and a few lesser luxuries. At Vatopedi we bought some toffee, and also a tin of boot-polish of that remarkable mauve hue which has lately been affected by the sartorial *élite* of English youth.

Aristarchus then reverted to his initiation as a monk. For a whole year he had been on probation in ordinary clothes, proving the genuineness of his call to the religious life by assisting to clean the church and undertaking any jobs that might offer. At length, surrounded by chanting fathers, he had stood in the middle of the church in shirt and pants to receive his robes. For the first year he had worked altogether in the church, and hated it. Now even mastering guests was too hard. What he meant was that it was too boring, that it gave no scope to his individual ambition. Soon, when he had enough money, he would be gone. Here at Vatopedi it was easy enough. You could always obtain passes up to six months to visit the mainland on business or to see friends. And even these might be renewed. In cenobitic monasteries, of course, it was impossible. And if they did turn you out, having no property, you were destitute. That would not happen to him. Would I give him my address, in case he ever reached England?

Certainly the world will know Aristarchus again.

Returning to the monastery munching from a handkerchief of grapes, I wandered slowly up the flagged slope of the court, buoyed on a flawless satiety of colour. Here, within this precinct four or five acres in extent, the artist sense of monkish generations seemed to have flowered its fullest; as, indeed, became this sheltered bay and its enclosing slopes of red cultivated earth. Yet despite the unceasing variety of architectural style and function; despite the disparity of nine centuries between contiguous buildings; no confusion, no studied diversity of period and period copy, broke the harmony. Underlying all, a single principle of colour-relation brought unity—a principle psychologically Byzantine, and standing in direct antecedence to that which rules in the twentieth century.

It will be recalled from those numerous hours devoted in past years at school to compulsory science, that if a ring of pink paper be placed upon a sheet of white, and gazed at, the white will eventually turn green. In the same way as that green, the colours of modern painting are non-existent. It is not of their own virtue that they strike the retina, but of their neighbours', who push them to it. Thus by the use of the dullest tones the most brilliant effects are obtained. And when, perhaps inadvertently, a bright tone of an inherently bright colour is employed in conjunction with com-plementary shades, the result may be such that the human eye involuntarily turns away, as from a bright light. This is something more than "crude," an adjective which implies an affection of the stomach rather than the optic nerve. It is the result of intention, something deeper than the gaudy taste of savages. That intention is not only to strike the eyes, but to leave within the brain an image that cannot fade.

This method of coloration is the outcome of that deliberate exploitation of mental processes practised in the present age. It is not sufficient to express this or that conviction full blown. Every stage of its genesis and expansion is fit material for the artist. Thus, analogous to this sifting of the mind's fundamental machinery, is the use of primary basic colours. Instead of blurring the paints with a prevailing tint, and presenting on the canvas a mellow, ready-made harmony, the modern artist seeks to clarify the elements of his picture, to create the harmony, not once, but a thousand times, in the perpetually shifting transition between the eye and the interplaying colours. Such a system, such a thing as a clean flat plane of one shade, must have seemed as indecent to Titian, had he seen it, as James Joyce's *Ulysses* to the author of that emotional hoax, *Hamlet*.

But before the age of Titian, before the Renaissance-Classical era, there existed, especially in Eastern Europe whence all mediæval culture came, a state of mind similar in many respects to our own. Preponderantly it was the aim of Byzantine art to represent not matter but emotion; and, further, to express it with such vigour as to stamp its message ineffaceably on the memory of the beholder. All emotion in those times was ultimately diverted to the channels of religion. And the Byzantine artist was as anxious to seek artistic expression for the mystic convolutions of his intellect as the modern for his analyses. Thus, though subject differs, the elements, form, line, and colour have remained akin. In architectural context, Athonite form and line have been discussed (cf. Chapter X). When it is remembered that Athos not only was Byzantine, but is, the colours of the buildings in addition add another wave to the creative affinity between ourselves and the mediæval Greeks.

It has been attempted, at the cost of iteration, to picture, as the circuit of the Mountain has revealed them, the ornaments of the different monasteries. As the landscape varies, so, it seems, have they. Thus the Lavra, old and storm-beaten, coats its church in crimson-tinted wallflower, withered and dying, while over the refectory door presides the grey and blue Virgin, hard and austere. Thus Chilandari, warm and soft, reflects the forest leaves of its environment. Thus Dionysiou, grey and ascetic on its cliff-hung crag, attains the final fantasy in a church of pillar-box vermilion. In the mind of the reader confusion has resulted—confusion which assails the visitor himself at first contact, and to which colour alone holds the map. For, of these innumerable walls, this is not old and that young, this Greek and that Turkish. Each is a clear,

smooth province, each a unit in a vast cycle of architectural complexion, each reacting on its neighbour and contributing to the
annihilation of that mellow textural beauty for which we norther-
ners treasure the passing of centuries. To monks emotionally
transfixed upon the future, the neutral contentment of age is no
virtue. Often the oldest buildings, being the most important,
preserve the most unflinching novelty. While the new grow old.
And the whole, instead of remaining like our Oxford and Cambridge colleagues, a haphazard collection of clashing styles, is
welded to a single artistic unity by the use of the traditional washes
on buildings whose disparity of age may amount to a millennium.

But it is at Vatopedi that the whole gamut of colour seems to
have coalesced in one gorgeous *ensemble*. Nowhere are the tones so
luxuriant, nor the principle of their application so clear. Loth to
lose the detail of its composition in a memory replete with the glory
of the whole, I made a plan. And from this can still picture to
myself the vivid magnificence of the scene: the violent contrast
of the snow-white campanile against the fevered, rust-coloured
church, smooth as silken velvet; the northern range of buildings,
light red and grey, their roofs covered with lichen of daffodil-
yellow and sprouting hosts of tall white chimneys against the blue
bay below; the high, curving rows of cells at the foot of the hills
behind, forming a background to the exquisite pink chapel of the
Holy Girdle near the gate, rising as a ship on a wave from the
sloping grass-grown flags; everywhere the inevitable Greek blue,
that chalky bluebell blue, covering shutters and window-sills,
outlining white buildings to make them colder, strawberry ones
to make them hotter; and over all the sun flashing on the leaded
cupolas and glittering down the lead ribs of the cones atop the
towers. In this lead roofing Byzantine building has excelled. With
no abruptness, yet without the ostentation of a definite pitch, the
vertical lines of the structure are brought gently to rest, and its
colours no wit disturbed by that soft grey which slowly gleams and
fades as the sun moves over the heavens.

Upon a hill above the monastery lies a many-windowed ruin
overgrown with elders and wild figs, which is known as the
Athonias. This was formerly a school, which was founded in the
middle of the eighteenth century, when the Greek world was

experiencing that revival in wealth and letters which preceded the Revolution. The prime movers in this attempt to provide the Mountain with that which it must always lack, a material *raison d'être*, were the abbot Meletios of Vatopedi and the Patriarch Cyril V. To its headmastership was summoned the noted scholar Eugenius Bulgaris; cells for 170 students were provided; and from Germany, Austria, and Russia, besides the Ottoman Empire, they flocked to learn in the traditional home of learning. But the school was partly under lay supervision; and the curriculum soared beyond the confines of mediæval ecclesiastics. Hence it became an object of detestation to the monks, who cast such aspersions on the morals of the headmaster that he sought an asylum in the Crimea, invited thither by Catherine the Great. She, like her distant predecessors of Kiev and Novgorod, was anxious to attract Greeks and Greek culture to the south of Russia. But her efforts were neutralised by those of her subjects, who starved the new colonists into flight. Meanwhile the career of the school, that brief shout of youth in the fastness of beards and miracles, was finally closed by the simple expedient of arson. Untouched since, it lay before me long and desolate as I climbed between the olives in the hot afternoon. But a thorough inspection revealed that it possessed no single feature of interest. Returning along the flat tops of stone walls to avoid the dust, I found David fresh from Caryes, boasting of a lunch off meat and beer. Aristarchus settled us to a cocktail on the balcony. But hardly had the glasses touched our lips than there bore upon us the vanguard of that social maelstrom in which our last ten days on the Mountain were to be engulfed.

Its hats we had already noted upon the couch, speaking, as hats do, of hellish possibilities: one, antique in pattern, companion to a cape; the other, taut and French, impregnated with brilliantine. Behold now their masters: Professor Papastratos, our acquaintance of Xenophontos, white-moustached and decrepit, occupant of 1,000 capes; and young Mr. Botzaris, an Athenian dandy, owner of a famous name and possessing fluent English. With them came the *epitropos* Cosmas, of entrancing rotundity, who made us many apologies for our work's interruption by the grape-harvest. All together we sat drinking on the balcony in the dark and smoking the cigarettes which the *epitropos* commanded. David and I discussed

[217]

Oxford in a corner. David, whose researches in anthropology—
anthropophagy it should have been—had procured him a minor
fellowship, rose in chivalrous defence of the Alma Mater to whose
alimentary cord he was still attached. I, who had approached my
first term full of historical promise and resolution, ventured to
question how far the broader culture was likely to be imparted
by men whose lives were given wholly to the study of the Anglo-
Saxon village; and how it was to be expected that any person with
an average sense of the passing of time should devote three precious
years to the memorising of facts as little relative to the origins
of our present civilisation, and the evolution of a historical
philosophy, as an early Bradshaw. David replied meekly that he
for his part had found the anthropological instruction absorbing.
We then moved to the neutral ground of metaphysics, and fell into
handclasps of agreement on the subject of those acquaintances
whom we had known to have sought a guiding principle in life from
the great thinkers. Either they had become demented, or were
now teaching the genitive of table to boys under thirteen. I admitted
to David's taunts that a sense of filial duty had provoked me to
qualify for a degree. But defended myself in as much as I had not
had it conferred, and had reclaimed with avidity the £12 which
my college had held over to that end. Did I, then, maintain that an
Oxford career was barren? No; each unborn son should enjoy
one, but conditionally on his displaying a mental activity independent of the mannerised sophistries of his preceptors. Years
later, I foresee, this passage will be hailed from obscurity and the
gates closed against him.

As the professor and the dandy were staying only a short time,
a joint tour of the monastery was arranged for the following
morning. We assembled first to drink coffee in the common-
room of the Synodico, the council-house, where the monks gather
at seven o'clock after the morning service. It was here, paralysed
with fear, that I had been formally introduced my second day on the
Mountain thirteen months ago. The rooms were comfortably
and normally furnished, and bore a pleasant air of nineteenth century
gaiety. We sat, as usual, on a balcony, ironwork of Greek blue
against the burnt strawberry walls, with the trumpets of morning
glory and dry purple everlastings growing from boxes. Below,

the sea lay like a pearl in the morning light. Only the derricks of a two-masted schooner could be heard creaking sacks of corn into a row-boat. Beside us the *epitropos* Cosmas added the radiance of his presence. Papastratos and Botzaris emitted information.

At length we started. On the way down the professor slipped and hurt his arm. Botzaris boasted of an *eicon* he had bought at the Russian *skiti* of the Prophet Elias for 6½*d*. Our lack of enthusiasm when he told us it was a copy hurt him.

First we visited the refectory, a late eighteenth century building, decorated in panels like the Piccolomini library at Siena. Adjoining was the buttery, stacked with ancient platters and mugs of silvered copper. While the others were examining an old print, David and I slunk away to the church.

This building, which was erected, like that of the Lavra, towards the end of the tenth century, exhibits the finest interior on the Mountain. It is very large—so large that David stood aghast at the task that lay before him. And the frescoes, painted by a master of the Macedonian school in 1312, are, with the exception of haloes, lettering, and occasional figures necessitated by the cracking of the plaster, unrestored. An extraordinary beauty pervades the whole, a kind of cold, misty light, shadowless and unbegotten, such as floats about London railway termini on Sunday mornings and constitutes the glory of St. Sophia. Spreading over the high vaultings and walls, the traditional scenes from the life of Christ are depicted on an immense scale. Most prominent are the Crucifixion where the delicately balanced resignation of the Christ contrasts with the rigid grief of the watching women; and the entry into Jerusalem, grey and blue broken by the red roofs of the town, with the background half filled by a tree, forerunner of Van Gogh, mobile with the emotion of the occasion.

Several days we spent in this church, watching the beams of the sun move slowly over the detail of buildings and figures, conjuring their beauty to full revelation, then leaving them to sink again into their mysterious world of long dead ink, where the eye must concentrate for minutes at a time to bring them out of hiding. And if the eye, how much longer the camera? Ladders of enormous dimensions were brought from a stack at the end of the *narthex*, with which Aristarchus, our self-appointed body-servant, set the

[219]

corona and all the chandeliers a-swinging in order to display his detestation of the holy place. But worse even than these fittings, the shafts of sunlight offered insurmountable obstruction. While some were necessary to light the church at all, one invariably thrust obliquely straight across the lens. We had almost given up hope of the large Crucifixion when Aristarchus, hurrying by unknown paths to the dome, nailed his gown over the offending inlet. Then, borrowing other gowns, he and I ran with ladders round the outside, adorning each window with these crêpe draperies. Even these were not sufficient; and finally my green dressing-gown was requisitioned to strike an ultimate *cri* upon the rust-coloured walls.

The floor, which is of the same nature as that of Chilandari, would seem by its unevenness of surface to be even older, and probably contemporary with the foundation of the church. Outstanding in the design are the large slabs of heavily figured pink marble bordered with dark green, the combination of which, both in colour and marking, much resembles tongue and spinach. From this rise four monolith columns of grey granite, the main supports of the building, and bound head and foot in brass. While the church of the Lavra, the only one which approaches this in magnificence, is disfigured by a screen of modern grey marble, here the furnishings are all old; the *eiconostasis* of wood minutely carved and gilded; the abbot's throne, dated 1619, of similar workmanship; and the main doors of ivory inlay—a craft temporarily unpleasing to eyes jaundiced by the imports of Anglo-Indian relatives, but in its setting decorative. These were finished in 1567, "the work of Lawrence and Joseph." Giving on to the courtyard are another pair of doors plated in early bronze reliefs, and said to have been brought from St. Sophia in Salonica. Both within the church and the cloister that abuts are various mosaics. Those within consist of two pairs of panels of the Annunciation, the Angel and the Virgin facing one another twice over in different parts of the church. One pair is coarse in execution and undeniably ugly; the other undistinguished. But in the semicircular *tympanum* over the door leading from the outer to the inner *narthex* is a very fine group of Christ enthroned at the Last Judgment between the Virgin and St. John the Baptist. Both from its technique and the evidence of a dedicatory inscription, this appears to belong to the eleventh century.

As we moved pleasurably round this sanctuary, there joined us the rest of the party, including Mark. With them came the priest and keeper of the treasures, a tall, intelligent monk whom we had met last year and who was now writing a book on the church and its possessions. Of the reliquaries and *eicons* that he showed us, it requires a more specialised study than we were able to give, to write in detail. Vatopedi has always been celebrated for its *objets d'art*. Dr. Covel has left a glittering account of the collection in the seventeenth century, mentioning, among other things, an *epitaphion*, the banner of the recumbent Christ that is carried in procession on Good Friday, carrying 12,000 dollars—£3,000—worth of pearls. This was doubtless looted in the Revolution, when much of the metal work also disappeared, either into the pockets of the Turkish soldiers or to be melted down for the national cause.

Directly behind the altar hangs the most revered of all the *eicons*, a *Panaghia*, and its renowned candle. These were thrown down a well during the Arab invasions of the tenth century, and, on their being retrieved, it was found that the candle was still alight. Thus it has remained ever since, a bolster of wax like a small sapling, and was seen by Dr. Covel in 1677 as by us. The picture itself is sheathed with successive plates of metal elaborately wrought in different ages. But along the bottom and up one side runs a series of small reliefs, scarcely two inches square and solid gold, which are, without question, of the very finest Byzantine workmanship. There is a breadth of treatment, maintenance of textural individuality, and strength of composition almost magical in such small spaces, where all but the greatest craftsmen would have confined their effort to the achievement of a graceful pattern and no more. It may be supposed that this continued insistence on the importance of all genuinely Byzantine work that dates from before the fall of Constantinople is due to personal mania. But its significance may be judged from the last two acquisitions in this province of the South Kensington and British Museums: an ivory panel of the eleventh and twelfth century, $8\frac{1}{2}$ inches by 6; and a circular enamelled reliquary of the same date, $1\frac{1}{4}$ inches in diameter; these two objects cost £1,200 apiece. Fine as they are, in the treasuries of the Holy Mountain their eminence would be small. The auction value, in crude terms, of many of the objects described in this book can be counted only in thousands and tens of thousands of pounds.

From a cupboard in the wall what is perhaps the most famous relic on the whole Mountain was now produced: the piece of the Virgin's Girdle presented to the monastery in the fourteenth century by King Lazar I of Serbia. This miraculous snippet of camel's hair—"she made it herself, I expect," remarked a monk—used habitually to be transported, and presumably still is when occasion arises, to the plague-stricken towns of the Near East; where even European writers have testified to its arrestation of the pestilence. There accompanied it now an old Serbian cross set with cornelians and four broad crystals, and presented by "Stephen and Lazar."

In a glass-fronted hanging cabinet other treasures were ranged on shelves. There were three portable mosaics, about 8 inches high each, representing the Crucifixion, St. John Chrysostom, and St. Anne and the Virgin. The last of these, though much earlier than the sixteenth century, was a gift from the Tsarina Anastasia, wife of Ivan the Terrible. Their fineness was such that it was necessary to peer closely to make sure that they were mosaic. Beside them stood two reliefs of about the same size in steatite, a composition marble, one of St. George, the other of scenes from the life of Christ. And thus, indeed, it would be possible to continue through every corner of the church; to dilate upon the painted *eicons*; upon the silvered *Panaghia* said to have been brought from St. Sophia in Constantinople; and upon the half-length of Christ blessing Peter and Paul, metalled and enamelled, and presented by that despot, Andronicus Palæologus, son of the Emperor Manuel II, who sold Salonica to the Venetians in 1423. But in the whole collection one object stands alone. This is the cup bestowed on the monastery by Manuel Cantacuzene, son of the Emperor of that name, who was despot of Mistra from 1349 to 1380. Standing about 10 inches high, it consists of a broad bowl of transparent, gold-flecked jasper, yellow, dark green, and red, which is mounted on a thick octagonal stalk of silver-gilt. From a bulge in the centre of this, two rhythmic tapering dragons spring off at a tangent, until, taking an acute-angle turn, they come to rest upon the metal rim, wings folded, heads supported by little pairs of clutching claws. The base is also octagonal. And on every other facet are chased the circular monograms of the donor:

Μανουὴλ   Δεσπότου   Καντακουζηνοῦ   Παλαιολόγου
Manuel   Despot   Cantacuzene   Palæologus

The last name is accounted for by Manuel's grandmother having been a Palæologina. I had spoken so much of this cup, that Mark and David could not conceal their distaste for it.

We then moved to the *narthex* to inspect the miraculous picture of the Virgin whence blood had been drawn by the blow of an angry deacon. He had been late for supper, and having been refused his commons, could contain his resentment against a controlling deity no longer. Stricken with remorse after the act, he ensconced himself in a dark corner opposite the affronted Mother of God, where he remained for the rest of his life—30 years. The offending arm had been immediately withered. And the bones of the limb are still contained in a glass-lidded box placed at the foot of the picture in eternal supplication. They seemed of considerable age.

Midday the heavens were lit by the return of Adrian from Salonica. Small of stature, flowing of robe, with a grizzled foxy beard, a fat, neat bun, and romantic, soulful eyes, there is a bounce in his walk as becomes the owner of a great fortune. For, in the old days before the confiscations, Adrian had taken fullest advantage of the system which allowed him, if he could outbid the other fathers, to farm the monastery's estates on his own account. Last year he had been *Protepistates*; and the effusion of his greeting had doubled our pleasure in arrival. He had sat with us at lunch in the inn at Caryes, holding his silver-headed staff and attended by the old Rip van Winkle. He had conducted us to churches and chapels; he had overseen our every comfort. Now, at Vatopedi, he came to us in the *salon*. What reunion, what emotion! And we sat for long talking, he throwing his arms above his head with a rustling of draperies, to express uncertainty or chagrin in his soft, quavering voice.

"You ought to come here in the winter. The weather is not so hot and the water colder. It is glorious then. There was a priest on my boat from Salonica who came from Plymouth, in England. He is a Roman Catholic, and is coming here." We shivered. "He speaks no Greek—not a word——

"As for the new constitution," he continued, "it is exactly the same as the old, save that the Governor gives his assent to official documents. . . .

"This—is this for me? It is most beautiful." And we handed him an illustrated treatise on campanology.

Our next meeting was in the *Synodico*, where we again assembled before visiting the library. On the latter, without technical knowledge, it is impossible to comment; though it was plain that, as a collection, the books of Vatopedi surpassed any on the Mountain. Historically the outstanding volumes were two: a small psalter, once the property of the Emperor Constantine IX Monomach, 1042–1054, and autographed in that imperial scarlet which posterity has chosen to term purple; and a great Gospels copied by the Emperor John V Cantacuzene, who retired to Vatopedi in 1355 and assumed the name Joseph, which he has appended to his manuscript: $Iωσαφ$. He had already visited the monastery in 1341, when he was still the Grand Domestic, and had built himself a house. It is thought, from a recorded though now lost inscription, that it was he who erected the beautiful double-pillared phiale which still stands outside the church.

Mark was sitting in the courtyard that afternoon when a voice behind him suddenly said, "Come and have a glass of grog." Looking up, he beheld a monk of 85 years leaning from a window. He was an old sailor, who assured him on entry that he "brewed it" himself. "It" proved extremely strong—another tribute to British methods. The great event of his life had been when he was eighteen and his ship had put in to Portsmouth. Walking along the quay, he and a friend came across two boys in a boat, to whom they gave some Turkish delight. The boys handed them cards in return, which revealed that they were none other than "the King's two sons." Perhaps he meant the Queen's.

The Beauty of Wealth

The following morning was a Sunday, and Adrian arrived early for his portrait. We nicknamed him "the young grandmother." Though unknown to us, the Governor and Evlogios had already decided between them on "the old girl." All four of us were sitting looking out to sea in utter content when there chugged into the harbour a small steam launch, which belonged, we were told, to a Cavalla merchant. Figures disembarked. And there irrupted on our calm two middle-aged Greeks, a very old one, palsied and unshaven, together with the threatened priest, sweat-stained and odoriferous, with a permanent stubble veiling the lower half of a face like a tousled cock sparrow. Adrian was appalled, and, gathering up his skirts, hurried away. Aristarchus was furious. We suggested that, for the sake of our rooms, it might be easier if we left the same evening. But, being Sunday, the mules were at their ease and could not be disturbed. Later in the day, even more of the party arrived overland from Caryes, including two Germans who used English as a common language in which to communicate with their Greek companions.

In the afternoon Mark and I sought refuge with Adrian. He occupied a large suite of apartments, to one of which was attached a minute conservatory such as leads off a Kensington back drawing-room, wherein flourished an enormous magnolia and several gardenia plants. Against the walls rested shelves of books; on the fringed table paperweights of golden quartz; and in the place of honour hung a gigantic red plush hair-tidy, blazoned in ornamental lettering with the word

ΚΑΛΗΜΕΡΑ

which means "Good morning." A serving-monk in another room was busy unpacking a Primus stove which Adrian had bought for his own use in Salonica. To this were attached nests of aluminium pannikins, which were scattered all over the flat.

Another monk brought us the usual refreshments in gilded cups and gilded glasses. The *ouzo* bottle was placed at our side. Gradually the conversation shifted to depths in which my Greek would hardly carry me.

"It is all," summarised Adrian, "a fight between the army of the

Devil and the army of God, with Christ and the Holy Ghost. One day God will win.''

This was his confession of faith, wailed out in the sheep's voice that hid, as I happened to know, a strain of innocuous but competent wolf. Afterwards we talked of the union of the Orthodox and Protestant Communions. It had been proposed this year, with a view to regulating the position of the White Russian and Balkan churches in relation to the Constantinople Patriarchate, to summon to the Holy Mountain the preliminaries of an Œcumenical Council; a council such as has not met since that of Florence in 1438; while even then the representation was faulty. I had pictured the magnitude of this event, and had planned to sneak out to its attendance in the train of a friendly dignitary. But, as preparations were progressing, the Turkish government suddenly announced that if the Œcumenical Patriarch once left Constantinople to preside over such a body, he should not be allowed to return. So there, for the moment, was the end of it. Adrian said that in the event of the council's materialising in the future, it was proposed that it should split into committees, each to deal with a different point of conflict and each to be billeted on a different monastery. But, as I suggested and he agreed with a puff of satisfaction, Vatopedi would probably be the centre.

Dinner, our last meal, was served, owing to the largeness of the party, in the guest refectory. There was meat, now that Friday was past. As might have been expected, the food during our stay had been profuse. But we could not boast the experience of Dr. Covel, who wrote of the monastery: "They gave us limpets, these thrice as big as owres in England and yellow, all cover'd with a fat yellow mosse which they eat either alone or with oyl; and tast well." We were fortunate, however, in having tasted πλυνυδνότι, a kind of light port served after the meal, which still retains its Byzantine appellation of "toothwash."

Conversationally the meal was lugubrious. The priest was determined to show himself a man of the world. Grasping such decanters as lay within reach, he emptied them. Nor were we long left in doubt as to his toleration of the grosser excesses. Though these, after the nature of Roman Catholics in the Levant, he was mainly concerned to fasten upon the monks who were his hosts. We, on the other hand, were equally resolved to show that, dog though he be, our interests lay elsewhere. Rebuffed by the atmosphere of a Puritan conventicle which greeted his sallies, he ceased. But confidential he remained till the end. Much was explained when he informed us that he was training at the English seminary in Rome. We had known others. . . .

Chapter XVII

FEAST

FOR THE last time Haralambos brought our water to the sink. For the last time Aristarchus laid our breakfast. We opened the last *pâté de saumon*; we carved the last tongue. And having pressed, despite the assurance of the Plymouth priest and his Greek companions that it was unnecessary, a gift upon the guest-master and a somewhat smaller sum to swell Aristarchus' private 7,000-drachma fund, we hastened to the *Synodico* to say good-bye. Adrian and the guest-master accompanied us to the gate, the former protesting that weight of years and rheumatism would never allow him to visit England. Amid a bowing and a waving we rode off, feeling that another of life's pleasures was behind us.

We were concerned to reach Caryes in time to wait on the Holy Synod in morning session. The ride was hot, and, to our sated sensibilities, dull. After two hours we reached the suburbs. Tangled fences lined the road. Rickety gates gave entrance to gardens and allotments. Turning a corner, we beheld the onion-shaped domes, green and gold, of the inflated Russian *skiti* of St. Andrew. We had intended originally to proceed to Coutloumousi, a pleasant monastery situated a quarter of an hour away over fields and stiles, which we had used as our town house last year. Its inmates are mainly from the Ionian Islands. For the monasteries have a system of regional recruiting, each choosing a separate district in the Levant. This is so far obeyed that to-day the novices of, for instance, Simopetra, whither members were formerly drawn from a district round Smyrna now emptied of Greeks, are still derived from that particular section of refugees from that district. As a result, a few of the older Coutloumousiots are English subjects; the Ionian Islands having been under British rule from the time of the Napoleonic wars to the accession of King George I of the Hellenes in 1862. The other monks used to hate them; for, while there was considerable popular agitation for the islands' reunion with Greece, the islanders themselves, in the event of any dispute, were for ever invoking their British passports. Matters reached a head in the middle of the century, when a difference of opinion with the monastery of Pantocrator over a territorial boundary led to the citation of the abbot of Coutloumousi before the Holy Synod. He, knowing himself to be in the wrong, retired behind locked doors, which were broken forthwith by the Synod guard and his person stripped in search of documents. He and his elders were then degraded from office. But an appeal was sent to Mr. Wilkinson, the English Consul at Salonica, who so persuaded the Turkish Pasha of the town that the latter enforced their reinstatement. Another history has survived of a Russian attempt to gain possession of the monastery by inducing the Patriarch to dismiss the Anglo-Ionian abbot in favour of a Russian creature. This was countered by similar means and the hoisting of the Union Jack. But it is perhaps only another light on the same incident. To-day the monastery is notable for the stupidity of its abbot and the colour of its church, a deep peony crimson. This contains one good *eicon*, of the Italianised island school, and presumably brought to the monastery by a former inmate.

Despite these attractions, there came upon us as we rode a sudden desire for freedom. We were irked with ceremonies and good behaviour, with the early shutting of the doors, the attendance of services, and the punctuality of meals. Physically and mentally, our resolution was waning. We were exhausted with lack of food, and our ribs stuck out like famine children's. We instructed the muleteer to go to the inn instead. Thence David and I hurried to the Synod house, to find the session over. Our attempts to elicit from a surly guard when the church of the Protaton or the chapel of the Prodrome might be open, were cut short with unconquerable finality by a demented monk who rooted himself at our side and started to shout.

Perforce content, therefore, with the assurance that the Synod would be sitting again at four, we sought Monsieur Lelis, the Governor. But he was away at Xeropotamou "for the feast." Being anxious to attend such a function ourselves, we decided to follow him if it were possible, and went to the post-office to consult him on the telephone. But it was not from the post-office we could telephone; we must go to the *konak* of Xeropotamou round the corner. After forcing ourselves by accident into a nest of surprised Russians, we reached the desired front door.

"Telephone from here?" said its opener. "Quite impossible. The *antiprosopos*"—the monastery's representative on the Synod— "is away."

"But we, I tell you, know that it is possible."

"Who told you?"

"The post-office."

"But why do you want to telephone?"

"We must speak to the Governor."

"The Governor?"

"Yes. We are friends of his."

"But it is impossible. The *antiprosopos* is not here."

And thus, like a recurring decimal, the argument began again. As it progressed, we gradually forced the gesticulating old man up a flight of stairs till we stood upon a landing.

"Now," we said, like a trio of Chicago gunmen, "where is it?"

The monk disappeared into a bedroom, whence sounded a noise like the inside of Big Ben at midday.

"There are three English here who want to speak to the Governor. . . . HE'S COMING. Take it!"

We rushed upon the instrument, throwing the earpiece from one to the other in the consternation of success. The conversation began in Greek, till I could explain who we were, when it continued in French. Monsieur Lelis was charming. He enquired feelingly after our work, hoped the photographs were satisfactory, and seemed delighted that we should follow him. Should we inconvenience the monastery, already full of guests?

"*Mon cher ami! Pour vous il y aura toujours de la place.*"

Purring under this euphemy, Mark and I said we would arrive about six. Only two? Yes, two. David, unfortunately, must stay behind to work.

It was now midday. The narrow, vine-hung streets, cobbled, and concave for the sake of drainage, were empty of the prowling black figures. The shop fronts, glazed or unglazed, were silent. Oppressed, we pattered back to the fleshly sanctuary of the inn.

The host, moustached and collarless, accompanied by his two youthful assistants, conducted us by wooden ladder and wooden balcony to the upper floor. Sick of the company of one another, we commanded three separate rooms, the two lesser at 1s. 3d. a night, the larger, an apartment of honour which was pressed upon us that it might not fall to the use of other and uncleanly visitors, at 2s. 6d. This latter was decorated in the Turkish fashion, with green plaster reliefs. Adjacent stood the bathroom, floored in lead and suspending from the ceiling a small watering-can with an inverted funnel-mouthed spout, which, when filled, would empty a seductive stream over the inviting back. The windows looked straight down the peninsula to the summit. This is the view that gives the visitor, on arrival in Caryes, his first inkling of what lies in store. Immediately in front, the surface of a great depression, a mile across, tilts down to the sea, thick with the varying greens of gardened squares and alternating trees, olives, cypresses, and Lombardy poplars. Beyond, forest and shrubs begin again, rising in short successive tiers, till only the phantom obelisk, white and unsubstantial, floats up and for ever into the unmeasured blue.

On descent, a lunch of macaroni, meat, and French beans was placed before us. We sat at one of the numerous rough tables on a bench. The whole ground floor was occupied by a low room, giving egress upon one side to the street and on the other to a kind of wooden staging hung with flowering creepers, and permitting through its cracks a view of unsavoury chickens. The meal finished, we demanded grapes.

"There are none," said the innkeeper.

Coincident with his words, I espied through the open door a jungle of thick, purple bunches in a garden ten feet above the street. Insane with ceaseless thwarting, I leapt the tables, scaled the wall with the bound of a chamois, and returned with the words "There are." Thenceforth there were. As we ate, a monk arrived with a telegram forwarded by Adrian from Vatopedi. It announced, to our excitement, that Howe and Simon were arriving on the morrow.

The frescoed monuments of Caryes are two. The more prominent is the church of the Protaton, half basilica, half Greek cross in form, which contains a cycle of early fourteenth century frescoes of the Macedonian school. This building dates from before the foundation of the first monastery in 963, when Caryes was already the centre of the Mountain's hermits. The other is the chapel of St. John the Baptist, or Prodrome, attached to the cell of Denys of Fourna, which was at present occupied by a monk of Coutloumousi named Meletios. Last year, to our disappointment, Meletios had been away. And not even the influence of Adrian had been sufficient to negotiate the barrier of locks and bolts that he had left behind him. Only to a vine-covered courtyard could we gain entrance. Thither ladders were brought. And perched precariously upon a strut among the grapes, we peered in through a window which could scarcely have emitted an arrow, only catching sight, as it afterwards proved, of some eighteenth century additions to the frescoes within. Now, David and I set out to find the chapel again. The streets had come to life. And, enquiring, we were told that Meletios was once more away. We set our teeth.

The sun told us that it was time to visit the Synod. Entering, we sat on divans among the dignified old men and made desultory conversation. When coffee had been handed, we broached our desire to photograph in the Protaton. Certainly. As for the Prodrome, what could they do? We might pay for a new door. But it was private property. And there was an end of it.

Seated now in the placid environment of the English countryside, with a warm fire and a south wind blowing a hint of primroses in at the window, a strange film overspreads the memory of our last days on the Mountain. The smallest action was a struggle; to rise from a chair needed determination; to walk down the road, effort titanic. We had become in a sense light-headed: partly, through some upset of mental equilibrium, result of contact with the unfamiliar forces accumulated through centuries, greedy of the novice and venturer from without; partly from physical deterioration. The difficulty of decision was overpowering. But, even more so, the maniacal, irrational obstinacy with which a decision, once made, was pursued. With the little breath that God had left us, we vowed that neither prison nor death should deter us from that chapel. And returned to the inn to seek advice.

Our host was stirred. It appeared that Meletios had only been gone a day. And it was possible that he was still upon the Mountain.

A messenger was sent to Coutloumousi; and another to Coutloumousi's arsenal, an hour away upon the shore. But these reported
that the monastery's boat had sailed for Cavalla last night. Then,
as we discussed the situation, the conversation was overheard in
passing by a nondescript man in a grey tweed suit, who came
running in to say that Meletios had left the key with Nicolaides.
Our hearts bounded. And continued to thump, while arrangements
were made for David to visit the chapel early next morning. It was,
of course, only the key to the courtyard—no farther than we had
penetrated before. None the less, half our elation remained. We
had at least an ally.

We had bought some dried figs at a neighbouring shop, and
were drinking tea, when the sound of hoofs reminded Mark and
me of our obligation to be at Xeropotamou, an hour and three-
quarters away, before the sun set. Stuffing some week-end trifles
into the saddle-bags, we rode over the ridge in the golden evening,
with all the chestnuts lit above us.

The gate was still open and the porter expectant. All around,
both in the courtyard and outside, reclined in the half-light every
variety of Levantine manhood, labourers, guards, policemen,
tramps, hermits, boys, and old men, assembled to celebrate the
Exaltation of the Cross—a ceremony not to be confused with the
Invention, but supposed to have originated with the dedication of
the churches built by Constantine in Jerusalem to commemorate
the latter event. Here at Xeropotamou is the largest piece of the
Cross on Athos, 13 inches long. Hence the special significance
which the occasion assumes.

It is a common witticism of cynics that if all the *soi-disant* wood
of the Holy Rood were collected, there would be sufficient to
build a town. The joke, however, is with the statisticians. It has
been calculated that a cross, to have borne a full-grown man, must
have contained not less than 10,860 cubic inches of wood. In
A.D. 326 Helena, mother of Constantine, made her famous discovery. And the Cross was left intact in Jerusalem. But, to the
agony of Christendom, it was carried off by the Persians in 615
and was not recovered till Heraclius captured Ctesiphon thirteen
years later. In order to preclude once and for all a recurrence of
this disaster, it was now divided into nineteen parts, which were

distributed over the Near East, Jerusalem retaining four and
Constantinople receiving three. In the assaults which the Levant
was to endure at the hands of both Europeans and Asiatics during
the next 1,000 years, the greater part of the wood was lost. And
out of the 10,860 cubic inches, there had survived in the middle
of the last century, when Count Riant surveyed the authenticated
reliquaries, not more than 244: sufficient, in fact, to build, not a
town, but a tea-caddy. Rome, Venice, Brussels, and Ghent possess
about 30 each, Paris 15. The Holy Mountain, therefore, with an
aggregate of almost 54 cubic inches, owns more of the true Cross
than any place in the world. The sceptic may question whether
the wood of these relics ever bore the body of Christ. But there
is no adequate reason to doubt that they are pieces of the Cross
which St. Helena found and which, with divine guidance, she distinguished from its two companions.

We were conducted by the guest-master to a clean double-
bedded room leading off a broad passage tiled in black and white.
There followed us the muleteer, a hireling, who was to proceed
to the port early next morning to meet the new arrivals and fetch
the box of plates that we had deposited at the shop on our way from
Simopetra to Russico. That there should be no mistake, we wrote
two letters, one to the shopkeeper, the other to Mr. Χαοῦ (Howe).
We were then conducted downstairs to a room brightly lit and
filled with a chatter of conviviality. And there, handing apéritifs
to the assembled company upon a silver tray, was dear long-lost
Father Boniface.

Last year Father Boniface had been in charge of Daphni, the port,
the property of this his monastery. Warned of our arrival, he had
prepared breakfast for two strangers who could then speak hardly
a syllable of his tongue. And it had been he who, upon the non-
arrival of the steamer by which we were to depart, had rescued
us from a night in the inn, had taken us to his house, laid us on clean
linen, fed us, and entertained our day—for there was now one
with us who could speak—with quizzical stories of his fellow-
monks. We had probed the very intimacies of monastic life; we
had seen him wash his face and beard; we had concocted messes
in his kitchen. He had once occupied an ecclesiastical position in
Jerusalem. But circumstances had obliged him, in old age, to accept

a subordinate position in an institution which he regarded with the critical eye of the outside world. He told how in the idiorhythmic monasteries the elders and *epitropoi* took all the money, while the younger monks went without clothes and were reduced to stealing. He talked of the favouritism that led to advancement. And he poured contempt on excessive religious observance.

"It is unfortunate," we had said, "that you have no church here in which to celebrate the liturgy."

"Unfortunate? Not at all. God gets drunk with too many people shouting at him."

Finally, on departure he gave us a melon, a small yellow fruit. It is the fault of melons that, while their flavour is delicious, it is vague. That of the one in question possessed the sharpness of a nectarine. Never since melon grew has earth borne such a one as this which it was our privilege to eat.

At our entry Father Boniface almost dropped his tray. His woolly-white beard, depending from round ruby cheeks, danced with delight as he heaped glasses upon us. Hardly, it seemed, were we in time; for we immediately filed into a gala dinner, sitting down with about thirty monks at one long table brightly lit with hanging lamps. The Governor had gone to Daphni to bid good-bye to a friend. Mark and I were alone in the forest of tall hats and rustling gowns. On our left sat a fierce *epitropos* at the head of the table, his iron-grey moustaches twitching with anger as he shouted orders at Boniface, who was acting *maître d'hôtel*. The food was of distinction. *Hors d'œuvres* of onions, tomatoes, and anchovies were followed by three courses of salt fish, the last covered with an excellent clove mayonnaise in which swam prunes like the grapes in *sole véronique*. As the meal progressed, the *epitropos*' temper cleared. He remembered me from last year. Where had I learnt my Greek? And why did I not drink? Why not?

"I am drinking."

"You are not."

"I *am*."

"But look at all the other decanters. They are empty. Yours is not half gone." And he filled my glass and almost forced it down my throat.

"Very well, I shall get drunk."

"Drunk? What does that matter? You must drink."

So drink we did, while the others belched heavenly repletion, varying their tributes with the sound of a rat in straw, the washing of wine on gums.

Coffee, accompanied by a light sweet wine in lieu of port, was handed in the other room, till it was time for the momentous service, which was to last all night, to begin. Did we wish to come to the church, or to sleep? Sleep, we thought. And the fierce *epitropos* saw us with all courtesy to our room. But sleep, for me at least, was not forthcoming. Through our open windows and the open doors of the church floated not the usual far-off wailing, but great volumes of sound, which so affected Mark's slumbering consciousness that to each burst he retaliated with a groan and a toss that encroached still further on the night. Being very tired, I persevered till an hour or two after midnight. Then, feeling that it was absurd to miss both the service and my rest, I dressed, felt my way downstairs, and crossed the starlit courtyard filled with black forms, praying, wandering, sleeping.

The church was not unknown to me. On the occasion of our previous visit, supposing that we were pressed for time on our way down to catch the steamer which did not arrive, we had hastened into the monastery and begged that, if possible, we might see the treasures at once. Vespers were in progress. But we were hurried, notwithstanding, through the crowded nave to within the *eiconostasis*, where the officiating priest, invested with stole and thurible, hooked the relics out of a cupboard in the intervals when his voice was not required to conduct the service. One was the famous piece of the Cross, enclosed in an ornate and comparatively modern casket; another a small but very ancient reliquary set with misshapen pearls and magnificent *cabouchon* emeralds. And the third a small ophite paten known as Pulcheria's cup. Ophite, like steatite, is a composition stone, of a greenish hue, while the other is buff. This object, which enjoys the reputation of boiling water without assistance, is possibly the finest Byzantine stone relief in existence. There is another not unlike it at Russico. But beyond these two there exists nowhere anything of the sort that can approach them for age or depth of workmanship. That of Xeropotamou, a shallow bowl not more than six or seven inches across, exhibits the Virgin and Child upright between two angels, encircled by a band of fifteen other full-length angels in arches, together with an outer series of prostrated apostles. An inscribed silver border makes it appear that the cup was a donation from the fifth century Empress Pulcheria. But this was not added till the eighteenth, and was one of an extraordinary series of forgeries, both of chrysobuls and stone reliefs, which sought to assign a spurious antiquity to the monastery's history. Among its supposed founders was the Emperor Romanus I Lecapenus, who died before any monasteries were yet in being. It is probable, however, that he has been confused with the Emperor Romanus III Argyrus, who reigned from 1028 to 1034 as the husband of that elderly siren, the Empress Zoë. This Romanus had a sister named Pulcheria. And it is likely, therefore, that the cup dates from the eleventh century and not the twelfth, as is usually supposed.

Another benefactor of the monastery was the Sultan Selim II in the latter half of the sixteenth century, who rebuilt and endowed it after a visit to the Mountain. Such instances of the followers of the Prophet seeking God through Christ have not been uncommon. Busbecq, a little earlier, records how the Turks used to delay their journeys till the Greek Church had given the sea its customary blessing. And Thevet, who visited Athos about the same time, encountered a monk who had escorted Bajazet II to Mount Sinai and had seen the sultan *"secrettement faire son oraison en ce mont."* Further, he had presented the monks with relics and ornaments.

As I entered the church, the *narthex* was in total darkness. Pressing shoulder to shoulder towards the east, in their effort to peer through the central doors, stood a compact multitude of fathers. They were of the lowest grade; and their smell of hot clovy hair, boot-polish, garlic, and unwashed linen, was overpowering. Imperceptibly, for they were all in a trance, I wedged through them. And my eyes reached the nave as the crisis of the ceremony began.

In contrast to the usual dim light, an exquisite shadowless radiance, bright as the stage of a theatre, only as different from electricity as rainwater from chalk, suffused the entire building. All the innumerable chandeliers, candlesticks, candle-brackets, candle-crosses, that had previously seemed but a superfluous obstruction, were now in play. Within the corona, itself a ring of flames, the central chandelier rose in a mountain of light. Beneath stood a stool, caparisoned in brocade. And on it, at this moment, borne aloft from out the *eiconostasis*, was placed the casket containing the Cross. From his throne, at the back of which I stood, stepped a bishop in a full red cope falling in folds from his shoulders and fastened at the ankles. From his head streamed the black veil which all the monks were wearing. In his hand was his staff, with the twin serpents' heads of ivory. There joined him two deacons in copes of green and gold; and two others in black. All but he carried candles. And, forming a circle, they began to pace slowly round the relic, while the singing swelled from soft accompaniment to the attack. Rhythm of chant and paces, that intrinsic rhythm independent of "time," caught the beholders from their human frames. The voices were no longer nasal. Once and again, a hundred and a thousand times, the *Kyrie eleison*, in limitless plurality, beginning deep and hushed, mounted the scale with a presage of impending triumph—to die off and begin again:

KYRIE ELEISON
KYRIE ELEISON
KYRIE ELEISON
KYRIE ELEISON
KYRIE ELEISON
KYRIE ELEISON

KYRIE ELEISON

while the figures stepped round and about. I was transfixed, like the monks, by this revelation of Orthodox observance, as different from the ordinary service as a country vicar's reading is from the Coronation.

When it was finished, the dawn was already flitting over the buildings outside. I breathed deep in the cold, mysterious air. The muleteers were waking beneath the trees and in the monks' summerhouse, a round edifice like a bandstand. Over the sea I looked to the southern point of Longos. But no steamer was visible. And I returned to shave. As I did so, the Governor, pretending not to see me, suddenly scurried past with nothing on but a shirt. He emerged a moment later in trousers to enquire after our night's rest and to regret that he must leave at once, as the Bulgarian *chargé d'affaires* had arrived in Caryes. Before he went, he attended a service that was now proceeding in the phiale outside the church. Thither the relic had been carried on high by the two deacons in copes. And the bishop, dipping a bunch of basil in the water of the fountain, was blessing those who put their heads within his reach. Owing to the necessity of simultaneously kissing the relic, I forbore.

By this time Mark was dressed, even out of the saddle-bags, with his customary aplomb. We watched the service and the crowd round the phiale till dispersal. Then walked to the gate. For us, underneath the ridge, the sun was not yet risen. But glinting in its reach out upon the sea was the steamer, making rapidly for Daphni.

We leapt to our bedroom, caught up towels, and with whoops and bounds threw ourselves down the hill, exchanging the laborious hairpins of the path for the dusty shoots between the olives. A quarter of an hour saw us at the bottom, over the broad bridge, and up another slope, panting for breath; till the coastline bore round to the left and a bay 500 yards across separated us from the jetty of the port. It was half a mile round by the path, and the steamer was almost in. Mark was behind, out of patience with this insensate excitation. Like the slave on the ice, I hurtled down the boulders to the water's edge; flung clothes upon the shingle; and, with a last shout that my pockets contained all the money remaining to us, dashed into the water. Being accustomed to proceed long distances only at my leisure, I am not a strong swimmer. But it was now as though a pink torpedo were thrusting over the surface of the still shadowed bay, where the reflection of the ridge was conscious to my straining eyes as they fixed on the sunlight beyond and the white crest of water at the steamer's bows, turning over like the earth from a plough. Two silent boatloads of tall-hatted silhouettes glided across my path. The rattle of an anchor sounded. I struck on, side and front, hidden from the passengers, who were looking at the approaching fathers. Rounding the bows, I bobbed up beneath the unseeing gaze of Howe and the correctly hatted Roman profile of Simon. Would they never notice? I paddled on. Other passengers, women—could they still exist?—were riveted upon this agitated and unseemly Poseidon spewed up from the waters of sanctity whence they had expected only hermits. At last: a start; a wave; a shout; a babble; a torrent of converse. And those who traversed the pages of our first adventure in the Levant will share the joy of the reunion.

Exhausted, sinking, I clung to the painter of a boat, its oarsmen eyeing me disdainfully. The delay was without end; the water cold and the sun no nearer. While the steamer, from a vent in its side, retched cinders, sewage, and cabbage-stalks upon my unprotected person. At length they were down the gangway. And we pushed off, leaving the argosy of civilisation to return to its world. The rowers heaved. I hung, anchor to their progress. We neared the quay. A crowd was there, and in the foreground Mark, wrapped neatly in a face-towel, together with the muleteer clasping the letter we had charged him to deliver. My feet touched bottom. But how emerge? A covering was produced from a suit-case: and a tweed cape, the ultimate affectation of 1922, was flung upon my shoulders. Shivering with cold, I ran barefooted in the wake of the others through the gaping ranks of monks and muleteers to the inn, where we sat beneath a row of oleanders, *ouzo* coursing through us like fire.

The newcomers themselves now wished to bathe. Affixing their luggage to a mule that our man had brought, and making sure that the plates had been retrieved from the shop, we walked along to where our clothes were lying and swam out again, this time to reach the sun. In it we sat and dried. So that by eight o'clock, when, after three-quarters of an hour's climb, the monastery's gate was reached, we were in a state of perspiration. We had thought that there might be difficulties about the reception of Simon and Howe till after the presentation of their letters at Caryes. But, it being a feast-day, the doors were open to all. In a dishevelled troupe, Howe looking like a race-meeting in my tweed overcoat—all but his shirt-sleeves having been left on the mule—we were ushered by Boniface into the monks' common-room, where the elders and more distinguished guests were assembled for the real festivities that were now to begin. At first we said that under no consideration could we stay to lunch. But when we learnt that it was timed for half-past nine, and that deep offence would be given if we left before, we changed our minds. The atmosphere was delightful. Bells were ringing; sunbeams battling with the blinds; guests and monks arriving; drinks being handed; tables laid. The room in which we sat was furnished with unusual variety: rocking-chairs rocking; tables groaning with a wealth of albums; walls hung with every sovereign that ever sat, including our own dear Victoria in the peerless ill-favour of her later years. Cocktail followed cocktail. We explained to Simon the ritual of their acceptance, and lent him a tie for the occasion. Then the meal was announced. And we learnt what is meant by a "Feast of the Church."

The tables were disposed up, across, and down, in the form of a rectangle missing one end. At them sat a company of 60 or 70. In the middle, at the top, presided the bishop who had conducted last night's ceremony, spare and dignified, whose diocese in Asia Minor had been annihilated in the war. By his side was Evlogios, handsomest monk on the Mountain, with his flowing iron beard and broadly chiselled aquiline features. The news had reached us at Vatopedi that he had just been appointed to the archbishopric of Tirana, and would thereby become Primate of Albania, an important post for a man of 47. But he was not certain, he said, whether he wished to exchange the idyll of Athonite existence for the turmoil of that uncouth political fiction.

The courses began with soup, and continued, four in succession, with octopus. There was octopus cooked amid segments of the garlic bulb, and octopus, more subtly delicate perhaps, alone. There was octopus with beans; and there was octopus again alone but for a hot gravy. Then followed roes, hard and round, an inch in diameter and three long. These were garnished with a yellow mayonnaise of beaten caviare. Their advent was pregnant with event; for, unaware of their resilience, I plunged my knife upon one, to see it fly over my elbow on to the spotless sheen of the gown of the father next me. He was ruffled. But, drying the spots with my napkin till they were invisible, I bathed him with such tears of remorse that he was restored to calm. The waiting, directed by Boniface, was faultless. And of the plenty of wine it is unnecessary to speak.

The climax was reached with snails. These, nine to a dozen on each plate, were served with the tops knocked off. They had to be wheedled therefore, not, as in the West, from the snail's own door, but by an adroit twist of the fork from above. Boniface, all those around us, and even Evlogios from his vantage-point, were so concerned lest we should fail fully to appreciate them, that we were at pains to acquire the proper motion. Delicious they were. Meanwhile we drank as though it were ten at night instead of in the morning. All did the same. The conviviality grew. We laughed and shouted and toasted one another across the tables. Then, headed by Evlogios and the bishop, the assembled company took each an empty shell between thumb and forefinger and blew a blast of whistles, as though ten thousand milk-boys were competing for a prize.

Dessert of apples and grapes was succeeded by coffee and the lighter wine. The sun was in the top of the heavens when, having bidden regretful farewell to Boniface, the fierce *epitropos*, and all the others, we started out for Caryes. Simon, unfamiliar with the wooden armchairs with which the Greeks furnish their mules, sat with a straight back and a grip at the knees, as became a man who hunts from Craven Lodge and wishes the muleteer to know it. Thus, with new dignity, we reached the capital.

Chapter XVIII

METROPOLIS

At the entrance to the main street of Caryes the muleteer bade us dismount. A blazing Indian summer had set in, to which, while the rest of those who had partaken of Xeropotamou's enormous meal were sleeping, we had been obliged to expose ourselves. Being exhausted with the heat and the activity of the previous night, I refused. There ensued a long altercation, in which the man explained that both he and I would go to prison if I were to persist. It was permissible to ride in from the other side and round to the inn, as we had done from Vatopedi. But no one had ever passed the Protaton and its sacred *eicon* of the Virgin except on their feet. As I had already done so twice on a mule's back, I thought his intention was simply to aggravate. But, as windows were beginning to fly up and the sun was on my shoulders, I gave way. This was fortunate, as he proved, on enquiry, to be right and my previous muleteers to have been criminally negligent in allowing such an infringement of the rules of the town.

In the inn we found David. He told a story that set our pulses beating.

Early that morning, as arranged, a little boy had arrived with a key. It was quite useless, he explained, to go down to the chapel, as this opened only the door of the yard. David persisted. Together they shut the street behind them. The entrance to the cell lay up a flight of wooden steps.

"That door," said the boy, "is shut."

David, summoning his few words of Greek, then delivered a meaningless and urbane conversation, nonchalantly fingering the lock and surreptitiously implanting his knee in a position of leverage. The boy, quieted by this apparent resignation, became almost sympathetic. When David, with unforeseen promptitude, suddenly disappeared inside. Screeching, the boy followed. In front stood

[243]

another door, padlocked. Grasping an opportune hammer, David, with the blood of the first wet upon his lips, removed the staple with a blow. He was now at the entrance to the chapel, fastened by iron-bound portals that would have kept Jack Sheppard in Newgate. The boy, alarmed lest at such opposition this monster should gnash the very bricks from their foundations, fled into the street for help. Simultaneously an unholy calm, the cunning of desperation, gripped the assailant. Searching walls and floor with rapid finger-tips, he discovered a crannied key. It fitted. And when the boy returned, accompanied by the man Nicolaides, it was to find a sedate and businesslike figure arranging his apparatus with the deliberation of a photographer in his studio. Nicolaides shrugged. For in the East, while they expect a man to bow to fate, when the West turns fate, they themselves bow to that as well. In cold blood the incident makes strange reading. But we were no longer, it must be remembered, in possession of our ordinary faculties.

From the inn David, Mark, and I proceeded to the next house down the street to take coffee with the Governor. His residence had originally been built as the central office of the Athonias, the burnt school above Vatopedi. Last year it had been empty, and we had used it as a place of repose during our day or two in Caryes. The upper floor where Monsieur Lelis now lived consisted of a large landing divided at the top end by a glass partition, behind which he sat. To either side of this were little bedrooms. He displayed much interest in Mark's drawings, appreciated their humour, laughed as we had laughed over that of Adrian, "*la vieille fille*," and begged that one might be done of himself. At the present moment he was on the point of leaving for Zographou with the Bulgarian *chargé d'affaires*. But we must dine with him to-morrow night, and also devote the afternoon to the cause of art.

David then took us to see the violated chapel. The boy, an infant of thirteen, screamed out to all the world as we arrived:

"This gentleman broke all the doors yesterday, and that's the truth."

Stifling his falsetto with drachmas, we went in and were comforted by a series of wholly remarkable frescoes, unlike any others on the Mountain and of great evolutionary significance in their connection with the mediæval West. Unfortunately, they had suffered from excessive restoration; and many had been altogether displaced by newer. This, combined with a patently spurious inscription, had led our precursors in artistic research to dismiss them as negligible eighteenth century.

As it was evening, we returned to the inn. The sleepless night, the hour in the water, the feast, and the midday ride, had induced in me that grandmaternal affliction, a migraine. White waves, hopeless and horrible, clouded the eyes to the hammer of a sick headache. I retired to bed, and lay thinking how easy, even pleasant, to die in this dramatic squalor: garments torn and stained strewing the uncovered floor; plaster falling from the ceiling and walls; a carafe of warm and cloudy water at the bedside; and only the effulgent pigskin of my suit-case to remind me of those pompous little islands lying off the north-west of Holland. From the street beneath came the clip-clop of mules, the hum of voices. The sunset streamed through the tattered petticoats of the windows on my tortured eyes. When it was dark, David brought me a plate of *pilaf*. It remained on the floor, where I found it, coagulated and grey, on waking next morning, restored but shaky.

Howe and Simon, having fallen asleep the previous afternoon, were obliged to rise early to catch the Synod in morning session and obtain their circular letter of introduction to the individual monasteries before proceeding to Vatopedi. David and I accompanied them, to remind the authorities of their promise that the Protaton should be open to the camera this morning. There was business on hand. But Daniel of Iviron, the *Protepistates*, emerged to say that the sacristan had been summoned and would be here in half an hour. We thanked him and retired. Whereupon David, ordinarily placid as a Hampstead pond, burst into a rage. Half an hour! Half an hour was half an hour! Did they think that the world offered nothing for him to do but wait half-hours on their disgusting pleasure? Let them open the Protaton. The Almighty in person should not drag him inside it after this. And, like a cyclone, he battled away down the street to the house of Nicolaides, with the syllables of "Half an hour" left hissing in the air behind him as I followed.

On our advent Nicolaides, in his turn, was seized with a blinding fury. Some devil possessed the morning. How could he spare the boy to look after us to-day? Was he there for nothing? There were grapes, and he had work. David ground and foamed, the skin of his face tight as a two-months-old corpse.

"Grapes?" I answered. "What are grapes, when we have spent 200 English pounds and journeyed across Europe in order to photograph these paintings? We will hire you another, a whole man, who will do twice as much work as the boy."

"I don't want a man. Only the boy knows where the jars are kept"; and he trailed off into domestic technicalities, while we snatched away the infant, delighted at the prospect of another sixpence. But David had only lifted the shutter of the first exposure when I returned, stronger even than God, to fetch him to the Protaton. I had met one of the Synod guard, who civilly told me it was open. On arrival, the sacristan let it be seen that he found his task plainly distasteful. He had work, food, and sleep to claim his attention during the day, he told us. Being anxious, now that David and I were reduced to subsisting on brandy and soda, that the work should not be prolonged, I muttered glibly of the presents that we customarily made to the churches whose frescoes we recorded. His demeanour then changed; for the Protaton seldom received gifts from visitors. From sitting half asleep in the stalls of the *antiprosopoi*, each one labelled in brass with the name of its monastery, he brought us ladders, helped them behind the *eiconostasis*, and even assisted David to a position on top of the *ciborium*. At midday he was obliged to return to his house, but promised to fetch us from the inn at two. This he did, a quarter of an hour early.

As it was Wednesday, the first fast day of the Athonite week, no meat might be sold by order of the *Epistasia*. This and other rules of that autocratic body, the Synod's executive, are strictly enforced. In every café, both in Caryes and Daphni, hangs a fixed tariff stamped with the seal of the community. And we heard of an instance where an innocuous game of patience while waiting for the steamer was peremptorily stopped by one of the guards. Revolted by the insipid macaroni that the innkeeper placed before us, Mark went shopping and returned with a dozen eggs, which he scrambled himself with the artistry of a chef. These, accompanied by a white fizzy wine, a hybrid between cider and ginger beer, made a meal which the acutest dyspepsia could not refuse.

It remained to make plans for departure. We were still intending to pay another visit to Dionysiou, in the hope, if Gabriel should have overruled the *epitropoi*, of seeing the Trapezuntine chrysobul. The board outside the steamship agent's told us that there was no boat to Salonica till Saturday. Hastening to the post-office, we found David, who had thought there was one on Friday, despatching telegrams to that effect. These we countermanded. And our plans were still further modified by a passing monk, who told us in casual conversation that Gabriel had been obliged to go to Cavalla. Without him it would be useless to return. But there was only the Saturday boat, and that we decided to take.

Mark and I then went to the Governor. He was posed in a corner of the divan against the windows, with the flaring patterns of draped curtain and painted blind framing not only him, but a view of the summit beyond. Thus we sat and talked, Mark busy with his pencil and he playing with a tasselled string of oranges, dried to the size and hardness of cherry-stones and sweet scented.

It was my purpose, during this conversation, to gain from the Governor a definition of the attitude of Greek bureaucracy towards the Holy Mountain. The question of status is settled. And the financial difficulties are not as pressing as they seemed. But there had existed last year an unconcealed friction between the monastic and lay authorities. Was this on the wane or the increase? Might it, in fact, constitute a danger that, if the Hellenic constitution, wherein the Mountain's autonomy is embodied, should at any time be overthrown by one of the dictators which are perpetually being washed up on the shores of the Mediterranean, the government of Caryes would lapse before the practical necessities of the modern state?

The foregoing chapters have aimed to picture Athos in every aspect as the composite and living memorial of a great civilisation, to which nature and man, history and religion, artist and architect, have contributed and contribute. Landscape and peak; buildings, coloured and convergent; paintings, forerunners of the twentieth century; manuscripts from the seventh; *eicons*, mosaics, reliquaries, and jewels; these, each in relation to the others, are the inheritance of a people whose vicissitudes of fortune since they entered upon the custody of the Roman Empire in 330 and became a nation, have risen to a glory and sunk to a depth experienced by no other country in Europe. And it is the preservation of this inheritance for which the Greek government is responsible to Greeks and to the world.

The misfortune, therefore, of ill feeling between Athens and Caryes can be appreciated. Of its existence last year we had been made aware in both places. And there were still signs that it was not wholly eliminated. The natural resentment at the confiscation of the estates was no longer so marked, save in the foreign monasteries. But there was another point of friction in the portable and inestimably valuable contents of the Athonite treasuries and libraries. No country in the world, not excepting Italy, has been so systematically plundered of her works of art as Greece. And long ago the law was passed to forbid all antiquities, whether classical or mediæval, from leaving the country. Already the enterprise of travellers such as Robert Curzon and Uspenski—of whom the latter's collection of *eicons* from Greek monasteries has been published, and is preserved intact by the Soviet government—had robbed the Mountain of many of its chiefest possessions. The process was not, indeed, new; Thevet reported in the latter half of the sixteenth century that all the good books were already gone. But till recent years it was lack of cultural education rather than venality which led the monks so easily to the dispersal of their treasures. To-day this is not so; their conception of their value may almost be said to be inflated; and the patriotic conscience, inert under the Ottoman rule, now beats with the vigour of the awakened sleeper. Should the Trapezuntine chrysobul or the Nicephorus Phocas Bible disappear, it were a national calamity. But to-day such events are unthinkable. In 1926 the monastery of Stavronikita announced its intention of closing down for lack of funds. Yet in the same year it refused any thought of parting with a psalter written in block letters of gold and a fourteenth century illuminated Gospels, the price of which—for I saw them—would have run into thousands of pounds sterling.

It is, on the other hand, a fact, of which the Athenian authorities are vaguely aware, that valuable objects continue very occasionally to disappear. In 1925 an early parchment liturgy in the form of a roll was believed to have fallen into the hands of a Salonica moneylender. And a year later, to my personal knowledge, an Anglo-American collector acquired a small but finely illuminated service-book, eleventh or twelfth century, in exchange for £400 cash down; an entertaining contrast to the price of £20 paid by Robert Curzon at Xenophontos in 1837 for the great Gospels autographed by one of the many Emperors Alexius Comnenus, which is now in the British Museum. The major part of the scandal lies in the fact that the £400 went, not into the coffers of a monastery, but the pocket of an individual monk. Again, in 1926 an official warning was conveyed through the British Legation in Athens to the effect that a well-known American firm of dealers was contemplating commercial descent on the Mountain. In which, it must be admitted, those concerned displayed no very great interest.

It is plain, therefore, that the solution of this particular difficulty lies in the formation of an official catalogue, whereby the existence and whereabouts of the treasures shall be finally registered. To this project, however, the monks are resolutely opposed, and threaten to hide or bury everything they possess rather than submit to it. If this is cussedness, it is only reciprocal. For it cannot be denied that the various Greek official propositions that have been put forward from time to time have been tactlessly expressed. The former dictator, General Pangalos, was loud in his determination to turn the Mountain into that pet resource of Mediterranean statesmen, a casino. While the Athenian savants have freely mooted invoking the authority of the Metropolitan of Athens to confiscate by force all the works of art on Athos for the Byzantine Museum, which at present contains only one object of first-class importance. Since Athos is spiritually subject only to the Œcumenical Patriarch, the legality of such a procedure would be indefensible. It is unlikely that either of these propositions was ever seriously contemplated; such is certainly not the case in the present time; but their advertisement, combined with a certain arrogance in Athens and a petty dignity in Caryes, led to a considerable disturbance of relationships.

But, with the appointment of Monsieur Lelis as second of the newly instituted governors, the oil of genuine tact and goodness of heart was necessarily poured upon the waters.

"I am here," he said, "only to ensure that the constitution which the monks themselves drew up, and which has been accepted in its entirety by the Greek government, is maintained. That is the extent of my duties. In the region of finance, it is not true to say that the government has *confiscated* the monastic farms. Compensation will be paid, and many of them are only rented for the space of ten years.''

He continued to enumerate the extraordinary privileges that the monks enjoy: the exemption from military service; and from all taxation, death-duties, and imposts on imported and exported goods.

''But,'' I said, quoting sources that I believed to be accurate, ''are not some of the poorer monks obliged to make a living by buying their coffee and sugar free of duty and then disposing of it on the mainland again at a profit, underselling the shops? And is it not a scandal that some monks grow privately rich, while their monasteries are falling to ruin and their lesser brethren in rags?''

''No, no,'' he replied, ''the monks are poor men, good and simple, leading sincere religious lives. Their duties are no sinecure. If there are exceptions, I have not met them.'' And he would have nothing of these scandals with which, as an irritated official, I had hoped to tempt him. This attitude was the greater tribute to him, since his dislike of the post was unconcealed.

''Tell me,'' he said, ''is there a woman in the world? Shall I ever dance again? Shall I ever reach Paris, where I was appointed, before my predecessor here—an old man who liked it—died suddenly?''

Thus, with the light and the portrait, the discussion closed. The Governor was right. Let the Athonite community be judged by the majority. Almost identical with his words were those of Sir Paul Rycaut, writing of the Mountain in 1679: ''. . . for the most part good simple men of godly lives, given greatly to devotion and acts of mortification. . . . We may, without overmuch credulity, or easiness of belief, conclude them not only to be real and moral good men, but such also as are something touched with the spirit of God.'' ''Overmuch credulity'': it is always that—the fear of being made a fool—which leads the observer to seek evil in simplicity.

We returned to the inn to ''dress.'' For we were to dine with Monsieur Lelis. At eight o'clock we presented ourselves. Bearing an unshaded lamp, he led the way to a recess in the landing. Cook and serving-man was Father Stephen, a grey ascetic who had resided on the Mountain without intermission since he was fourteen.

"*On ne peut à peine y croire,*" the Governor informed us, "*mais c'est la vérité: il est vierge. Il m'a demandé l'autre jour comment les femmes sont faites. Je lui ai dit que j'en amènerais une pourqu'il puisse voir.*

" '*Ici,*' *s'écria-t-il,* '*sur la terre sainte?*'

" '*Oui, et de plus, je la mettrai dans votre chambre.*' "

"*Il faillit en mourir.*"

Whatever Father Stephen's inexperience of worldly pleasures, he was not insensible to the needs of civilised digestion. Macaroni was followed by rissoles with tomato sauce and salad. We ate to bursting, and afterwards talked behind the glass partition, playing with Father Stephen's cats, Bijou and Coco. Outside, jackals howled in the vineyards and crickets chirped without ceasing.

I awoke next morning with an inflamed throat that would neither open nor shut.

"This," I said to myself, "is typhus. There are no drains in the town. I leave Caryes to-day if I sleep under a bush."

Running along the balcony, I poured my intention upon David. He, too, he said, preferred to make a last bid for life. And even Mark, hitherto in buoyant health, was reduced to acquiescence. For the moment, however, we were engaged to breakfast with Evlogios at the Lavra *Konak*, whither we were escorted by the Governor, who said that the prospective archbishop was his greatest friend on the Mountain. Though he speaks only Greek, Evlogios reads French and German. The conversation ranged over Byzantine culture and its modern interpreters.

"The French," said he, "are Slav propagandists. They are always trying to attribute the best paintings and buildings to Slav artists and Slav architects." Which is, as he pointed out, curious, since all Slav culture emanated directly from Constantinople, and was usually inferior.

Breakfast, which was served by an ill-kempt youth called Nicola, who was hoping to become a monk in three months' time and was much puffed up of it, consisted of tea, rusks, tinned butter, and jam. In the middle the telephone rang; and Evlogios and the

Governor held a long conversation with our old friends of the Lavra, Nicodemus and Dr. Spyridon. There had been a fire at Kerasia, actually at the Holy Apostles', where lived Andreas and Basil, who had conducted our ascent of the summit. But it was only in the forest, and no buildings had been burnt.

From the Lavra *Konak* we continued to a bookbinder's, a hot walk down steep wooded paths interrupted by streams. The bookbinder was Father Niphon, whose sunken cheeks, furrowed brow, and eyes staring into the beyond, we had seen a hundred times among the frescoed saints in the churches. He showed us his workshop, his tools, his different leathers, and his German and Russian presses. There was always occupation. At present he was engaged on a sumptuous photographic facsimile of the *Codex Sinaiticus* for the library of the Holy Synod. We afterwards sat eating grapes. I was anxious to return, as numerous inscriptions remained to be copied in the chapel of the Prodrome before we left. But the Governor could only repeat: "Leave Caryes to-night? Ridiculous! Impossible! You shall not!"

The heat was stifling in the little chapel when I ultimately reached it. David, who had worked there since eight o'clock, left at two. I remained till three, when he returned to fetch me; since the innkeeper, in order to make up for a meatless Wednesday, had cooked us a chicken which he refused to serve till we were all there to eat it hot. As we did so, decision seized us. We would leave, not only the capital, but the Mountain. Our work was done. And there was a boat calling on the way to Cavalla the following morning. Though this was exactly opposed to where we wished to go, being on the way to Turkey, it would at least enable us to avoid the industrial fair at Salonica and also to motor over part of Macedonia. The mules were ordered; the unwashed clothing packed; the bill paid; the youths tipped. After waiting twenty minutes while the Governor was closeted with the *anti-prosopos* of Iviron, we bade him good-bye, promising to meet again in other more accessible capitals whither his diplomatic profession might call him.

It had been our intention to spend the night at Xeropotamou. But such had been the delay in starting that it was already nearly dark, and it was plain that the doors would be closed. Having replaced the fastenings of the chapel and left compensation with Nicolaides for any damage that Meletios might detect, we rode from the town. The muleteer, whom we had beaten magnificently in a bargain-drive, had purposely forgotten to provide our saddles with rugs. This omission, much against his will, he was forced to rectify while we waited, and the twilight closed.

Sad at this last evening, even in pleasure at the prospect of new comfort and new health, I climbed the ridge alone. The stars came out. The trees stood about me in black aisles. At the top Mark's mule ran away. The saddle, girthed with a single thread, turned round and he was precipitated into the dust. Thenceforth he walked, while I rode. The moon, paring of a crescent, only intensified the murk. And the animals, whose masters' prided boast it is that they see in the dark, tripped and slid about the cobbles with torturing uncertainty. Their owner, sulking at the lateness of the hour, the bad bargain, and the rugs, walked ahead, leaving us to manage as we might. To our bodies no worse could come. But in front lurched the baggage-mule bearing the fragile outcome— 200 glass plates—of all our plans and effort. Unthinking of my own's inept paces, I rode with my eyes fixed upon the tail of the other. If it stopped to nibble, so did I. If it strayed from the path, I drove it back. At one point it fell with a sickening crash into a ditch higher than itself. I, on top, worked with feverish wiles to urge it to the mouth. David meanwhile sat humped and desperate, oblivious of the disasters that were impinging on his life's work.

At Xeropotamou, a twinkling quadrangle of lights, the muleteer, who was gleefully aware of our plight, was confident that we should at least attempt an entrance. But, rather than endure yet another loading and unloading, we would have ridden down the Matterhorn. To the song of his curses we embarked on the steepest descent on the Mountain. We reached the bridge, climbed the next hill, and rounded the bay. Suddenly, with one eye still on the luggage, I caught sight of David's body prostrate by the roadside: motionless; too late. Dismounting to retrieve it for burial in the old Cotswold churchyard, there greeted my touch a fearful spasm, and then— let a veil be drawn. The mules had continued with their fellows. Supporting one another, we staggered down to the port like the two grenadiers.

The ground floor of the inn, low and dirty, was full of indiscriminate labourers and fishermen. With difficulty we distinguished the host, unshaven and hard-faced, in a white and collarless sweater. We asked for food. To which he replied:

"At present I am eating, and I shall eat for a little."

Incensed, we picked the biggest *ouzo* bottle from the counter and disappeared into the night with it. He was therefore obliged to follow. Food we wanted, did we? Well, there was neither bread, nor fish, nor meat, nor vegetables, nor fruit, nor wine. How true is the proverb that a Greek will grow fat on what will starve an ass. David and I could do no more. But Mark rose like a Florence Nightingale. In a basket he discovered two dozen eggs. He relit the fire; called for pepper and salt, set out plates, spoons, and forks; and at length—we dined. As we ate, our eyes rested on the inn's official designation, ostentatiously placarded on the wall opposite:

ΚΑΦΦΕΖΥΘΕΣΤΙΑΤΟΡΙΟΝ

καὶ

ΞΕΝΟΔΟΧΕΙΟΝ ΥΠΝΟΥ

COFFEE-ALE-EATING-HOUSE

AND

HOTEL OF SLEEP

Upstairs, two rooms awaited us. One was empty; the other to be shared with a snoring and odorous fellow. From him we dragged the spare bed next door. I lay down. And it was hard to think that any man had lain in precisely such a bed before. Within one hour the sheets were strewn with the corpses of 22 broad red bugs, each of which had added a spurt of alien blood to the varying contributions of my predecessors. As long again brought the figure up to 63. I then threw half the mattress out of the window, where it stuck in a vine. Sleep, which I had thought impossible, came at last, despite the tickling. And I awoke feeling completely restored. There was evidently ground for the ancient practice of bleeding. In the light of day, the total was brought by Mark's practised eye up to 95. It was disappointing that we did not reach the century.

Dressing-gowns a cynosure, we bathed with the rising of the sun; we breakfasted as we dined; at ten o'clock we sighted the steamer; and at half past we were on board, the skirts of the other sex fluttering about us, and the tale of our luggage, plates and all, complete.

Instead of returning past the other fingers of Chalcidice to Salonica, we sail close in along the shore, prior to rounding the base of the summit and striking across to the coast-line of Thrace. We sit on the upper deck. A steward in a white jacket brings us iced drinks upon a tin table. And before us the whole promontory unfolds; high up, Simopetra, crag and building casting black shadow down the gulley; perched low at the water's edge, Gregoriou; Dionysiou, materialising suddenly from its green marble cleft; St. Paul's set far back at the apex of a slope, with the summit borne upward from its tower; the *skiti* of St. Anne clinging to the corner cliffs; and then the corner. The ship lurches. A breeze strikes up. Spray spatters on the deck. Mighty cliffs, fantastic humps, sugar-loaves and pyramids, beetle from the waves as we caracole their crests. Still, we keep close in. The walls of rock rear up and topple out of sight. Trees and shrubs make tentative approach from above, then recede before declivities of shale. Suddenly a wooded ravine, dark and steep as a pipe, drops to the water. At its foot an island; at its top, 2,000 feet up, the red wall of the Holy Apostles'. Thence we ourselves had once looked down on the deck of a passing ship such as this, a tiny dot on the peacock rim, unreal, enigmatic in parvitude. Now we are small, mortals without mark in a world of ponderous concerns. And over all, filling the sky, rules the peak, massive and obtuse to our inferior vision. A mile and a quarter it stands from the water by cliff and ledge; till the trees dot away and only the white marble dances up the blue to the music of the cold morning sun.

The wind drives past; the waves grow bigger; the boards of our Leviathan pitch to the east, roll to the north. At the farthest angle, the tower of the Lavra arsenal stands white; and, with the turn, the monastery of Athanasius itself lies low and scattered on an upper platform. The peak is hidden by the cloud above it. We strike out into the open sea. This is good-bye.

Afternoon passes to evening. And a calm descends as we sail

within the lee of Thasos. The prow points for the hills, smoky purple, as the falling sun plays gold on the downy breasts of the clouds. Cavalla is in sight, a white blur; houses, churches, minarets; trams, hotels. There is a lament in the wind's talk to the marrows of life. Turn south, it says, astern, where the dark is moving up from the water. There, carried high on a bank of clouds, hovers a shape, a triangle in the sky. This is the Holy Mountain Athos, station of a faith where all the years have stopped.

INDEX

Index

A

Adeney, W. F., 202 note
Adrian of Vatopedi, 210, 223–4, 225–6, 228, 244
Afforestation, 62
Aghia Roumeli, Crete, 196, 198
Akakios of Xenophontos, 161, 164, 168, 169–72
Albania, 241
Alexander II, Tsar, 146
Alexandra Feodorovna, Tsarina, 146
Alexandria, Patriarch of, *see* Meletios
Alexis, Tsar, 69
Alexius III Angelus, Emperor, 203
Alexius Comnenus, Emperor, 249
Alexius I Comnenus, Emperor, 57
Alexius III Comnenus, Emperor of Trebizond, 115, 118
Chrysobul of, 116–18, 247
Amalfitans, Tower of, 70
Amalia, Queen, 37, 105
American Archaeologists, 108
Dealers, 249
Greeks, 127, 192
Anastasia, Tsarina, 222
Andreas of Kerasia, 91–102, 252
Andronicus Palaeologus, Despot, 222
Andronicus Palaeologus, Emperor, 87
Angora, 212
Anne, St., 103
Antony of Volinsk, Archbishop, 154
Architecture, *see* Byzantine Civilisation
Aristarchus of Vatopedi, 211–14, 219, 220, 228
Asia Minor, 98, 109, 114, 166, 212, 241
Athanasius of Athos, St., 56–7, 59–60, 75–9, 255
Athens, 33–7, 108, 142, 173–4, 187, 188, 248, 249
Metropolitan of, 41, 117, 249
Athonias, 216, 244
Athos, the Holy Mountain, 39, 40, 41, 47–187, 199 *ff.*
History of:
The Hermits, 54
First Chrysobul, 55
Foundation of Monasteries, 55–7
The Vlach Shepherds, 57
Latin Conquest, 57
Idiorhythmy, 57–8
Surrender to the Turk, 58

Athos, History of:—*contd.*
Intellectual Revival, 58
The Revolution, 58
Confiscation of Properties, 59
Russian Aggression, 149–51, 154
Treaties of St. Stefano and Berlin, 150
Deliverance from the Turk, 152–3
Treaty of London (1913), 154
Treaties of Sèvres and Lausanne, 155
Austria-Hungary, 154
Averof, Cruiser, 104, 153

B

Bajazet II, Sultan, 237
Balcony, 113–14
Barlaam of Gregoriou, 124, 127, 133–4
Bartholomew of the Lavra, 75, 81, 82, 89
Basil I the Macedonian, Emperor, 55
Basil II Bulgaroctonos, Emperor, 68
Basil III, Oecumenical Patriarch, 40, 41, 51, 117, 133
Basil of Kerasia, 101–3, 109, 252
Basil, St., rule of, 55
Basil, sweet herb, 110
Belch, 199–200
Belon, P., 74, 163
Benedict, Papal Legate, 57, 185
Benedict, St., 55
Berlin, Treaty of, 56, 59, 150, 155
Bessarabia, 184
Bessarion, Cardinal, 116
Boniface of Montferrat, 57
Boniface of Xeropotamou, 47, 234, 241, 242
Bouboulis, Monsieur, Governor of Macedonia, 45
Boulatovitch, Antony, 154
Bowen, Sir George, 176
Braconnier, Jesuit, 107, 176
British Museum, 221, 249
Brussels, 234
Broussa, 92, 109
Buddhist Monasticism, 137–8
Bulgarian *Chargé d'Affaires*, 239, 244
Monastery, 63, *see* Zographou
Bulgars, 149, 168
Bulgaris, Eugenios, 217
Buondelmonti, Cristoforo, 5, 163
Busbecq, Imperial Ambassador, 199, 237
Byron, Lord, 105

[259]

Index

Index

[262]

Index

Index

Index